TEN STUDIES IN TACITUS

TEN STUDIES
IN
TACITUS

BY

SIR RONALD SYME

CAMDEN PROFESSOR OF
ANCIENT HISTORY

CLARENDON PRESS · OXFORD

1970

Oxford University Press, Ely House, London W.1

GLASGOW   NEW YORK   TORONTO   MELBOURNE   WELLINGTON
CAPE TOWN   SALISBURY   IBADAN   NAIROBI   DAR ES SALAAM   LUSAKA   ADDIS ABABA
BOMBAY   CALCUTTA   MADRAS   KARACHI   LAHORE   DACCA
KUALA LUMPUR   SINGAPORE   HONG KONG   TOKYO

MADE AND PRINTED IN GREAT BRITAIN BY
WILLIAM CLOWES AND SONS LIMITED, LONDON AND BECCLES

PREFACE

THE TEN PAPERS saw the light of day at intervals during a period of fifteen years, 'grande mortalis aevi spatium', from 1949 to 1964. The reader may wish to know in what relation they stand to *Tacitus*, itself a nine years' labour, which was handed to the Press on a day in September of 1956 (between a visit to Moscow and a sojourn in Cambridge, Massachusetts, each for the first time), and was published in April of 1958.

The ten are diverse in origin, content, and scope. The first three and the tenth were lectures of a general character, delivered respectively at Vandœuvres (1956), London (1955), Liège (1952), Hannover (1961). Vestiges from several of the early chapters in the book will be found in the second; and five pages of the third were taken with little change from what is now Chapter XXXIV (cf. *Tacitus*, p. 453).

For the rest, Chapters IV, V, VI in the present volume, studies in historical detail (but also concerned with textual problems), emerged during the composition of the book. Chapter IV, 'Marcus Lepidus, *Capax Imperii*' is in fact the earliest of all the ten: it goes back to 1948, but was not published until 1955. Next, Chapter IX, 'The Friend of Tacitus'. Discussing Fabius Justus, it provides the argument to support a brief paragraph in *Tacitus* (p. 74): it was composed in 1956/7.

Chapter VII, written in the near sequel, enabled me to deal adequately with the engaging subject of obituary notices, to which I had devoted only a page, highly compressed (p. 313). Chapter VIII, 'The Historian Servilius Nonianus', is an attempt to elucidate one of the predecessors of Tacitus. It is independent, but has a precise and necrological link with Chapter VII.

The function of the *Addenda* is strictly limited: to rectify matters of detail and to register new items of information. General topics are eschewed, with one exception. Chapter X, the sparse annotation of which was confined to the ancient sources, is now equipped with two brief pieces of commentary designed to clarify controversy about the date of the *Annales* and the origin of the historian.

R.S.

September 1, 1969.

CONTENTS

I

THE SENATOR AS HISTORIAN*

ELECTIONS of magistrates and the passing of laws, the allocation of *provinciae*, wars, triumphs, and the building of temples, such is the annual register of the Roman State; and the 'res populi Romani' continue thus to be narrated when the magnitude of the events threatened to burst the structure (as in the last epoch of the Republic), when the Republic gives way before the Monarchy, and when the Monarchy has endured for a century or more. Sallustius Crispus decided to begin, not with Sulla's resignation of the dictatorship, but with the consulate of M. Lepidus and Q. Catulus (78 B.C.), while Asinius Pollio chose for his exordium the year that saw the compact of the three 'principes', heralding the armed conflict a decade later—'motum ex Metello consule civicum'. As for Cornelius Tacitus, his *Historiae* led off precisely with the first day of January, A.D. 69, Ser. Galba and T. Vinius being consuls. His second work went further back into the past (in more senses than one). The books have for title (or perhaps sub-title) 'ab excessu divi Augusti', according to the *Codex Mediceus*. After short and prefatory remarks ('pauca de Augusto et extrema'), the story of Rome under the successors of Augustus is narrated year by year.

Posterity knows the work as the *Annales*. Why *Annales*? Or, let it be asked, why not? Commentators in antiquity, such as the scholiast Servius, draw a distinction: 'annales' (they say) chronicle events in the past, whereas 'historia' is the record of a person's own time and experience. The distinction is not helpful, and it may be fallacious. It has not always been noticed that Tacitus himself nowhere employs the word 'historia' with the meaning of 'history'. In his usage, a historian is an 'auctor' or an 'annalium scriptor'. If he evokes the 'praecipuum munus annalium' (III. 65), it is to enounce the principal function of all history; and when he refers to 'annales nostri' (IV. 32), he simply means 'the history I am writing'.

In the beginning, history was written by senators (first a Fabius, and

* Reprinted from *Histoire et historiens dans l'antiquité*, Entretiens Tome IV, Fondation Hardt.

Cato was the first to use the Latin language); it remained for a long time the monopoly of the governing order; and it kept the firm imprint of its origins ever after. The senator came to his task in mature years, with a proper knowledge of men and government, a sharp and merciless insight. Taking up the pen, he fought again the old battles of Forum and Curia. Exacerbated by failure or not mollified by worldly success, he asserted a personal claim to glory and survival; and, if he wrote in retirement from affairs, it was not always with tranquillity of mind.

Sallust had been a tribune of the plebs, active and turbulent in a year of anarchy, the third consulate of Pompeius Magnus; he was expelled from the Senate by the censors of 50 B.C.; he saw warfare and governed a province for Caesar. His career being terminated (and a fortune amassed), he proposed to put his leisure to good employ, cured (so he professed) from the errors and ambition of his earlier life, a wiser man, and liberated from the spirit of party. To go in for hunting or practise agriculture was ignoble: he would write history. After the two monographs, Sallust embarked on an ample narration. The subject of his *Historiae* might be described as the decline of that oligarchy which Sulla had brought back to power, with Pompeius Magnus at first and for a long time the enemy of the *Optimates*, then their false friend, and leading to catastrophe.

Sallust had not got further than the year 67 when he died. Asinius Pollio took up the tale, a commander of armies and a diplomat in high or secret negotiations, a partisan of Caesar and of Antonius but professing to be a Republican at heart. Soon after his consulship (40 B.C.), Pollio forswore politics, turning to letters. He composed tragedies on mythological subjects (no trace survives), but soon found a more congenial occupation in recording the transactions of his own time, a theme which was also the fall of the Roman Republic, 'periculosae plenum opus aleae'.

Tacitus came to history in the same season of life as Sallust and Pollio. His experience was comparable. Not, it is true, the long agony of the civil wars, but the equivalent—'saeva pax' and a precarious equilibrium. He was *consul suffectus* under Nerva in 97, holding the *fasces* for a term of two months somewhere in the second half of that year. A few months pass and he comes forward with a monograph on his wife's father, Julius Agricola, consul and governor of Britain. A first essay, for he intends to go on and narrate the reign of Domitian, the fifteen years of silence and humiliation, 'quindecim annos, grande mortalis aevi spatium', to stand as testimony of past enslavement and present felicity.

The political events and arguments of 97 lie behind the *Agricola*. Tacitus pays due homage to the happy epoch now dawning: 'felicitas temporum'.

As would be expected, the treatise is an attack on the dead tyrant. It is also an attack on political extremists, namely the party of the opposition, the intractable men and the martyrs, who perished with no advantage to the 'res publica'. Tacitus in a passionate outburst goes out of his way to assert that a man can do his duty to the Commonwealth even under bad emperors. That is a defence of the cautious and virtuous Agricola. Also a defence of Cornelius Tacitus, who had made a good career under Domitian. Also (it can be divined) a defence of somebody else, none other than M. Ulpius Traianus, commander of the army of Germania Superior, who had been adopted by Nerva as his son and successor in October of 97.

That is not all. The year 97 (it can be argued) is also behind the *Historiae* of Tacitus. As the subject of his projected work, the eloquent consular announced the reign of Domitian. As it happened, he went back to 69. The reason is plain. The brief reign of Nerva had brought the past to life again, sharp and terrifying. The parallel between Galba and Nerva was inescapable—a weak emperor, the threat of civil war, the rôle of the Praetorian Guard, and an adoption in extremity. The one act failed, the other succeeded. Galba's choice was foolish and fatal, but Nerva elected a man who was 'capax imperii'. Consul in 97, Tacitus witnessed the disintegration of a government, the menace from the army commanders and the veiled *coup d'état* that brought Trajan to the power.

The theme of the *Historiae* is the murderous story of civil war and despotism—the rapid events of 69 followed by the twenty-seven years' rule of the Flavian emperors. Enough, perhaps, for one man's achievement. An interval elapsed. Tacitus went out to Asia as proconsul (112/13, summer to summer). At some time after his return he set himself to a second task.

It would be entertaining to speculate about his reasons (personal and political), and perhaps fruitless. We know very little about Cornelius Tacitus. Yet one supposition could be hazarded. In the late years of Trajan, a man could stand at a point of vantage, with a long perspective backwards. The time had come to ask when it was that the Principate took an evil turn, and why, to trace the decline of the dynasty from the Principate of Tiberius Caesar to the despotism of Nero, to analyse a process which was at the same time the decline and fall of the Roman aristocracy.

Tacitus proposed to narrate the story of the Caesars according to the canons and manner of the Republic. Hence the traditional and annalistic structure. That method labours under sundry disadvantages. On the one hand, it breaks the unity of large subjects and disperses the interest. On the other, it produces a catalogue of heterogeneous items. Tacitus himself comes out with sporadic complaints, and modern scholars have not been slow to fasten upon the defects and constraints of the annalistic framework.

By contrast, it is the signal advantages that ought to be emphasized. First, and patently, chronology. How dispense with dates? Sallust tried in the *Bellum Jugurthinum*, and the result is not at all encouraging. Under the Empire, it might be urged, new and better types of dating offered. Reflection inspires a doubt. There were various complications in computing the regnal years of emperors, for example by the *tribunicia potestas*. Moreover, eras of that kind would be repulsive to a senator. It was the aim of Tacitus to write about Rome and the Senate, not merely the dynasty. He did not want his Roman annals to degenerate into a sequence of imperial biographies.

Let us be grateful for eponymous consuls. The schema came as a blessing to a compiler, a copyist, or a mere 'exornator rerum': it saved him from many of the errors, inherent in his ignorance or his lack of a living interest in the 'res publica'. But it could not hamper a bold, vigorous, and selective writer. Knowledge of government, artistic skill and architectonic power would prevail.

Tacitus had abundant information, and he operated with great freedom. About his sources in the *Annales*, there has been interminable debate, not all of it wise or profitable. To take the first hexad. Tacitus claims or plainly implies that he had read all the authors who dealt with Tiberius Caesar, and he can be believed. The question arises, what value and credit did he accord them? We have his condemnatory verdict on the writing of history under the Caesars—the living adulated, the dead defamed (I.1). One might therefore be tempted to refrain from conjuring with names and the unknown. Still less the phantom of the 'Single Source'. Or rather (let it be postulated) there is a single source and a straight path—the archives of the Roman Senate.

Many scholars have doubted whether Tacitus had recourse to the *acta senatus* often, or at all; and peculiar argumentation has been adduced. Was not the answer before their eyes, in the matter and structure of the Tiberian books? Observe the sheer mass of senatorial transactions, debates reported at different stages, debates that lead to no conclusion—and the long strings of personal names attesting the diligence of documentary enquiry and the ever-vigilant interest of a Roman senator. The years 20, 21, and 22 (III. 20–76) are instructive and convincing. A full record, though nothing much happened. For the plan of his work Tacitus needed to fill up the interval between the prosecution of Cn. Piso, the governor of Syria (that is, the aftermath of Germanicus), and the death of Drusus Caesar, the son of

Tiberius. Other historians might have passed quickly from the one event to the other.

Having command of material from the *acta*, Tacitus can expand or contract, select or omit. And he has free scope with supplementary devices.

First, the speeches. The pronouncements of Tiberius Caesar were of paramount value, not only for matters of state but as a clue to the secret nature of that enigmatic ruler. And the style was not uncongenial. Commenting on the oratorical performance of the Caesars, Tacitus pays an expert's tribute—'Tiberius artem quoque callebat qua verba expenderet, tum validus sensibus aut consulto ambiguus' (XIII. 3). It could be supposed that he followed the imperial orations fairly closely; and it might not be fanciful to look for traces of Tiberius' manner, and even of his diction. Tiberius is perhaps the most impressive orator in the *Annales*.

Tacitus can also invent. He produces a petition from the imperial minister Aelius Seianus, asking for the hand of a princess in marriage, and the Emperor's answer, cautious and temporizing, but with a note of encouragement towards the end and an amicable hint of plans for Seianus' benefit not yet quite ripe for disclosure (IV. 39 f.). No reward (he said) was too high for the virtues and the loyalty of Seianus: which he would not hesitate to proclaim to Senate or People, when the time came.

Similarly, speeches from senators. A historian, Cremutius Cordus, threatened with prosecution, enters the Senate and delivers a noble oration on history and liberty (IV. 34 f.). Not, one suspects, to be discovered in the *acta senatus. . . .*

Next, the digressions. The author was free to enlarge on all manner of topics that engaged his attention. For example, when a proposal is made in the Senate to modify one of the Augustan laws about marriage, the *Lex Papia Poppaea*, Tacitus subjoins an excursus on the history of legislation from the beginning down to the third consulate of Pompeius Magnus—which consulate he links to the laws enacted in 28 B.C. when Augustus in his sixth consulship established the Principate (III. 26–8). That was the beginning of more rigorous control—'acriora ex eo vincula'. Again, when an attempt was made to saddle Tiberius with a programme of measures against luxury and extravagance, Tiberius in a dispatch to the Senate deprecates any action of the sort; he points out that the laws of Augustus were unsuccessful, and he implies that they were misconceived (III. 53 f.). The historian reinforces the speech with a digression. He affirms that luxury flourished unabated all through, from the War of Actium to the fall of Nero; and he adds a diagnosis, explaining the more sober standards of life and conduct that prevailed in his own time (III. 55).

Speech and digression, carefully selected incidents or unobtrusive comment, Tacitus compensates for one of the disadvantages of beginning a history with the year 14: he is able to introduce references to what preceded, with criticism of Augustus, insidiously. At the funeral of Augustus the men of understanding, the 'prudentes', expatiate upon the life and works of the Princeps (1. 9 f.). Praise is the smaller portion. The comments of Tacitus later on in the hexad perhaps add up to something much more deadly and subversive.

As has been said, senatorial business in the *Annales*, by its selection and arrangement, indicates the senator. Also the frequent names, as witness the seven men of rank whose 'sententiae' are registered by the historian after the suicide of an alleged conspirator, the silly Scribonius Libo—'quorum auctoritates adulationesque rettuli ut sciretur vetus id in re publica malum' (II. 32).

A sharp eye for personal and family history surveyed the record of Roman public life in the days of Tiberius Caesar. First, the *nobiles*, whose names evoked the old Republic: many still extant in the early Principate, having survived the wars of the Revolution, but destined to be destroyed by the dynasty of Julii and Claudii. Next, families that had come to recent prominence through the patronage of the Caesars, and were conspicuous in the historian's own time. He would be alert to discern their earliest emergence, which was not always honourable—avid careerists, ruthless prosecutors, or adherents of Seianus. Many names, and the need for accuracy: he wrote for a subtle and malicious audience. It is clear enough that a history of Tiberius' reign composed by somebody not a senator would be very different from the *Annales*.

Not merely a Roman senator is there revealed, but precisely Cornelius Tacitus, consul, *XV vir sacris faciundis* and proconsul of Asia. It might be worth looking for the trace of his predilections in odd items—and especially where the subject matter was not imposed but selected. That is to say, in speeches and digressions. The *Annales* disclose a keen interest in the religious antiquities of the Roman State. Tacitus by the time of his praetorship (in 88) was one of the *quindecimviri* who kept the Sibylline Oracles and had the supervision over cults of extraneous origin. A member of that college knew all about prophecies, numerical calculations and certain official ceremonies—and (let it be added) he acquired fresh reasons for a sceptical attitude towards the conduct of men and governments.

Again, the full documentation about the affairs of Asia. Debates about temples and the right of asylum or the vicissitudes of proconsuls (a prosecution or even a murder) help to certify the ex-consul who had held the twelve *fasces* in that province.

Lastly (and perhaps most important) Roman oratory. Tacitus had been a great speaker, among the first, if not the first, in that age. After the prosecution of Marius Priscus in 100 he bade farewell to public eloquence. Oratory was finished. The *Dialogus* conveys his renunciation and furnishes a diagnosis, not without irony. Oratory flourished in periods of political freedom, and turbulence. In a well ordered state it is not needed any more. One man holds the power, and he is the wisest ('sapientissimus et unus'); there is no need for long debates in the Senate, for men of good sense come quickly to the right decisions (*Dial.* 41). The *Annales* (it can be contended) supply an outline history of Roman eloquence under the Principate down to the historian's own time or memory. It is rendered through significant names or through specimens of oratory. One can adduce, for example, the son of Messalla Corvinus whose ease, grace and tolerance is intended to convey the manner of his illustrious parent (III. 34); L. Vitellius, the crafty minister of state, blandly explaining to the Roman Senate that Claudius Caesar needs a wife to help him, has deserved a wife by his blameless conduct, and ought to be united in matrimony to his brother's daughter, Agrippina (XII. 5 f.); the prosecutors Suillius Rufus and Cossutianus Capito, in invented discourses that are savage and aggressive to the point of parody (XIII. 43; XVI. 22); and the venerable consulars Cassius Longinus and Thrasea Paetus, grave, dignified, and a little old-fashioned when they speak in defence of tradition and the honour of the governing order (XIV. 43 f.; XV. 20 f.).

So far the structure and matter of the *Annales* (with especial reference to the first hexad). The style is in keeping. That the manner and words of Roman historians would tend to reproduce an earlier age is a natural assumption, even if history had not so often been written by politicians in retirement, acrid if not resentful, and prone to exalt the past to the detriment of the present. The Empire enhanced the appeal of antiquity.

With the first six books of the *Annales*, the style of Tacitus reaches its peak—less eloquent than in the *Historiae*, stronger and tighter, more archaic and more Sallustian. The advance on the *Historiae* can be easily documented. Likewise the different manner that becomes more and more perceptible in the course of the third hexad as extant (XIII–XVI). Various reasons could be assigned. Perhaps the author failed to revise, or was cut short by death. However that may be, there is another reason that could be given some weight. To a contemporary of Trajan, Tiberius Caesar belonged to a past already far distant; born in the year of Philippi, he was an anachronism, and was proud to be such; under his principate there still subsisted 'quaedam imago rei publicae'. Nero, however, was imperial and contemporary—alarmingly so, if one reflected on who was to succeed Trajan.

There is something else. With Sallust, Roman history came to maturity in an age that was filled, if not nauseated, with political oratory. Sallust felt an antipathy towards Cicero. That does not need to be contested, or anxiously played down. It finds its expression, and its best expression, in hostility to the voluminous periodic structure with its predictable conclusions, in the choice of a brief, harsh, abrupt style that subverts eloquence and asserts the truth, bare but discordant. Not, indeed, that the Sallustian style can or should be defined merely as anti-Ciceronian. It suited the man and the age. It became a fashion, quickly, as the discerning Seneca observes—'Sallustio vigente amputatae sententiae et verba ante exspectatum cadentia et obscura brevitas fuere pro cultu' (*Epp.* 114. 17). It also became classic, and a model for history ever after.

Asinius Pollio, archaic in his oratory, though not perhaps in his history writing, used with deadly effect the plain style of one who knew and distrusted the professions of men and governments, detesting any manifestations of the romantic and improving view of history. With Pollio and Sallust for precedent, the writers of the revolutionary age, it is no surprise that Tacitus avoids the edifying phraseology which, exploited by politicians in the last epoch of the Republic, had been annexed by Caesar Augustus and degraded by governmental use ever after.

His vocabulary betrays his aversions. Instead of 'auctoritas' he prefers the revealing 'potentia', its pejorative synonym. 'Aeternitas' had come to be attached, not only to the Empire of Rome, but to the divinity of the emperors: the word is admitted once only in the *Annales*, in reported discourse (XI. 7). Tacitus has a proper dislike for 'pius' and 'felix'; and 'felicitas' is found only twice, each time in reference to the resplendent success of the same *novus homo*, namely Seneca (XIII. 43; XIV. 53). 'Providentia' occurs once, and that in derision—for nobody could help laughing when the funeral oration on dead Claudius passed on to an allusion to his 'providentia' (XIII. 3). The senator furnishes a useful (and necessary) antidote to the legends advertised on coins.

Matter and style reflect the senator, likewise tone and sentiments. The rule of one man was installed at Rome to abate strife, control the armies and hold the Empire together. That was clear, and conceded (*Hist.* I. 1; *Ann.* I. 9). The non-political classes acclaimed the new order everywhere, with enthusiasm, but no senator could bring himself to confess a joyous acceptance: he was resigned, or bitter (and none the less bitter if he had recently come to high status). What the Princeps gained, the Senate lost—honour as well as power, and the imperial administration steadily encroached. Not despotism, to be sure, but the Principate, so it was proclaimed. The senator will be alert for the contrasts of name and fact, contemptuous of sporadic subservience or the manifestations of organized loyalty.

On the face of things, Tacitus might be claimed a Republican—if it were clear what substance could be given to that term under the Caesars. One layer deeper, and he is revealed, like so many others, as an opportunist, advocating the middle path in politics and hoping that chance or destiny would bring forth some ruler who might be better than the worst. Men and character matter, not system or doctrine. Hence the preoccupation with the theme 'capax imperii'.

'Urbem Romam', with these words the *Annales* begin. The City appears to be at the centre of a senator's interest, as under the Republic. That is not, however, the anachronism it might seem. Rome is still the seat of power, however much the Palace, the bureaucrats and the managers of secret influence may tend to supplant the Senate and the senatorial order. Tacitus is a political historian. Provinces and armies have their proper place—they will come into the narrative when they count (as they would in Book XVIII of the *Annales*.)

Otherwise, the subjects of Rome and foreign nations (like the lower classes) have a minor place. The inherited pride of an imperial people speaks through the mouth of Tacitus, with scorn and distaste for the foreigner, notably the Greek and the Jew (and for the Greek an aversion that exaggerates almost to parody the attitudes of old Romans). On the other hand, he knew and valued the northern barbarians; and, despising the conventional apologia for Rome's dominion over the nations, he insists on showing up the violence and oppression.

No senator could refuse to pay homage to the tradition of Rome and the Republic. The word 'priscus' exercises an irresistible appeal. Praise of the past was normal and necessary. It did not always blind a man to the times he lived in, or influence his conduct overmuch. In a debate about the wives of proconsuls, Valerius Messallinus speaks for the modern and humane view, deprecating the rigour of traditionalists: the 'duritia veterum' was out of place (III. 34). The author himself, in the digression on luxury, puts in a quiet plea at the end—'nec omnia apud priores meliora, et nostra quoque aetas multa laudis et artium imitanda posteris tulit' (III. 55).

2—T.S.I.T.

The writings of Tacitus are fierce and gloomy. That also (it should seem) is in the tradition, Sallust having set the tone, and no reason for dissent emerging subsequently in the history of Rome. Even without the fifteen years of the Domitianic tyranny, there was enough in the senatorial existence to predispose a man to a general suspicion of human behaviour and motives, a distrust of comforting beliefs, a propensity to the darker side. Yet it cannot with any confidence be assumed that Tacitus was not a robust, balanced, and cheerful character. The writer and the man are not always the same person.

For, it must be asked at the end, who is Tacitus? Not only a Republican, an imperialist, a conservative, a pessimist, but also a descendant of the ancient *nobilitas*, so some have fancied. On what grounds? The *Annales* show Tacitus preoccupied with the vicissitudes of aristocratic families. Further, he has sundry remarks in dispraisal of Roman knights and *novi homines*—for example, Aelius Seianus, paramour of a princess of the dynasty, is styled 'municipalis adulter', and the lady is taken severely to task for bringing disgrace on herself, her ancestors and descendants (IV. 3).

All of that need indicate one thing only: the writer conforms to Roman tradition and assumes the manner and the pride of the Roman *nobilitas*. Not, therefore, one of the patrician Cornelii. The truth may be such as would have appealed to the irony of Cornelius Tacitus himself. He has fooled posterity.

The *patria* of the historian may be in the provinces of the West, and further even, his ultimate extraction not colonial but native. Perhaps from Forum Julii in Narbonensis, the home of Julius Agricola, his wife's father; possibly from Vasio of the Vocontii, that elegant and prosperous city. The *novus homo* and senatorial historian stands in the line of succession that goes back to Asinius Pollio of the Marrucini, whose grandfather fought for Italy against Rome in the great rebellion, to Sallustius Crispus from Amiternum in the Sabine country, to Porcius Cato, the 'inquilinus' from Tusculum, consul and censor.

II

HOW TACITUS CAME TO HISTORY*

IT IS A question worth the asking, at what season in his life a man comes to the writing of history, with what equipment for the task and under what compulsion. Cornelius Tacitus did not discover his vocation until he had passed the age of forty. Was that late or early? Late, in the opinion of some scholars, late and almost anomalous. Gaston Boissier avowed his surprise on the first page of his *Tacite*, a book published in the year 1903, and held in merited esteem for its combination of elegance and judgement. And, more recently (in 1947), Ernst Kornemann, the last survivor of that notable company, the pupils of Theodor Mommsen, affirmed it as an axiom that Tacitus came late to history.

Impressive testimony, but it derives from misconceptions. One can easily divine what was in the minds of those men—and one can discover their national prepossessions. Literary talent is an early blossom in the favouring climate of France, whereas Germany in the modern world created the schools and system of historical research. The professional historian begins when young his apprenticeship to the trade, acquires the tools for research, masters what is euphemistically called the 'literature of the subject', and, working to direction, will no doubt produce before long a solid contribution to learning.

Rome was very different. History took its origin from political life, and from the political class. It was first written by senators, and it continued for a long time to be the jealous preserve of the governing order. They drew upon mature experience of men and affairs, they fought again the battles of the Forum and the Curia. If they composed in retirement, it was not always in tranquillity, or tempered with charity. They knew too much to be hopeful; and pessimism might be sharpened by personal rancour.

Political vicissitudes can be the making of an historian. Sallust almost confesses it in his first work, the *Catilina*. In his youth, he says, he responded to the call of action and honour and glory. But the times were

* A lecture, delivered in the University of London on 3 November 1955; reprinted from *Greece and Rome* IV (1957), 160–7.

evil, and he had been corrupted by ambition. Now at last he had come
out of the turmoil. He was cured ('ubi animus ex multis miseriis atque
periculis requievit'), and had resolved to pass what remained of life far
from politics. He would put leisure to good use. Not hunting or agricul-
tural pursuits. He would write history.

Sallust had been a turbulent tribune of the plebs; he incurred feuds,
and he made enemies. Expelled from the Senate, he came back as a
partisan of Caesar, commanded troops, nearly perished in a soldiers'
mutiny, and ended his career as governor of a province in Africa. When
Sallust retired, it was to a palace, to the gardens on the Esquiline that
perpetuate his name in imperial Rome. On a cool estimate Asinius Pollio
can also be reckoned among the profiteers of the revolutionary age. An
orator, a soldier, and a diplomat, he forswore politics soon after his
consulate in 40 B.C., and refused to take sides ever again. Sallust was in
his middle forties when he wrote his first historical monograph, and some
time elapsed after Pollio's consulate before Pollio embarked on that
famous history of his own epoch, 'motum ex Metello consule
civicum'.

To Sallust and Pollio there could be no greater contrast than Livy.
He had no share in the *res publica*, no public office that established his
dignity, deepened his understanding—and justified the writing of Roman
history. He came from a private station, from the schools of rhetoric,
where he learned the craft of words, and perhaps taught it.

Livy did not like the Sallustian manner of writing. And indeed, if
Sallust's style was detestable, that was not the worst thing about him.
The politician who turned moralist, the Sabine sermonizer of dubious
conduct, the comfortable author of a pessimistic history—a disquieting
figure. And Pollio the consular was little better: a Republican who survived the Republic, enjoying riches and esteem under a régime he professed to disavow, but proud, savage, and censorious.

Livy was repelled by those detractors of humanity; and, while ac-
knowledging the exciting appeal of recent and contemporary history,
he prefers to turn aside and seek consolation in ancient and happier times,
escaping from 'the tribulations which our age has witnessed through so
many years'. He trusts that the annals of an earlier Rome will prove
salubrious and edifying. Writers like Sallust and Pollio had been eager
to show up the dark and devious ways of men and governments. . . .

There are other contrasts. Livy was young—only about thirty when
he began (if the traditionally accepted date of his birth, 59 B.C., is to be
followed). He had not been anywhere: there is no sign that he had ever

left Italy, and he seems to have spent most of his long life quietly, in his native Patavium.

It follows that Livy in a number of respects is an eccentric in the line of the Roman historians. Cornelius Tacitus, however, was a senator and a consul. His career as a senator before the consulate coincides almost exactly with the fifteen years of Domitian's reign (81–96). Not only was he familiar with the political and social life of the capital—he had been abroad at least once in the service of the State, for three or four years (and perhaps more than once). Tacitus knew the provinces and the Empire.

If any testimony be needed of the benefits of foreign travel, let Edward Gibbon be cited, who, bringing his continental tour to a suitable climax explains how he first came to conceive the great design—'it was at Rome on the 15th of October 1764, as I sat musing amidst the ruins of the Capitol, while the bare-footed friars were singing Vespers in the Temple of Jupiter'. Gibbon was then twenty-seven. It was in the same season of life that an illustrious historian in a later age contemplated in the vale of Sparta the majestic panorama of civilizations.

The resemblance might amuse a philosophic mind (for here a Gibbonian phrase is in keeping)—and the contrast. And it may happen that the retrospective memory embellishes a little, or a project is postponed. Three years later we discover Edward Gibbon writing not about Rome, but about the Swiss Republics. . . .

With Tacitus the announcement of the historian's purpose and vocation emerges sharp and immediate, bound up with his first work, and evoked by political experiences. Towards the end of 97 (or possibly at the very beginning of 98) he produces a biography of his wife's father, Julius Agricola, who had died four years before. The monograph acclaims the dawn of a new era. Domitian having been removed, despotism and oppression are over, and men can speak freely at last. Nerva, the new ruler, combines 'libertas' and 'principatus'; and, with every day that passes, Trajan, whom Nerva has chosen as his associate in the power, augments the general happiness—'felicitas temporum'. Tacitus proposes to contribute his share. He will write the record of the recent past, to demonstrate what Rome suffered under the tyranny, and what Rome has now regained—'memoriam prioris servitutis ac testimonium praesentium bonorum'. That is his design. For the moment he offers the monograph on Agricola, which *pietas* will commend or condone.

The *Agricola* has been variously appraised, and it is variously vulnerable. Participating in the nature of a delayed funeral oration, it is an encomium. Other generals had paved the way for Agricola's conquests in the northern parts of Britain, namely Cerialis and Frontinus. That is not the theme. Other generals may have been no less circumspect when they explored some river's estuary, no less sagacious when they encouraged the untutored natives to study the liberal arts or adopt a refined and urban way of life; and the modest assiduity with which Agricola in the earlier stages of his career (as military tribune in Britain and as legionary commander) so advantageously brought himself to the favour of his superior officers might suggest unfriendly imputations.

That need not matter much. There is something worse. The panegyric of Agricola is also an attack on Domitian. Tacitus was an orator of majestic power, the greatest perhaps in that age, and he musters all the arts of the advocate, using his own malice to prove Domitian's malice against Agricola—for the Emperor feared and hated the great general, the conqueror of Britain. There is no point in citing the various allegations. A more urgent duty should engage our attention.

The *Agricola* turns out to be much more than a laudation of one man's father-in-law, or an attack on a dead tyrant. Commending the patience and forbearance of Agricola when shabbily treated by the Emperor, Tacitus deviates into a violent attack on a whole class of unnamed persons. They are described as 'admirers of that which is wrong': 'quibus moris est inlicita mirari'. He proceeds to read them a lesson. 'Let me tell them', he says, 'that there can be great men even under bad emperors, that duty and discretion, if coupled with energy and a career of action, will bring a man to no less glorious summits than are attained by perilous paths and ostentatious deaths with no advantage to the Commonwealth.' The fervour and acerbity in this outburst belies the normal gravity of the Roman and the senator. There lies the clue. Tacitus is referring to certain victims of the tyranny, and to a whole party of the opposition, namely that party which began with Thrasea Paetus in the reign of Nero and was continued by Helvidius Priscus and his son, and by Junius Rusticus. After the assassination of Domitian there was a loud call for vengeance, and some took up the cry whose claim or tie was distant and tenuous. They were frustrated, but they made a great fuss. Tacitus proclaims his dislike for the noisy advocates of the heroes and the martyrs.

Agricola had not been of that company. He had practised 'obsequium', which means obedience to legitimate authority—from the higher expedience, from loyalty to Rome and the Empire, whoever the Emperor might be. Tacitus is defending Agricola. He is also defending himself. Where, and with whom, had the senator Tacitus stood during Domitian's reign? Fifteen years of silence, he asserts. Those who survived the tyranny were maimed and dazed and blunted, only shadows and relics of their former selves. Yet the whole reign had not been of one colour, and horror. Not everybody had been condemned to silence, and senators advanced in the career of honours, some unobtrusively, others (especially in the last years) by leaps and bounds. What is the grievance of Tacitus? He puts every emphasis on Domitian's jealous grudge against Agricola, but he cannot pretend that his own career suffered any set-back.

A casual detail provides a corrective. The historian himself supplies it later, in the *Annales*. When praetor in 88, he was already in possession of a priesthood. He was *quindecimvir sacris faciundis*. Member, that is to say, of one of the four highest in esteem of the sacerdotal colleges. It was rare for a man without ancestors to win a dignity of such eminence before the consulate. Tacitus must have been high in favour with the Emperor, or with the managers of patronage. Furthermore, he was *consul suffectus* in 97. It is generally (and conveniently) assumed that he owed the consulate to Nerva and to Nerva's friends. He might, however, have been on Domitian's list, designated already in 96.

So far Tacitus in relation to the *Agricola*. There is somebody else, who likewise was not conspicuous among the enemies of Domitian (while Domitian lived): M. Ulpius Traianus, whom Nerva adopted in October of 97. Nerva's choice fell not upon some aristocrat of ancient lineage, but upon a member of the new imperial aristocracy. Like Agricola Trajan was one of the new Romans from the provinces of the west. Like Agricola he knew the Empire and the armies, and had practised the virtue of *obsequium*. The two men are linked in Agricola's biography: Agricola by his death was spared many tribulations, but frustrated of one felicity. He had hoped and prayed to see Trajan as *princeps*.

Trajan was the right man, 'capax imperii'. That phrase is not found in the *Agricola*, but it occurs elsewhere in the writings of Tacitus more than once, and it is highly significant. To the least percipient of readers in the modern age the phrase will evoke the Emperor Galba, whom the insurrections in the west that brought down Nero conveyed to the power for a brief tenure ending in disaster, 'omnium consensu capax imperii nisi imperasset'. And Galba became startling and contemporary when history repeated itself less than thirty years later, when another dynasty ended abruptly.

The elevation of Galba was an accident, the product of the confused events before and after the fall of Nero. The armies acquiesced, but some were sullen and angry. In Upper Germany the legions had offered the purple to their commander, Verginius Rufus, who refused: only the Senate, he said, was competent to confer the power. Verginius affirmed a principle, and embellished his fame thereafter. In truth the power was beyond his reach—being the first of his family to enter the governing class, he lacked prestige and alliances.

Galba had birth, wealth, and a reputation. Empire found him out. In desperation he chose an associate, whom he adopted as his son and heir. Not a man who knew government and the armies, but a young aristocrat of blameless character, Piso Licinianus—who had lived long in exile. A bad choice, and in any event too late. The legions on the Rhine already had proclaimed an emperor of their own, Vitellius. Galba perished but not in battle against Vitellius: he was killed in the Roman Forum by the Praetorian Guard, whose candidate was Otho. A sequence of wars and proclamations began, with Otho and Vitellius destroyed in turn before the year was out.

When a generation had elapsed and the dynasty of the Flavii went the way of the Julii and Claudii, past history came to life again, sudden and menacing. How far would the resemblance go? The conspirators had been able to produce an emperor, M. Cocceius Nerva, whom birth and social elegance commended, with a long experience at court and all the diplomatic arts. But Nerva had never seen a province or an army. How long would he last?

Despotism was abolished, and Rome was born anew. 'Libertas' and 'Roma renascens' duly appear on the currency—and other legends that recall 68 and 69. Thus 'concordia exercituum', announcing that the armies are of one mind in loyalty to the government. That assertion was sinister, and suggestive. The armies had yet to speak. It was everybody's secret since Nero's end that an emperor did not have to be made at Rome.

In the course of the year 97 rumours were going about—the governor of Syria might be the next emperor. Nothing happened, and the great armies in the zone of the northern frontiers on Rhine and Danube showed no overt menace. In the month of October the storm broke. It originated in the city of Rome.

The Guard rose in mutiny. The soldiers besieged the Palace, calling for vengeance on the assassins of Domitian. Nerva complied, and he was forced to render solemn and public thanks to the troops. He had forfeited all authority, and his government was tottering to its fall. He could not escape to the armies, but there was one remedy, and he took it. Mounting the Capitol, he stood before the altar of Juppiter Optimus Maximus, there to announce that he took a partner in the power. He nominated one of the generals, Trajan, the governor of Upper Germany. All disturbance abated, and everybody was happy.

Galba and Nerva: the parallel of an adoption in extremity was patent —the outcome by contrast felicitous. There were aristocrats available, among them Calpurnius Crassus whose pedigree carried names of ancient power, the dynasts Crassus and Pompeius (and he was nephew of the Piso chosen by Galba), but Nerva passed them over. Trajan belonged to the new aristocracy of the Empire.

And there were other parallels of scene and of character between 69 and 97. Now Tacitus was consul in 97, a fact of vital importance in his conversion from oratory to the writing of history. Of his actions in the tenure of that office only one thing stands on record. A letter of his friend Pliny narrates the obsequies of the venerable Verginius Rufus, who died after a long illness at the age of eighty-three. Verginius was accorded a public funeral, the laudation being spoken by the consul Cornelius Tacitus: 'nam hic supremus felicitati eius cumulus accessit, laudator eloquentissimus'.

Verginius Rufus survived the emperors whose hatred and suspicion he incurred. Producing his encomium Tacitus cannot have failed to see that another great and good man might be honoured in like fashion— Julius Agricola, who died before the truth could be told. To discover the link between Verginius and Agricola requires no effort or ingenuity. It is there. Pliny towards the end of his letter echoes and adapts the peroration of Tacitus' *Agricola*.

In a laudation upon Verginius Rufus the bare facts were sharp and vocal—the end of a dynasty, the claimants for the power, the temper of the generals, and the sentiments of the armies. An orator whose talent combined majesty and subtlety, though constrained perhaps to curb his gift for damaging innuendo, will not have missed the chance to deliver a sermon on obedience to the *res publica*, a solemn prophecy on the august theme 'capax imperii'.

It would be worth knowing, for more reasons than one, precisely when Tacitus was holding the *fasces*. The list of consuls for 97 was a long one (many of Domitian's designations being kept for concord, along with the candidates of the new government). A fragment of the *Fasti Ostienses* recently discovered reveals the names of several *consules suffecti*—but Ostia still withholds the name of Cornelius Tacitus. It is clear enough that his tenure falls in the second half of the year—and it might well have embraced the momentous month of October. If so, Tacitus could have been present at that cabinet council which ratified, if it did not enforce,

Nerva's decision to adopt Trajan: when Galba adopted Piso, a consul and a consul-designate were present.

However it be, Tacitus witnessed the disintegration of a government, and was in a position to learn the true story behind the adoption. Of that transaction the best evidence, and almost the only evidence, comes from an official oration, the *Panegyricus* of Pliny. The orator affirms that Nerva acted under the direct inspiration of divine Providence. It may be surmised that other agencies were at work, while Trajan stood at Moguntiacum, the chief place of arms in Upper Germany, waiting while the Roman government grew weaker, and ready to march if no summons came.

That is, a veiled *coup d'état*. It had become abundantly clear that the next emperor after Nerva would be a military man, either after a civil war, or averting a civil war. The adoption was tantamount to an abdication, so the orator concedes—and Nerva conveniently died about three months later.

Nerva's reign was a theme to excite any historian—but the truth was too dangerous to be told, and perhaps it would never be published. Tacitus (it can be argued) felt the impact of what had happened, and reveals it by his *Historiae*, and in his *Historiae*. In the *Agricola* he announced the reign of Domitian as his subject. Some years pass, and when the *Historiae* begin to see the light the design has been modified. Not Domitian. He went farther back for a beginning, but not to the fall of Nero. He chose the first day of January 69: the day on which the legions at Moguntiacum refused allegiance to Galba. The topic of adoption is thrown into initial prominence by an oration from Galba; and the other three speeches in Book 1 are allocutions to the Praetorian Guard. Let it be maintained against Cornelius Tacitus that one year of Nerva was better schooling for an historian than the fifteen years of Domitian.

The theme of the *Historiae* of Tacitus is the murderous story of civil war and despotism. For his models he went back to the classic historians of Rome. For style Sallust and Livy were the paramount pair, equal in rank but totally diverse—'pares magis quam similes'. For that is the epigrammatic verdict transmitted by the judicious Quintilian, not his own, but coined by one of the imperial historians, Servilius Nonianus, consul and proconsul of Africa.

Sallust and Livy. It was the ambition of Cornelius Tacitus to surpass them both, more splendid in his writing than Sallust, more concentrated than Livy, more penetrating, and more ferocious.

III

TACITUS ON GAUL*

ACITUS ON GAUL. The title seems paradoxical, for the name of the historian of imperial Rome is linked for ever with a small work he composed concerning the land of Germany, its tribes and their habits.

The *Germania* is a precious opuscule. It is unique—yet it is not original. The *Germania* of Tacitus belongs to a recognizable type, the ethnographical excursus or essay, and it had models and precursors. As one would expect, the *Germania* exhibits various defects of the genre, especially the use of conventional and inherited motifs. Furthermore, not all of the historical information is up to date. It looks as though Tacitus recorded what he had read in books, not what he had seen and observed. It seems pretty clear that he followed his source very closely, not adding many details.

Much has been written about the *Germania* of Tacitus, perhaps too much. It has appealed to students of literature, and to historians, to researchers in European origins, to patriots and to politicians. It may be a change and a relief to turn instead and enquire what Tacitus has to say about Gaul. Something may emerge about the history of Imperial Rome, about the historian himself—his art, his methods, his predilections.

It is often alleged that Tacitus' acquaintance with the Roman world was narrow and imperfect: he knew little, and he cared little, about the provinces. Some critics have even taken him to task quite sharply. Tacitus, they say, would have been a better man, and a better historian, if he had gone more widely about the lands of the Empire. Travel would enlarge a man's sympathies, it would diminish his pessimism, and take him out of the miasma of metropolitan corruption into the pure atmosphere of provincial morality.

Such opinions are hasty and superficial. They depend upon deductions from the writings of the historian, especially from the *Annales*, the story

* A lecture delivered at the University of Liège on 13 March 1952; reprinted from *Latomus* XII (1953), 27–37.

of the Caesars from Tiberius to Nero.[1] And, at first sight, that work seems narrow in scope, being concentrated mainly upon Rome, the emperors and the Senate. However, let it be recalled that Tacitus is a political historian. Rome is the seat and centre of the imperial government, and Tacitus' central theme is the relations between the Caesars and the senatorial aristocracy.

The provinces hardly seem to come into his narrative. Spain does not attract the author of the *Annales*, there is little about the Danubian provinces, the Balkan lands, or inner Anatolia.

And why should there be? In normal times the provinces are almost wholly devoid of identity, for the true units throughout the territories of the Empire are tribes or towns. It is not to be expected or tolerated that a Roman historian should compose tribal, local, or municipal history.

For long years in the long imperial peace, most regions are devoid of incident or notoriety. Spain was a vast area, embracing three provinces. In the past it had bulked largely in the wars of Rome, foreign or civil, from the days of the Scipiones down to the final pacification under Caesar Augustus. Yet Spain contributes nothing to the *Annales* (so far as preserved) except the assassination of one governor and the prolonged absence of another.[2]

Towns and tribes and provinces lead a quiet indescribable existence, remote from history. When civil war comes, they enter the orbit of great events, their power and resources will turn the scale. As a form of government, the Principate itself took its origin in the provinces, and the *imperatores* implanted at Rome the absolute power that they had exerted abroad. There was a great secret of empire, 'arcanum imperii', says Tacitus, referring to the civil wars after the fall of Nero: an emperor did not have to be made at Rome.[3] But, surely, it was not a secret. It had been anxiously covered up, but everybody knew the dangerous truth.

The provinces, it is agreed, are not prominent in the *Annales*. A vital fact, however, has been omitted. The *Annales* as we have them are incomplete. The work breaks off in Book XVI, in the course of the year 66. That was not the end determined by the historian. His plan can be conjectured—and why should he not have lived to complete it? A work of eighteen books in three groups of six. Namely, six for Tiberius Caesar, six for Claudius and Caligula, and six for Nero.

---

[1] The present argument will therefore be confined to the *Annales*.
[2] *Ann.* IV. 25 (L. Piso); VI. 27. 3 (L. Arruntius).
[3] *Hist.* I. 4. 2: 'evulgato imperii arcano posse principem alibi quam Romae fieri'.

Nor is it idle to add a further conjecture about the missing conclusion of the *Annales*. What were the main subjects treated in Book XVII and in Book XVIII? The answer is clear. First, Book XVII: the tour in Greece organized by the emperor who was devoted to all things Greek, and to every kind of display and pageantry. Also the insurrection of the Jews. Second, Book XVIII: the risings in the western provinces, the fall of Nero and the catastrophe of the Julio-Claudian dynasty (A.D. 68).

The first move against Nero came from one of the Gallic provinces. Julius Vindex, the governor of Lugdunensis, raised a rebellion but was defeated in battle by Verginius Rufus, commander of the army of Upper Germany. Rufus stood loyal by Nero, but Nero lacked spirit and energy.

Vindex the insurgent had tried to induce other governors to join the revolt. Only one of them would listen to him. It was Sulpicius Galba, the legate of Hispania Tarraconensis; and, although Galba's position seemed hopeless after the defeat of his ally Vindex, Nero also gave up hope, and through a chain of accidents and misunderstandings Galba became emperor after all.

Such, in brief, would be the climax of the *Annales*. Tacitus as a writer is not only a master of style and colour, of movement and drama. He has a supreme gift for arrangement and architectonics. He sees the field in front of him and knows how to prepare his effects in advance. The rising of Julius Vindex is not merely the initial action that provokes the overthrow of Nero: it is a climax and turning-point in the relations between the Roman government and the peoples of Tres Galliae.

There was a Gallic problem in the early Principate, and Tacitus was well aware of it. What was its nature?

The Gaul which Julius Caesar had invaded, crushed, and conquered remained tranquil on the whole. Yet the Roman government was vigilant and distrustful. The land was large and populous, with an old tradition of martial glory. The Gauls were a collection of tribes, not a nation; yet the resistance to Julius Caesar had called forth a national spirit. It might still be very dangerous.

The invasions of Germany in the time of Caesar Augustus helped to support Roman rule in Gaul. Rome could claim to be the protector of the Gauls, their ally in a war which for the Gauls (who remembered Ariovistus and others) was a war of revenge. The chieftains of Gaul and the levies of Gaul marched with the Roman legions into Germany (and perhaps did much of the fighting).

But the conquest of Germany had been abandoned. The revolt of Arminius and the loss of three legions was a sharp lesson to the Roman government—and might be an incitement to the peoples of Gaul. How was the Roman government to deal with the problem?

No legions were stationed in the interior of Gaul. At first sight a sign of confidence. In truth, there was a strategic reason. Eight legions stood along the Rhine, from Vetera (Xanten) to Vindonissa (Windisch, near Bâle). They seem to face Germany, to repel attack or to resume the conquest of that country. But they can face both ways—Gaul as well as Germany.[1] That indeed is the special function of two of the four legions in the Upper German command, those at Argentorate (Strasbourg) and Vindonissa. There were hardly any Germans in Baden and in the Schwarzwald. No: the legion at Strasbourg is ready for war—but not against Germans. The legion will march by Saverne on Metz and Reims. As for the other legion, from Bâle it is a short step, by the Gap of Belfort between Vosges and Jura to Besançon and then to Dijon, at the strategic centre of the whole country. Any Gallic insurrection will be crushed with promptitude.

Gaul under the early Empire remained very much as it had been before. Though men come down from the old *oppida*, and cities are founded in the plain (thus among the Aedui the new town Augustodunum takes the place of Bibracte), though the cities themselves prosper, though commerce flourishes and education spreads, the social structure subsists. Gaul is still rural rather than urban, feudal rather than municipal. It is a land of tribes and tribal chieftains, of large estates, country houses—and much of the population in serfdom or close to it. In short, a medieval stage of civilization: the manorhouse and the village.

The evidence provided by Caesar in the *Bellum Gallicum* can be regarded as still valid. Caesar shows perfect examples of the Gallic baron. First, Orgetorix of the Helvetii—'longe nobilissimus fuit et ditissimus'.[2] This man had an establishment, a *familia*, of ten thousand men. And in addition, a large number of 'clientes obaeratique'.[3] With the help of these retainers and dependants, Orgetorix was able to do as he pleased and to baffle the process of justice among the Helvetii.

Second, the Aeduan chieftain Dumnorix, the friend and ally of Orgetorix. The facts about Dumnorix are the classic text for dynastic marriages

---

[1] *Ann.* iv. 5. 1: 'sed praecipuum robur Rhenum iuxta, commune in Germanos Gallosque subsidium, octo legiones erant'.

[2] *BG* i. 2. 1.

[3] *BG* i. 4. 2: 'Orgetorix ad iudicium omnem suam familiam ad hominum milia decem undique coegit et omnis clientis obaeratosque suos, quorum magnum numerum habebat, eodem conduxit: per eos ne causam diceret se eripuit'.

among the *principes* of Gaul.[1] Dumnorix had extended his power far and wide, and he had not confined his operations to taking a wife from among the Helvetii, the daughter of Orgetorix. He had made his mother marry a 'homo nobilissimus ac potentissimus' among the Bituriges; and he had used his half-sister and his female relatives to contract matrimonial alliances in other tribes.

By contrast, the old *provincia*, Gallia Narbonensis, which is organized on the municipal system. The population was mixed in origin, and perhaps not Celtic by predominance; hardly any of the tribes (except the Allobroges) had a national memory of wars against the Romans; by climate and products it was a Mediterranean region; there was a tendency to live in towns; and, Roman civilization supervening upon the Hellenic, the *provincia* might have grown and developed upon the Italian model even if there had been no colonies established there of Roman veterans.

'Italia verius quam provincia.' So was Narbonensis designated.[2] Facts confirm the phrase. The inhabitants of the Narbonensian province are recruited for the Roman legions, and even, at an early date, for the Praetorian Guard—but they are hardly ever found in the auxiliary regiments. The young men of the municipal aristocracies enter the imperial service as officers in the legions (*tribuni militum*) and go on to financial posts as *procuratores Augusti*. And, the next stage, these families produce Roman senators.[3] A number are attested in the early Empire. The first consul from the western provinces was Cornelius Balbus in 40 B.C., a man from Gades in Spain: a portentous and isolated phenomenon of the revolutionary age. The second comes in the reign of Tiberius Caesar in A.D. 35—Valerius Asiaticus from Vienna (which had once been a tribal capital, the city of the Allobroges).[4]

Narbonensis, therefore, belongs with the civilized parts of Spain—and with that zone of northern Italy that can be described as 'provincia verius quam Italia', namely Italia Transpadana. Climate, history, organization, and administration, everything separates Narbonensis from Tres Galliae.

To return, therefore, to Gaul properly so called. The natives are not normally permitted to serve in the Roman legions, but only in auxiliary

---

[1] *BG* I. 7. 3 ff.

[2] Pliny, *NH* III. 31: 'agrorum cultu, virorum morumque dignatione, amplitudine opum nulli provinciarum postferenda breviterque Italia verius quam provincia'.

[3] The prime example is the family of Julius Agricola—'utrumque avum procuratorem Caesarum habuit, quae equestris nobilitas est' (*Agr.* 4. 1).

[4] As recently revealed by a fragment of the *Fasti Ostienses, Inscr. It.* XIII. 1, p. 188.

formations;[1] and the chieftains command tribal regiments, but only seldom occupy the position of *tribunus militum* in the Roman legions or find employment as *procuratores* in the service of the Roman government.[2] And, being tribal chieftains, the Gallic *principes*, despite their wealth and education, cannot expect to have access to the governing class of Rome, like the families from the *coloniae et municipia* of Narbonensis or Spain.

The facts about the social structure of Tres Galliae are plain and patent. On the one hand, the chieftains, of old dynastic families, great owners of property; on the other, a large population, tenants or even serfs. Clearly not a region that could be readily amalgamated with the regions of town governments—Italy, Narbonensis, and the more civilized parts of Spain.

What then was to be the destiny of Gaul? An important part of the Roman Empire, rich and populous, yet not integrated with the more vital parts and not contributing to the imperial administrative class. And Gaul might also prove troublesome.

Trouble might originate either among the barons or among the depressed class. Like their ancestors, the Gallic nobles were proud and bellicose, rejoicing in splendour and display. Hence quarrels, extravagance, and debts. Their pride would be injured by subjection to the Roman rule—and they might envy the opportunities of the Narbonensians, who had admittance to the Roman governing class. And they resented the burden of Roman taxation.

Such were the grievances of the rich. Discontent among the country population threatened a social revolution that would easily and perhaps inevitably take the form of a national rising against foreign rule. And nationalism might be fanned by superstition.

There were Druids—but what are Druids precisely? The old priestly and aristocratic class of Druids known from Caesar seems to have faded out.[3] Why was this? Presumably because the nobles had quickly abandoned the traditional education, turning with eagerness to the dominant

---

[1] The total of Gallic legionaries discoverable in the first century of the Empire does not reach even a dozen. A single group of eight in III *Augusta* in Africa, of the Flavian period, furnishes almost all the evidence (*Inscr. lat. de l'Algérie* 3115, 3116, 3117, 3118, 3120, 3125, 3535 [Theveste]; *Inscr. lat. de l'Afrique* 152 [Ammaedara]).

[2] The notable exception is C. Julius Alpinus Classicianus, appointed procurator of Britain at the time of Boudicca's rebellion, cf. *Ann.* XIV. 38. 4, and the inscription at London, *CIL* VII. 30 + *AE* 1936, 3. His wife is called 'Iulia Indi filia Pacata I[ndiana]', presumably daughter of the Treveran noble Julius Indus, who was loyal to Rome at the time of the rising of Florus and Sacrovir (*Ann.* III. 42. 3).

[3] The class is represented by Diviciacus the Aeduan, with whom Cicero had converse (*De Div.* I. 90).

language and culture of the civilized world. When that happened, the old religious and magical beliefs sank into the lower classes and retained their potency there. If the name of the Druids survived, it now adhered to village sorcerers and rural magicians.

Druidic practices, we are informed, were officially proscribed by the Roman government in the time of Tiberius Caesar.[1] For what reason? Was it the abominable rite of human sacrifices? Perhaps. Yet it is not at all likely that the ritual was still being carried out in Gaul.[2] The belief in witchcraft, however, still kept much of its strength. And witchcraft might not always be harmless. It might operate as a subversive and revolutionary force among the credulous and fanatical population of the countryside, and, working upon social discontent, lend fuel to a nationalist insurrection against the Roman rule.[3]

The danger that Gaul presented to the Roman government now becomes clearer. It arose precisely from the social structure. A discontented noble would have allies among his own class and kin—but he could also gather a large following of clients and serfs among the depressed country population.

Such in brief is the Gallic problem. Tacitus in the *Annales* expounds it in three episodes concerning the *principes* of Tres Galliae.

The first episode belongs to the year 21.[4] It is an insurrection. Two

---

[1] Pliny, *NH* xxx. 13: 'Gallias utique possedit, et quidem ad nostram memoriam. namque Tiberii Caesaris principatus sustulit Druidas eorum et hoc genus vatum medicorumque'. The statement is precious. Pliny, born in 23 or 24, had lengthy equestrian service on the Rhine (for a large part of the period 47–58), and was later procurator of Gallia Belgica, so it appears, about 74 or 75 (cf. *NH* xviii. 183). Pliny also reports the Druidic superstition that proved fatal to a Roman knight (from the Vocontii in Narbonensis) under Claudius (*NH* xxix. 54). Suetonius, who assigns to Claudius the abolition of Druidism (*Divus Claudius* 25. 5), cannot compete.

[2] Human sacrifices had been suppressed by the Romans, according to Strabo the geographer (iv, p. 198). Strabo's testimony is valid for a much earlier period than the latest dated incidents in his work (A.D. 18 and 19) might appear to indicate. Pomponius Mela (iii. 18) refers to an innocuous vestigial remnant: 'manent vestigia feritatis iam abolitae, atque ut ab ultimis caedibus temperant, ita nihilominus, ubi devotos altaribus admovere, delibant'. This author was writing precisely in the year 43 (cf. iii. 49). But there is no sign that he is referring to a contemporary or recent cessation of ritual murders.

[3] The abject superstition of the rural population among the Aedui is shown by the episode of Mariccus in 69. This person claimed to be a god and gathered about him a 'fanatica multitudo' of eight thousand followers (*Hist.* ii. 61). In the next year Druids emerged, and, encouraged by the burning of the Capitol, announced the imminent fall of the Roman power, so Tacitus affirms (*Hist.* iv. 54. 2). The testimony of a Roman consular ought not to be ignored or discarded.

[4] *Ann.* iii. 40 ff.

3—T.S.I.T.

chieftains started it, Julius Florus among the Treveri, Julius Sacrovir among the Aedui. The historian provides a full and detailed account—how the two *principes* formed the plot, and gathered great hosts of followers. Among the Aedui Sacrovir had forty thousand men at his back, but this was not an army, only a vast multitude, few of whom were properly equipped with weapons.

The Roman legions on the Rhine intervened, and the revolt was crushed. Not, however, before it had caused great alarm at Rome. It was even believed that all the tribes of Gaul had risen.

Next, the second episode, in the year 48. Not in Gaul but in Rome, and in the Senate House. And the sharpest possible contrast. The Emperor Claudius admits to senatorial rank a number of the *principes* of Tres Galliae, and he explains and justifies his policy by an oration to the high assembly.

The speech is extant, almost complete. It is preserved on a bronze tablet at Lugdunum.[1] One of the most precious of all historical documents, it carries the authentic language of Claudius Caesar and reveals not a little of his psychology.

Yet the oration is not altogether satisfactory as an exposition of imperial policy. Remorseless in erudition and in pedantry, Claudius insists on delivering a long lecture on early Roman and Etruscan history; and when he comes to the point, certain of his central arguments are hasty, superficial, and fallacious.

Tacitus shows more skill and insight. He proceeds in two ways.[2] First, he invents a speech in reported discourse, giving the arguments employed against Claudius Caesar in private by the members of his Council. And, a remarkable feature, those arguments are trivial and emotional. They appeal to national prejudice and ancient history. The Gauls, exclaim the counsellors of Claudius, are foreigners, and nothing less than the hereditary enemies of the Roman People. Why, their ancestors captured the city of Rome.

Second, Tacitus produces an improved version of the *Oratio Claudi Caesaris*. He purges and prunes the imperial discourse, he strengthens and ennobles it. The argument acquires proportion, coherence, and power.

The third episode produces another surprise. Twenty years after Claudius had brought Gallic chieftains into the Roman Senate, Julius Vindex rose in revolt against Nero. Julius Vindex was not only a Roman

[1] *ILS* 212.   [2] *Ann.* XI. 23 f.

senator and governor of one of the Gallic provinces—he was a Gaul himself, a descendant of kings in Aquitania.[1]

There has been much debate about the rising of Julius Vindex. Was it a move to dethrone a tyrant—or was it a native insurrection against the Roman rule?

What impelled Vindex in the first instance will never be known. Perhaps some small incident or personal motive. However, whatever the cause, whatever the programme announced by Vindex in his revolt against Nero, that revolt quickly took the form of a native insurrection. Other chieftains joined him, and he acquired a host of followers, a hundred thousand, it is said.[2] But this too was not a regular army. The fate of Florus and Sacrovir was re-enacted. The Rhine legions duly marched against him, and Vindex was defeated at Vesontio (Besançon).

The rising of Julius Vindex led to the fall of Nero. It had another result. It seemed to demonstrate that a Roman senator from Gaul was still a Gallic baron. It was Claudius who argued that such men would be useful members of the Roman Senate. What happened now seemed to refute and condemn the Emperor—and justify the opposition of his counsellors.

The lesson was not lost. In the next age there can have been very few Roman senators from Tres Galliae. Instead, the Emperors continue to recruit the governing class from Spain and Narbonensis. The process spreads quickly to Africa and to the Greek East. Men from the cities of Asia become senators, and Galatians, of Celtic ancestry, the descendants of kings and tetrarchs.[3] But Gaul is missing.

To return to Cornelius Tacitus. He skilfully causes the Gallic problem to unfold in three episodes—Florus and Sacrovir, the Emperor Claudius, and Vindex. Taken altogether, those three episodes permit and encourage three deductions.

First, he has precise knowledge about Gaul. Note, for example, in the account of Florus and Sacrovir the phrase 'obaerati et clientes' or the detail about Augustodunum, the city of the Aedui—it was a centre of polite studies for the aristocratic youth of Gaul.[4]

---

[1] Cassius Dio LXIII. 22. 1. His father had been a senator, presumably one of those admitted by Claudius in the year 48.

[2] Josephus, *BJ* IV. 440: ἅμα τοῖς δυνατοῖς τῶν ἐπιχωρίων. Plutarch (*Galba* 8) gives the total of a hundred thousand followers.

[3] As C. Julius Severus is styled (*OGIS* 544: Ancyra).

[4] *Ann.* III. 43. 1: 'nobilissimam Galliarum subolem, liberalibus studiis ibi operatam'. Notice also how Tacitus in his version of the speech of Claudius emphasizes the cultural contribution of the Gauls: 'iam moribus artibus adfinitatibus nostris mixti' (*Ann.* XI. 24. 4).

Second, Gaul has captured his interest. He gives a very full account of Florus and Sacrovir. Other writers might not have followed this procedure.[1] Above all, Tacitus is the only author to mention the admission of the Gallic chieftains by Claudius Caesar. There is not a word about it in Suetonius, Seneca, or Cassius Dio.[2]

Third, his sympathy. Tacitus has no high opinion of the Emperor Claudius. Yet he is clearly on the side of the Emperor against his counsellors. Claudius' speech is noble and sensible, whereas the arguments of the objectors are prejudiced and ridiculous.

This is encouraging. We seem to be on the way towards making an important discovery about Tacitus as a man and a historian. How is this combination of knowledge, insight, and sympathy to be explained?

Now it is a common opinion, as has been stated above, that Tacitus was not much interested in the Roman provinces. That opinion appears groundless. Those who criticize Tacitus have not always taken into account the official career of a Roman senator. Tacitus might easily have acquired personal knowledge of Gaul and the Rhineland.

First, in the earliest stage of the *cursus honorum*. The aspirant to senatorial honours normally spends a season as military tribune in a Roman legion. Tacitus was born about A.D. 56: his military service, falling about the year 76, might have been passed on the Rhine.

Second, most senators who wish to reach the consulate hold the command of a legion not long after their praetorship. Tacitus was praetor in 88, consul in 97.[3] Shortly after his praetorship, so he states in the *Agricola*, he was absent from Rome for the space of four years.[4] Perhaps as *legatus legionis* somewhere. Let us not be deterred by the pronouncement of Theodor Mommsen who described Tacitus as 'the most unmilitary of historians'.

So far his official career. Some have supposed that Tacitus when abroad in the period 89–93 was governor of Gallia Belgica. That post in a senatorial *cursus* falls, not after a man's praetorship, but just before his consulate. That is to say, it would have to be in the period 93–6 or 94–7.[5]

---

[1] The only other record is the brief allusion in Velleius Paterculus II. 129. 5.

[2] The history of Dio is fragmentary, it is true, but Suetonius devotes a chapter to the acts of the censorship (*Divus Claudius* 16). Seneca emphasizes and derides Claudius' lavish grants of the Roman citizenship (*Apocol.* 3. 3).

[3] For the date of his praetorship, *Ann.* XI. 11. 1.

[4] *Agr.* 45. 5.

[5] At that time Belgica was being governed by Glitius Agricola, who passed to the consulate in 97 (*ILS* 1021: Augusta Taurinorum).

And now, to conclude. There is something else. Where was Tacitus born? A precious detail about his parentage is preserved by the Elder Pliny in his *Naturalis Historia*. He states that he knew a Roman knight called Cornelius Tacitus who was imperial procurator of Gallia Belgica.[1] When was that? Perhaps in the period 55–8 about the time of Tacitus' birth. Pliny spent a large part of the period 47–58 in three officer positions, each of them with the armies of the Rhine.[2]

The procurator of Belgica was an important person. Upper and Lower Germany were included in his province, and he was thus paymaster-general for the armies of the Rhine. Officials generally had their wives with them. The future historian of Rome and the Empire may have seen the light of day in some city of Belgica or the Rhineland—Trèves, Reims, or Cologne.[3]

But the place where a man happens to be born is a mere accident. It is not his *patria*.[4] Where is the city of origin of the Cornelii Taciti? Not perhaps in Italy, but somewhere in the provinces of the Roman West. Could it be one of the cities of Narbonensis? But that subject would demand another investigation.

[1] *NH* VII. 76.

[2] As emerges from various passages in the *Naturalis Historia*. Cf. also his nephew's statement (*Epp.* III. 5. 4), and the phalera found at Vetera, *CIL* XIII. 10026[22]: 'Plinio praefec(to)'.

[3] Tacitus records under the year 58 a peculiar conflagration in the territory of Cologne (*Ann.* XIII. 57. 3). Notice also the sympathetic treatment of that community in his narrative of the year 70 (*Hist.* IV. 65).

[4] Thus the Emperor Hadrian was born at Rome, but Italica in Baetica was his 'patria' (HA, *Hadr.* 1. 3; 2. 1).

IV

MARCUS LEPIDUS, *CAPAX IMPERII**

T HE THEME 'capax imperii', immortalized by Tacitus' verdict on the Emperor Galba, runs through his writings, and imparts a unity to the record of conspiracies and civil wars. It emerges quickly in the *Annales*. Augustus, so an anecdote alleges, discussed the matter when his end was near, and made play with the names of three men. M. Lepidus, he said, had the capacity but no desire; Asinius Gallus was eager but not good enough; Arruntius, however, was not unworthy and might make a bid. Moreover, according to Tacitus, some versions named Cn. Piso instead of Arruntius.[1] There it might rest, a happy invention, or at least an unverifiable report, did not the story raise a problem of historical identity. Who was the Lepidus whom the dying Princeps rated so highly, Marcus or Manius ? The *Codex Mediceus* has 'M. Lepidum': all modern editors alter the *praenomen* and read 'M'. Lepidum'.

This passage is only the beginning of the trouble. Two Aemilii Lepidi of consular standing recur in the *Annales* and annoy the conscientious reader. They are not at all easy to keep apart, despite the operations of scholars since Justus Lipsius. Those operations have been considerable. Following Lipsius' lead, Borghesi and Nipperdey evolved a doctrine about the two Lepidi which won rapid and general acceptance, with hardly a murmur of dissent anywhere, and it now stands canonical both in editions of Tacitus and in the works of reference.[2] It involved an alteration of the manuscript reading, easy and trivial to all appearance—the substitution of the abbreviated *praenomen* M'. for M. That change was

---

* Reprinted from *JRS* XLV (1955), 22–33.

[1] *Ann.* I. 13. 2: 'M. Lepidum dixerat capacem sed aspernantem, Gallum Asinium avidum et minorem, L. Arruntium non indignum et si casus daretur ausurum. de prioribus consentitur, pro Arruntio quidam Cn. Pisonem tradidere; omnesque praeter Lepidum variis mox criminibus struente Tiberio circumventi sunt.'

[2] Nipperdey's doctrine was clearly formulated in his long note on III. 32. 2. For modern works it will be enough to adduce Groag in *PIR*², A 369. Nobody, it appears, gave heed to G. H. Walther, who in his edition (Halle, 1831) had put the case for M. Lepidus as 'capax imperii', using the right arguments. That scholar has generally been undervalued: he was firm and pertinacious against emendations.

made, not only in the passage in Book I about the 'capaces imperii', but in seven other places, no less. In consequence Marcus Lepidus dwindles miserably and is all but blotted out, whereas Manius is augmented and exalted. The time has come to challenge the legitimacy of the procedure, and to look at the results.[1]

I. Two branches of the Aemilii Lepidi survive the revolutionary wars and show consuls in the time of Augustus. A certain M'. Lepidus became consul in 66 B.C.[2] Unobtrusive in his conduct of that office, he is mentioned only twice thereafter, until the outbreak of the war between Pompeius and Caesar.[3] In January and February, 49 B.C., Lepidus was much in the company of certain other consulars, Cicero among them, whose doubts about the war and about the strategy of Pompeius Magnus he shared and perhaps intensified, reluctant to follow the Republic and its ostensible champion across the seas.[4] By the middle of March M'. Lepidus, reflecting in his attitude the course of events, was ready to return to the capital and attend in the Senate House at Caesar's bidding.[5] Nothing more is heard of this pliable and inconspicuous character. His son Q. Lepidus reached the consulate in 21 B.C. after keen and bitter competition with a rival, L. Silanus, and was proconsul of Asia.[6] No descendants are known.

The other line, by its tenacious ambition to recover primacy for the Aemilii, makes history and comes more than once within reach of the supreme power. There had been a great Marcus Lepidus, twice consul (187 and 175), censor and *princeps senatus*. It was his grandson, M. Lepidus, consul in 78 B.C., who raised civil war in Italy to overthrow the ordinances of Sulla the Dictator.[7] The younger son of the rebel, brought forward by

---

[1] Marcus in I. 13. 2, not Manius, was postulated (briefly) in *Roman Revolution* (1939), 433— and reiterated in *JRS* xxxix (1949), 7. Not having seen, however, that the emended items are vulnerable, each and all, I accepted the standard attribution of IV. 20. 2, to Manius Lepidus (*Rom. Rev.* 517: rejected in the reprint of 1952). The present paper was composed in 1948, the annotation added in 1955.

[2] He is M'. f. by filiation (*Inscr. de Délos* 1659). The parent can be the *monetalis* M'. Aemilius Lepidus (*BMC, R. Rep.* II. 291, no. 590=E. A. Sydenham, *The Roman Republican Coinage* (1952) 74, no. 554); and the presumed ancestor may be M. Aemilius M'. f. M'. n. (*cos.* 158).

[3] In 65, as one of the five consulars who testified against C. Cornelius (Asconius 53, cf. 70); and in 57 (*Ad Q. fratrem* II. 1. 1).

[4] *Ad Att.* VII. 12. 4, etc.

[5] ib. IX. 1. 12. He was dead by 44, cf. *Phil.* II. 12.

[6] *PIR*[2], A 376. The inscription on the Pons Fabricius (*CIL* I[2]. 751=*ILS* 5892) furnishes his filiation and shows that he could not be a son of the Triumvir.

[7] A grandson, cf. *Phil.* XIII. 15. The intermediate generation is represented by a Quintus: only an item of nomenclature.

Caesar's revival of defeated causes and predilection for patricians, found himself in a position of unexpected advantage when the Dictator was assassinated, and, in the alliance of the other Caesarian marshals, he attained an eminence above his capacities as one of the Triumviri ruling the Roman world. The Triumvir had several children. His son Marcus, detected in conspiracy by the vigilant Maecenas shortly after the battle of Actium, was put to death.[1] Another son, Quintus, has left no trace behind.[2] As with certain other *nobiles* in the time of Augustus, his existence has to be deduced from nomenclature. Quintus is the parent of Manius Lepidus, *consul ordinarius* in A.D. 11, whose style is 'Q.f.M.n.'.

Manius Lepidus is one of the perplexing pair of consulars that constitute the subject of this inquiry. He is introduced by Tacitus under the year 20. Aemilia Lepida, a profligate lady of birth and station, on trial for a variety of offences, was defended by her brother—'Manio Lepido fratre'.[3] The historian expounds her lineage and circumstances. A great-granddaughter of Sulla and of Pompeius, Lepida had been the intended bride of L. Caesar (the grandson and adopted son of Augustus). When the prince died (A.D. 2) she was given to the upstart P. Sulpicius Quirinius, a loyal servant of the dynasty. It also emerges in the course of the narrative that she had once been married to the aristocratic Mam. Aemilius Scaurus (*cos. suff.* A.D. 21), great-grandson of the *princeps senatus*, an illustrious orator but no paragon of conduct.[4]

The surprising details about the ancestry of Aemilia Lepida permit and encourage a genealogical reconstruction. It may be surmised that a Cornelia, daughter (otherwise unattested) of Faustus Sulla and Pompeia (the daughter of Magnus), married the insubstantial Q. Lepidus, son of the Triumvir.[5] Odd facts like these, and necessary surmises, reveal important ties of kinship in the *nobilitas*, especially among certain of the great houses which, defeated in the wars, form a depressed class in the earlier and middle years of the Augustan Principate, but emerge again and acquire prominence in its last decade—not without support, many of them, from Ti.

---

[1] *PIR²*, A 368. More things than one are questionable in this 'conspiracy', variously reported by Livy, *Per.* CXXXIII; Velleius II. 88; Appian, *BC* IV. 50. It is absent from Dio's narration, but alluded to subsequently under 18 B.C. (LIV. 15. 4).

[2] Unless he be the Q. Aemilius Lepidus in a list of sudden deaths taken by Pliny from Verrius Flaccus (*NH* VII. 181). That person, however, might be the parent of the consul of 78 B.C.

[3] III. 22. 1.   [4] VI. 29. 3: 'insignis nobilitate et orandis causis, vita probrosus'.

[5] cf. Groag's stemma of the Cornelii Sullae in *PIR²* III, facing p. 362. Aemilia Lepida is therefore a first cousin of Sulla Felix (*PIR²*, C 1463), the father of Faustus Sulla (*cos.* 31) and of L. Sulla Felix (*cos.* 33). Mam. Scaurus also comes in here, being both the uncle and the stepfather of a L. Sulla (*Ann.* III. 31. 4), i.e. probably the consul of 33.

Claudius Nero, who is now Ti. Caesar.[1] It is also, presumably, a link with
the offspring of Faustus Sulla and Pompeia that helps to explain how
L. Arruntius (*cos.* A.D. 6), though his father was the first consul in the
family, comes to rank among the men deemed worthy to rule.[2] Tacitus
when introducing Arruntius did not overload the anecdote with genealogical annotation: the pedigree was going to matter after the accession of
Claudius when a certain Camillus Scribonianus rose in armed rebellion.
This man was the son by blood or adoption of L. Arruntius.[3] Along with
the resuscitated glory of an ancient patrician house, the Furii Camilli, the
pretender asserted against Julii and Claudii the Sullan and Pompeian claim
to the Principate.

Such being the facts, M'. Aemilius Lepidus (*cos.* A.D. 11) could clearly
qualify as 'capax imperii'—at least on grounds of lineage, since he is not
only the grandson of M. Lepidus the Triumvir but carries in his veins the
blood of Sulla Felix and Pompeius Magnus. Pedigree against pedigree,
how does he stand when matched with the other consular Lepidus in the
Annales of Tacitus, M. Lepidus (*cos.* A.D. 6), who is the grandson of the
Triumvir's elder brother, L. Aemilius Paullus (*cos.* 50 B.C.)?

A venal character, and not likely to be swayed by principle or spirit,
Aemilius Paullus kept clear of the Civil Wars and, though proscribed by
the Triumvirs (his own brother among them), came to no harm, but escaped, took up his residence at the city of Miletus, and preferred to stay
there.[4] The son, Paullus Aemilius Lepidus (*suff.* 34 B.C.), more than retrieved all that the father had forfeited. Like some other astute young men
of the ancient patrician houses, he attached himself to the fortunes of
Octavianus about the time of the *Bellum Siculum* and soon found his fore-
sight rewarded with the consulate.[5] More significant perhaps was the
marriage he contracted in those years. His bride was a Cornelia, of Scipionic ancestry, as Propertius affirms in the lament he composed when she
died in 16 B.C.:

> testor maiorum cineres tibi, Roma, verendos,
> sub quorum titulis, Africa, tunsa iaces.[6]

---

[1] For depressed *nobiles*, *Rom. Rev.* 377; for the 'Pompeian' affinities of Tiberius, ib.
424 f.; for the mixed character of his following discernible after A.D. 4 (aristocrats and *novi
homines*), ib. 434 f. Cn. Cinna Magnus, who came late to the consulate in A.D. 5, is close
kin to the descendants of Faustus and Pompeia—being, indeed, the son of Pompeia by her
second marriage.

[2] Arruntius, like Mam. Scaurus, is described as a 'propinquus' of L. Sulla (III. 31. 3).

[3] Presumably by adoption, cf. Groag in *PIR²*, A 1140. Hence a further link with the
line of Magnus, attested by the name 'Scribonianus'. The son of the pretender Scribonianus
is described as 'a[bnepos]' or 'a[dnepos]' of Magnus (*ILS* 976).

[4] Appian, *BC* IV. 37.   [5] cf. *Rom. Rev.* 237 ff.   [6] Propertius IV. 11. 37 f., cf. 29 f.

If that were not enough, Cornelia, being daughter (by an earlier marriage) of Scribonia, was half-sister to Julia, the daughter of Augustus.[1]

The connection with the dynasty enhanced and maintained the distinction of the Aemilii. Paullus became censor in 22 B.C. Nor did the death of Cornelia sever the alliance with the family of Augustus. Paullus speedily married a niece, the younger Marcella.[2] Then the Aemilii rose to a dangerous height. The marriage of Paullus and Cornelia had produced two sons. The elder, L. Aemilius Paullus, married Julia, granddaughter of the Princeps, and became consul in A.D. 1—no doubt with some remission of the age limit. The Aemilii now stood close indeed to the succession. A mysterious catastrophe, designated as conspiracy against Augustus, consigned Julia's bridegroom to destruction.[3]

The younger son of Paullus is M. Aemilius Lepidus (*cos.* A.D. 6), whose qualifications must now be weighed against those of M'. Lepidus (*cos.* A.D. 11). As for pedigree alone, noble and patrician, the value it bore under the Republic of Augustus was exorbitant, greater surely than in the last age of the genuine Republic. Scipionic blood was a rare quality, with no Scipiones left in the direct succession after Cornelia's brother, P. Scipio (*cos.* 16 B.C.).[4] Descent from Sulla and Pompeius, also in the female line, was barely comparable in splendour. Yet social distinction did not always connote political importance. How does the balance move on this item? An answer can be given. The Cornelii Sullae, their relatives, and their allies are not permitted, so it seems, to achieve distinction for the greater part of the Principate of Augustus. Thus a shadowy Sulla, son of Faustus and Pompeia, does not reach the consulate.[5] Aemilia Lepida, it is true, is betrothed to L. Caesar, perhaps a significant hint of their re-emergence: the dynasty, in the absence of Ti. Claudius Nero at Rhodes, was building up support for itself in the families of the *nobilitas* that hitherto had been

---

[1] Scribonia's husbands are a pretty problem. Suetonius, mentioning her marriage to Octavianus in 40, calls her 'nuptam ante duobus consularibus' (*Divus Aug.* 62. 2). Hardly correct, cf. Groag in *PIR*², C 1395. The parent of Cornelia should be a P. Scipio, for her brother is P. Cornelius P. f. P. n. Scipio (*cos.* 16 B.C.). The *Fasti* of the *Magistri Vicorum* (first published in 1935) disclosed a P. Cornelius, suffect in 35 B.C. This ought to be the man, cf. *Rom. Rev.* 229 f. But other problems remain—who was his father?

[2] *PIR*², C 1103.

[3] Suetonius, *Divus Aug.* 19. 1, cf. the scholiast on Juvenal VI. 158. There is no other evidence. The incident may fall in A.D. 8, cf. *Rom. Rev.* 432. E. Hohl suggested A.D. 1 (*Klio* XXX (1937), 337 ff.).

[4] *PIR*², C 1438. That Scipionic descent may, however, derive from Lentuli Marcellini, cf. Groag's remarks under C 1395.

[5] The presumed parent of Sulla Felix (*PIR*², C 1463), and grandfather of the consuls of 31 and 33. His sister Cornelia is likewise only a genealogical construction, wife of Q. Lepidus M.f. (likewise not consul).

kept at a distance. This betrothal, however, can hardly compare with the ties that already bound the other Aemilii to the reigning house, and it was soon annulled by the death of the young prince. M. Lepidus, however, was a cousin of the Princeps' grandchildren, and his brother (L. Aemilius Paullus) was actually married to one of them, namely Julia.

There remains personal capacity and achievement, not to be neglected even under an aristocratic monarchy that was expected to bestow the consulate as of right on a *nobilis*, even the nastiest or the most incompetent.[1] Marcus Lepidus, the consul of A.D. 6, stands out as a paragon from the sloth and pretentiousness that was a traditional reproach against his class, and was exemplified by many aristocrats of that age, to the shame and anger of Tiberius Caesar.

When the great rebellion broke out in Illyricum and continued for three long years (6–9), Marcus Lepidus did not remain at Rome, to pass the time in indolence, in intrigue, or in frivolous criticism of the generals. He undertook military duties of high responsibility. At Siscia in the winter of 8 Lepidus was in charge of the army while Tiberius went to Rome; and in the next year he led the army southwards across Bosnia to Dalmatia, and shared in the final conquest of the country. For his services Lepidus was awarded the *ornamenta triumphalia*.[2] He may, or may not, have stayed to become the first governor of Illyricum superius (i.e. Dalmatia), when the province was divided on the termination of hostilities. Nor is it known whether he accompanied Tiberius to the Rhine. He is next heard of in 14. When the Princeps died, the armies were in the safe hands of men loyal to Tiberius Caesar. Lepidus held Hispania Tarraconensis with three legions.[3]

II. Birth, the dynastic connection, and *virtus*, such was Marcus Lepidus. Velleius Paterculus, writing in 29 or 30, styles him 'closest to the name and station of the Caesars'.[4] Surely, therefore, the 'capax imperii'. And here one inquiry might find its term, having established the *prima facie* case for

---

[1] Seneca, *De ben.* IV. 30. 1. He goes on to discuss Fabius Persicus and Mam. Scaurus.

[2] Velleius II. 114. 5; 115. 2 f.; Dio LVI. 12. 2, cf. 17. 2.

[3] Velleius II. 125. 5: 'at Hispanias exercitumque ⟨in iis cum M. Lepidus, de cuius⟩ virtutibus celeberrimaque in Illyrico militia praediximus, cum imperio obtineret, in summa pace et quiete continuit'. The supplement is due to Madvig. An inscription at Uxama honours a M. Aemilius Lepidus as 'patronus' (*CIL* II. 2820).

[4] id. II. 114. 5: 'autumno victor in hiberna reducitur exercitus, cuius omnibus copiis a Caesare M. Lepidus praefectus est, vir nomini ac fortunae Caesarum proximus, quem in quantum quisque aut cognoscere aut intellegere potuit, in tantum miratur ac diligit tantorumque nominum quibus ortus est ornamentum iudicat'. The *praenomen* 'M.' is one of the improvements (from the lost *Codex Murbacensis*) added by Burer to the *editio princeps* of Beatus Rhenanus.

rejecting the traditional and canonical emendation 'M'. Lepidum' in the first book of the *Annales*. It will be desirable, however, in the light of this experiment (and indeed necessary, if certainty is to be attained) to investigate the seven other instances where the consensus of scholarship acquiesces in the alteration of the manuscript reading.[1] Some of the changes might be wrong, perhaps all of them.

Even if the identity of the 'capax imperii' be waived for the moment, enough has been said to define the extraction and the personality of the two Lepidi. In the third book of the *Annales* the problem becomes acute. In two related episodes a Marcus Lepidus is mentioned. What is said about each excludes their identification. These two passages have always been the starting point of discussion about the two Lepidi.

Early in the year 21 Tiberius sent a missive to the Senate: as Tacfarinas had resumed his depredations in Africa, the Princeps suggested that the Senate should depart from the normal procedure of balloting and choose a proconsul with military experience and in sound health.[2] Whereupon one of the consulars, Sex. Pompeius (*cos.* 14), inspired by personal enmity (and eager no doubt to accelerate his own prospects for one of the two proconsulates), seized the chance to make an attack on Marcus Lepidus (the *praenomen* is here written out in full, 'Marcum Lepidum'). Lepidus, he said, was lazy and impoverished, a disgrace to his ancestors: he ought to be debarred from competing for the province of Asia. The Senate, however, took Lepidus under its protection. They held him to be not a slothful character, but gentle rather; his straitened circumstances were an inherited disability; he had sustained his rank without reproach, and that should count towards his repute, not against. The upshot was that Lepidus went to Asia, the decision about Africa being left to the Princeps. Proceedings then deviated into a debate about the propriety of governors taking their wives with them.[3]

When the Senate next assembled, Tiberius wrote complaining that all responsibility was thrust upon his own shoulders. He put forward two names for the proconsulate of Africa—'M. Lepidum et Iunium Blaesum nominavit'.[4] Lepidus, however, did his best to get out of it. He alleged the state of his health, the tender years of his children, a daughter of age to be married. There was one reason which he chose to dissemble—Blaesus was the uncle of Seianus. Blaesus was appointed.[5]

---

[1] viz. III. 11. 2; 35. 1; 50. 1; IV. 20. 2; 56. 3; VI. 5. 1; 27. 4.
[2] III. 32. 1.   [3] III. 33 f.   [4] III. 35. 1.
[5] Q. Junius Blaesus (*suff.* A.D. 10), succeeding L. Apronius (*suff.* 8), who had a triennial tenure, and to be replaced, after two years, by P. Cornelius Dolabella (*cos.* 10).

In the one or the other of the two instances, 'Marcum Lepidum' and 'M. Lepidum', the manuscript reading must be altered to produce the other Lepidus, Manius. The accepted remedy is to keep the first and alter the second, and easy it is, to 'M'. Lepidum'. The result is then that M. Lepidus went to Asia in 21, whereas M'. Lepidus was deemed by Tiberius suitable for special appointment, for military needs, to the proconsulate of Africa.

That will not do. It makes nonsense of all that can be established, in an independent fashion, about the two Lepidi. First, military experience. Manius had none, so far as is known, whereas Marcus had been Tiberius' legate in Illyricum. Next, personality. The man whom Sex. Pompeius attacked and the Senate defended ('Marcum' in the text) is not an active or illustrious character. With all the license of personal invective at Rome, it is not possible to tax as slothful and degenerate a consular who has commanded armies in active warfare and governed the province of Tarraconensis; and, on the other side, the friendly Senate's defence, gentle manners and no wrong-doing—'nobilitatem sine probro actam'—is equally ludicrous as an apologia on behalf of a 'vir triumphalis'.

The conclusion is inescapable. The correction of the *praenomen* should be made in the first case, not in the second. Reading there (III. 32. 2) 'Manium Lepidum' instead of 'Marcum Lepidum', all is in order. Manius (*cos.* A.D. 11), the inert fellow, after a public discussion of his personality and capacities, which even on the most favourable interpretation cannot be called resplendent, succeeds in maintaining his claim to a proconsulate by lot, and goes to Asia. Marcus (*cos.* A.D. 6), the military man, was put forward by Tiberius, his old commander, for Africa.[1]

The correction from 'Marcum' to 'Manium' can be supported by an argument about Tacitus' practices in the matter of nomenclature. If the *Codex Mediceus* is to be trusted, the *praenomen* of Marcus Lepidus does not appear elsewhere in the *Annales* written out in full, but only in the abbreviated form, 'M.' 'Manius,' however, is a *praenomen* of an archaic type. It is an old *nomen*.[2] Though not so rare and remarkable as 'Appius', 'Mamercus', and 'Servius', which are confined almost exclusively to certain patrician houses, it is none the less an uncommon *praenomen*, and may, like the others, have shown a tendency to resist abbreviation.[3] Now in the

---

[1] cf. G. H. Walther's note—'virum Tiberius quaerebat gnarum militiae et bello suffecturum', etc. He had duly cited Velleius in support of 'M. Lepidum' in I. 13. 2. He therefore altered the received text in III. 32. 2, printing 'M'. Lepidum'.

[2] cf. F. Münzer, P-W XIV. 1147.

[3] For unusual *praenomina*, and for the writing out of *praenomina* in full, see *JRS* XXXVIII (1948), 124 f., in comment on H. Fuchs' text of *Ann.* I–VI (*Editiones Helveticae*, 1946). Fuchs

only other passage of the *Annales* which indubitably refers to M'. Lepidus, his *praenomen* is in fact written out in full: the account of the prosecution of his sister Aemilia Lepida contains the parenthesis, irrelevant to the vicissitudes of the lady (which are expounded at some length), but precious and essential for identifying M'. Aemilius Lepidus by name and descent— 'defendente ream Manio Lepido fratre'.[1] To judge by all the discussion about the two Lepidi (and eight emendations of the text thought necessary to bring them into order again), Tacitus must have been a prodigiously casual writer in that he did not make it at once clear which was the greater Lepidus and which the less.

The *praenomen* 'Manius' written out in full seems to offer a clue. If the emendation proposed above is accepted, then Manius Lepidus is the lesser man beyond doubt, and he appears only twice in the *Annales*. The first occurrence serves to establish his lineage—in himself he is only a parenthesis attached to his colourful sister, and nothing that he said or did is recorded. The second proves him a nonentity, opprobriously in the invective of Sex. Pompeius, but no less forcibly in the excuse and extenuation— a quiet man who had done no harm. Tacitus then is vindicated. He has in fact provided the indications requisite to distinguish the two Lepidi. Not only that. The *Codex Mediceus* is also vindicated in this, that only one emendation is needed, not eight.

The consequences are serious.[2] A redistribution of references in Tacitus to the two Lepidi is involved. Manius gains one—and that by the emendation—namely words about his character in the Senate in 21 and, despite all the unpleasantness, his proconsulate of Asia.[3] Marcus on the other hand is liberated from this incongruity, and eight passages, including 'capax imperii', are retrieved from Manius and go to build up a character of great moment in the transactions of the time—and in Tacitus' conception of history and politics.

Manius Lepidus may be quickly dismissed. All that Manius did was to defend his sister (unsuccessfully) in 20, and go out, in virtue of rank and seniority, as proconsul of Asia for the tenure 21–2. His predecessor, holding the province in 20–1, had been C. Silanus (*cos.* A.D. 10).[4] Who followed

introduces a consistent system of abbreviation, obscuring indications in the *Codex Mediceus* that might be valuable: thus 'M. Lepidum' in III. 35. 2, instead of 'Marcum Lepidum', and 'M'. Lepido fratre' in III. 22. 1, for 'Manio Lepido fratre'.

[1] III. 22. 1.

[2] They will affect *PIR²*, A 363; 369; 422. Also two recent lists of the proconsuls of Asia, those produced by S. J. de Laet, *De Samenstelling van den Romeinschen Senaat* (1941) 240, and by D. Magie, *Roman Rule in Asia Minor* II (1950), 1581.

[3] III. 32. 2.   [4] Prosecuted and condemned in 22 (III. 66 ff.).

M'. Lepidus in Asia, as proconsul for 22–3, has not been recorded. In 22, when Blaesus' tenure of Africa was prorogued, Ser. Cornelius Maluginensis, the *flamen Dialis* (*suff.* A.D. 10), alleged that his own name ought to be admitted to the sortition for Asia despite his sacerdotal office, but this was disallowed.[1] The next attested proconsul after M'. Lepidus is C. Fonteius Capito (*cos.* A.D. 12) in 23–4, prosecuted but let off in 25.[2] Ten or eleven years from a man's consulate seems at this time to have become something like the normal interval before the proconsulate of Asia or Africa. That M'. Lepidus was in fact proconsul of Asia happens to be confirmed by an inscription.[3] As for Marcus Lepidus, he too governs Asia—but, as will be disclosed in the course of what is said about that man, independent facts prove that he cannot in any case be the Lepidus who went out in 21. Those facts have deliberately not been adduced in support of the emendation of 'Marcum' to 'Manium': it is powerful enough if it stands on its own merits.

III. So much for Manius Lepidus. Marcus by contrast now occupies the rank and rôle in the history of Tiberius' principate that should belong to Scipionic ancestry and personal distinction. As has been argued, eight passages in the *Annales* should be taken from the inferior 'Manius' and restored to their rightful owner;[4] these, along with three others where Marcus is named or alluded to (without the *praenomen*) combine to build up the picture of a senior statesman.[5]

Lepidus' life and actions in so far as they find mention in the first six books of the *Annales* will now be set forth in brief space. Of the *consulares* under Tiberius it is in fact Asinius Gallus who gets mentioned on more separate occasions than any other; Marcus Lepidus comes next, and behind Lepidus, appropriately enough, is L. Arruntius. Measured in words and chapters, the largest space, it must be conceded, goes to Cn. Piso, but that is really a single episode, from his appointment to the governorship of Syria down to his trial and death, lavishly narrated and artfully enhanced by the historian because it is the story of the fate of Germanicus and the vengeance for Germanicus. Otherwise Cn. Piso is not a significant figure.[6]

---

[1] III. 58 f., cf. 71. 2 f.   [2] IV. 36. 3.

[3] *CIL* III. 398 = 7089, attests M'. Aemilius M'. f. Pal. Proculus, the *praefectus fabrum* of a M'. Lepidus. Disallowed, on inadequate grounds, by Magie, o.c. 1362 f.

[4] I. 13. 2, and the seven items registered in n. 1, p. 36 above.

[5] II. 48. 1; III. 72. 1 (where most editors insert 'M.'); VI. 40. 3 ('pater Lepidus').

[6] He occurs in I. 74. 5, and II. 35. 1. Note also 'in sententiam Pisonis' (I. 79. 4), where he must be intended (despite the doubts of Groag, *PIR*[2], C 287), for no other Piso has yet been mentioned. If a *praenomen* has fallen out, it should be 'Cn.', not 'L.' If 'L.', the context would

Gallus, Lepidus, and Arruntius (or Piso instead of Arruntius, so some held), these were the three 'capaces imperii'. When Tiberius Caesar, requiring the Senate to make a clear admission that the stability of the Roman State and the Roman Empire demanded the principate of one man, and that he was in fact that man, initiated a debate on this high matter, by the devious but necessary profession of his own inadequacy to bear the whole burden unaided—'solam divi Augusti mentem tantae molis capacem'[1]— and went on to speak of dividing the power, Asinius Gallus asked an abrupt and awkward question, 'interrogo, Caesar, quam partem rei publicae mandari tibi velis?'[2] Deliberate malice, it should seem, not a mere lack of tact, though Gallus proceeded to explain what his question meant— namely to make Tiberius admit the necessity of one man's rule—and he added praise of Augustus and of Tiberius. Arruntius also gave offence, so Tacitus says, by a speech of like tenor.[3] The incident provides Tacitus with an excuse for inserting Augustus' verdict on the three *principes*: after that digression the debate resumes with two more speakers intervening, Q. Haterius and Mamercus Scaurus.[4] Lepidus is not named in the debate—he was absent in Spain. Had he been present in the Senate, it is a pleasing fancy that the good sense and balance, for which the historian later commends him, would have discovered some elegant formula for bridging, or disguising, the gap between appearance and reality in the ambiguous nature of the Roman Principate.

Lepidus is not mentioned again until 17; and then it is in a trivial matter. Tiberius transferred to Aemilius Lepidus the property of Aemilia Musa, a wealthy woman who had died intestate; for, he said, Lepidus needed money to support his rank.[5] That M. Lepidus' fortune (like that of Manius Lepidus) was by no means ample, will appear from a subsequent passage. M. Lepidus is next named among the *patroni* who undertook the defence of Cn. Piso in 20.[6] Then, at the beginning of the next year occurred those transactions in the Senate as a result of which Manius Lepidus was allowed to stand for the proconsulate of Asia, and Marcus, though nominated along with Seianus' uncle by the Princeps himself for a military task in Africa, prudently drew back and facilitated the choice of the other candidate.[7] Towards the end of the same year M. Lepidus intervened in a senatorial debate with the plea of mercy for Clutorius Priscus, who in his folly and

---

not reveal which of the two homonymous consulars is meant, the *pontifex* (*cos.* 15 B.C.) or the *augur* (*cos.* 1 B.C.).

[1] I. 11. 1.   [2] I. 12. 2.   [3] I. 13. 1.

[4] I. 13. 4: 'etiam Q. Haterius et Mamercus Scaurus suspicacem animum perstrinxere,' etc.

[5] II. 48. 1 ('Aemilio Lepido').   [6] III. 11. 2.   [7] III. 32; 35.

vanity had composed in verse a premature obituary on a prince of the imperial house.[1] Lepidus' intervention was fruitless—only one of the consulars supported him. The incident, though disquieting, was unimportant. Yet Tacitus reproduces the speech of Lepidus. He was perhaps more concerned with Marcus Lepidus than with the fate of Clutorius Priscus.

In the next year (22) Marcus Lepidus asked permission from the Senate to repair at his own cost a public monument that was also a family monument, the Basilica Aemilia.[2] Designated 'Lepidus' in the manuscript, without the *praenomen* (which is added by most editors), he cannot have his identity impugned. The Basilica had been remodelled by his grandfather L. Aemilius Paullus (*cos.* 50 B.C.), and repaired more than once since then. Tacitus commends this example of a virtue that had become very rare, and adds that the means of Lepidus were in fact modest—'quamquam pecuniae modicus'. Standards of wealth are difficult to estimate, likewise the nature of the repairs, when no statistics are available but only expressions of opinion. In any age the impoverishment of the rich is an ambiguous theme. M. Lepidus' fortune, as has been seen, deserved augmentation in the estimate of Tiberius Caesar. As for the other Lepidus, 'Manius,' he was derided by Sex. Pompeius as poverty-stricken, 'inops.'[3] The standards of Sex. Pompeius would not be a fair guide—he was a millionaire, with great estates in Campania, Sicily, and Africa.[4] Yet there is a small puzzle about Sex. Pompeius. When Lepidus set about repairing the Basilica of his grandfather, Tiberius promised to deal himself with the Theatre of Pompeius, which had been destroyed by fire: though the name of Pompeius was not extinct, no member of the family possessed the means for that task.[5] Some have supposed, in view of the opulence of Sex. Pompeius, that Tacitus' statement is erroneous. Sex. Pompeius did not, it is true, belong to the direct line from Magnus, being a descendant of his paternal uncle, but that is surely irrelevant.[6] The rebuilding of a massive structure like the Theatre of Pompeius might well have daunted the possessor of enormous wealth.

In 24 M. Lepidus again took the moderate and merciful line about penalties when a lady called Sosia Galla was condemned. Tacitus' admiration, foreshadowed by the sagacious speech he reported in the matter of

[1] III. 50.
[2] III. 72. 1: 'isdem diebus ⟨M.⟩ Lepidus ab senatu petivit ut basilicam Pauli, Aemilia monimenta, propria pecunia firmaret ornaretque. erat etiam tum in more publica munificentia'.
[3] III. 32. 2.   [4] Ovid, *Ex Ponto* IV. 15. 15 ff.; 5. 9 ff.   [5] III. 72. 2.
[6] The descent is from the Sex. Pompeius of Cicero (*Brutus* 175; *Phil.* XII. 27), through Sex. Pompeius Sex. f. (*cos.* 35 B.C.). A Sex. Pompeius Cn. f., suffect consul in 5 B.C., is adduced by R. Hanslik, P-W XXI. 2265. He never existed.

4—T.S.I.T.

Clutorius Priscus, invokes solemn and moving language, with an exordium not merely (and patently) reminiscent of Sallust in its studied simplicitly and archaism, but lifted bodily from that great exemplar: 'hunc ego Lepidum temporibus illis gravem et sapientem virum fuisse comperior.'[1] Behaving with dignity and discretion, Lepidus enjoyed the esteem of Tiberius and carried great weight with him. The example of Lepidus elicits from the historian one of his most significant reflections on men and affairs. It compelled him to doubt whether the favour of princes depends, like all things, on fate and predestination, to wonder whether a man's own prudence might not count for something, and enable him to steer a safe and honourable course in public life, equally removed from the extremes of abrupt defiance and degrading servility.[2]

Though Marcus Lepidus commanded armies and governed the province of Hispania Tarraconensis, he had never held the proconsulate of either Asia or Africa, the peak and consecration of a senator's career—as is demonstrated by the fact that his name was put forward for Africa by the Princeps in 21: there is no case known in the early Empire of a man's having both proconsulates. Now, at last, from an incident of the year 26, emerges the fact that Asia has fallen to M. Lepidus: an additional *legatus* is appointed under Lepidus for a special task in Asia.[3] That M. Lepidus was proconsul had long been known from coins.[4] An inscription records his tenure as biennial.[5] The decisive value of this document does not seem to have been discerned. It provides indirect but conclusive vindication of the thesis argued above, that the Lepidus who went out to Asia in 21 was not Marcus, but Manius. Marcus it cannot have been, for the two years would run from summer 21 to summer 23, whereas Marcus Lepidus was indubit-

[1] IV. 20. 2. cf. Sallust, *Jug*. 45. 1: 'Metellum . . . magnum et sapientem virum fuisse comperior.' The author of the *Annales* nowhere else employs the verb in the deponent form. Observe also, a little farther down, 'pergere iter,' cf. *Jug*. 79. 5. Further, Lepidus in his oration is made to refer to the poet Clutorius Priscus in Sallustian phraseology—'studia illi, ut plena vecordiae, ita inania et fluxa sunt' (III. 50. 3).

[2] IV. 20. 3: 'unde dubitare cogor fato et sorte nascendi, ut cetera, ita principum inclinatio in hos offensio in illos, an sit aliquid in nostris consiliis liceatque inter abruptam contumaciam et deforme obsequium pergere iter ambitione ac periculis vacuum'.

[3] IV. 56. 3: 'censuitque Vibius Marsus ut M. Lepido, cui ea provincia obvenerat, supra numerum legaretur, qui templi curam susciperet. et quia Lepidus ipse deligere per modestiam abnuebat, Valerius Naso e praetoriis sorte missus est.' The Latin and the situation are misunderstood by Magie, who states (o.c. 1362) that the Lepidus in question (whom he identifies with Manius) was 'chosen by the Senate as a special commissioner to supervise the building of the new provincial temple at Smyrna . . . but declined the appointment'. He goes on to deny that this Lepidus was proconsul of Asia.

[4] Coins of Cotiaeum, *BMC, Phrygia* 263, nos. 26 f.

[5] *AE* 1934, 87 (Cos), registered by Groag in the addendum to *PIR*[2], A 369 (III, p. XI).

ably at Rome in the year 22, repairing the Basilica of Paullus.[1] Therefore Marcus Lepidus' proconsulate is to be set in 26–28.

The lapse of years since his consulate (A.D. 6) might arouse disquiet. It will be recalled that the procedure of allocating the consular proconsulates was subject to fluctuations and perturbations. Thus, while a five-year interval seems to come into operation fairly early in the Principate of Augustus, it becomes abbreviated before long, but begins to expand again towards the end of the reign and reaches ten or eleven years under Tiberius in the period A.D. 20–2, as has been demonstrated above. Various factors operated to modify (or even derange) the order of seniority among the ex-consuls admitted to the ballot. One man might be privileged because of the number of children, another debarred for some delinquency, or gently persuaded to withdraw his name in favour of a candidate more acceptable to the masters of patronage. Above all, deaths of consulars or their absence on other tasks might shorten the list. Now when the Senate early in 26 proceeded to arrange the ballot for the two proconsulates, hardly any of the consuls of the years 12–15 may have been available, for one reason or another; and it can be observed in passing that the names of four consular legates in the imperial provinces at this time elude inquiry.[2] In such a situation, a junior ex-consul might receive promotion—or a senior who had previously missed his turn might be admitted. Examples of the latter practice can be discovered. One will suffice. In 2–1 B.C. the proconsul of Asia was Cn. Cornelius Lentulus, consul in 14 B.C.[3] In that period the normal interval was much less than twelve years. It might even be surmised that when Lentulus would have been expected to qualify, *c.* 9 B.C., he was absent on a provincial command.[4] Now in A.D. 14 Marcus Lepidus was legate of Hispania Tarraconensis. Lepidus had been *consul ordinarius* in 6. One of the *suffecti* was L. Nonius Asprenas—and Asprenas reached the proconsulate of Africa in 12, holding it for the triennium in 12–15.[5] Lepidus,

---

[1] IV. 72. 1. Not noticed by Groag, who, citing the inscr., stated 'itaque Asiam rexit a. 21–23 p.c.' Magie sought to evade the difficulty by putting M. Lepidus in Asia in 22–4 (o.c. 1581)—or perhaps in 23–5 (o.c. 1363). In vain: a Lepidus certainly went out in 21—'igitur missus in Asiam' (III. 32. 2). The operations of this scholar have only confused the problem (cf. p. 42, n. 3).

[2] viz., the commanders in Pannonia, Dalmatia, and the two Germanies.

[3] *SIG*³ 781 (Nysa). He is designated Γν[αί]ῳ Λέντλῳ Αὔγορι—which is important for identification.

[4] His Danubian command (*Ann.* IV. 44. 1; Florus II. 28 f.) could be put 9–6 (as consular legate of Moesia), cf. *Rom. Rev.* 401, instead of A.D. 1–4 (Illyricum), as suggested in *JRS* xxiv (1934), 125 ff.

[5] *AE* 1952, 232 = *IRT* 346 (the inscr. of his grandson). The proconsulate of L. Aelius Lamia, *cos.* 3 (*AE* 1936, 157 = *IRT* 930; 1940, 69), will be put next, in 15–16: a retardation due no doubt to his service 'in Germania Illyricoque' (Velleius II. 116. 3).

as the transactions of the year 21 show, had not previously held either pro-consulate. There is no difficulty in supposing that he was admitted to the lot—or specially appointed—in 26. Twenty years had elapsed since his proconsulate—but he need not have been very elderly. Lepidus' tenure was in fact prolonged. Twenty years in A.D. 26 is no more exorbitant than twelve in 2 B.C. And indeed, almost at once, very strange things began to happen to these proconsulates. In Africa C. Vibius Marsus (*suff.* 17) is attested from 27 to 30, succeeded by M. Junius Silanus (*cos.* 19) who held the post till 35.[1] Asia had one governor for six years, presumably 29–35, possibly 30–6: he was P. Petronius (*suff.* 19).[2]

It is evident that negative arguments based on seniority or a supposed normal interval between consulate and proconsulate are extremely hazard-ous. If any doubts are felt about the identity of the Marcus Lepidus attested in the *Annales* as proconsul designate of Asia in 26, there is only one remedy, and it will have to be stated firmly: another Marcus Lepidus, un-known to Tacitus and unknown to history, will have to be invented.[3]

Marcus Lepidus spent two years in Asia; his tenure may even have been prolonged to a third year.[4] And now supervened a series of catastrophies at Rome—the ruin of Agrippina, widow of Germanicus, and her sons, the conspiracy of Seianus, and all the judicial murders or suicides. Though his daughter was married to Drusus, the son of Germanicus,[5] Marcus Lepidus

[1] The *triennium* of Vibius Marsus is shown by *CIL* VIII. 10568; 22786 f.=*ILS* 9375. In the dedication to the man 'praefecto fabrum |M. Silani M. f. sexto | Carthaginis' (*ILS* 6236: Tibur) the six years may be calendar not proconsular; for the successor of Silanus is C. Rubellius Blandus, proconsul 35–6 (*AE* 1948, 1=*IRT* 330).

[2] Dio (LVIII. 23. 5) reports *sexennia* for Asia and Africa, without names. The sixth year of Petronius is proved by coins of Pergamum (*BMC, Mysia* 140, nos. 253 f.)—and the fifth has recently emerged on a Caunian dedication to Plautia A. f. (i.e. the 'Plautia P. Petroni' of *CIL* VI. 6866), the proconsul's wife, published by G. E. Bean in *JHS* LXXIV (1954), 91 f. His tenure is generally assigned to 29–35 (e.g. Magie, o.c. 1581), but there is nothing against 30–6. Petronius was back in Rome in 36, cf. VI. 45. 2 (late in the year), where he is men-tioned in the same context as Rubellius Blandus (proconsul of Africa in 35–6, cf. the pre-ceding note).

[3] That is, 'M. Aemilius Q. f. Lepidus,' as a consular son of either the consul of 22 B.C. or of the parent of M'. Lepidus (*cos.* A.D. 11). A place could perhaps be devised in A.D. 13. For the problems of that year, see A. Degrassi, *Epigraphica* VIII (1946), 34 ff.; A. E. and J. S. Gordon, *AJP* LXXII (1951), 283 ff. The latter writers argue that the item 'C. Silius A. Caecina Largus' should be split into two persons, an *ordinarius* and a *suffectus*.

[4] If M. Lepidus is accepted as proconsul in 26–8, the list for 20–30 will have to be radically revised. To the attested proconsuls mentioned above (p. 38f.), add Sex. Pompeius, *cos.* 14 (Valerius Maximus II, 6, 8). Perhaps also M. Aurelius Cotta Maximus Messallinus, *cos.* 20 (*Forsch. in Ephesos* III, 112, no. 22), though he might belong in 35–6.

[5] VI. 40. 3: 'Aemilia Lepida, quam iuveni Druso nuptam rettuli.' The item will have been registered in Book V. Drusus was probably born in 7: he assumed the *toga virilis* at the begin-ning of 23 (IV. 4. 1). His first betrothed was a daughter 'vixdum nubilis' of L. Salvius Otho

had kept clear of the struggle for power between the family of Germanicus and the faction of Seianus, unimpaired in repute or influence. He is next named in the year 32. Cotta Messallinus, at variance with Lepidus and Arruntius over a money matter, complained of their 'potentia' ('potentia' is the pejorative synonym of 'auctoritas').[1] Once again Lepidus and Arruntius occur in conjunction. At this time the other member of the three 'capaces imperii', Asinius Gallus, was held in public custody, incriminated because of Agrippina.[2]

Gallus perished in 33, it was uncertain whether by his own hand or not.[3] The same year witnessed the death of Marcus Lepidus. The obituary could be concisely formulated. Tacitus observes that the prudence and moderation of Lepidus had been adequately documented in the earlier books. His birth called for no advertisement—the Aemilian house had always produced a number of 'boni cives', and even the wicked Aemilii were illustrious.[4]

The historian left Arruntius to proclaim and perpetuate his renown in his own dying utterances. Scorning to endure through the last days until the end of Tiberius Caesar, the noble consular took his own life, in dignified protest against the abominations of the present, with prophecy of a worse tyranny to come. What happened after proved that Arruntius did well to die.[5]

IV. Such was the fate of Gallus, Lepidus, and Arruntius. Touching Lepidus, the historian gives detail enough from first to last to explain and justify his prominence. It might seem strange that he says nothing about the Scipionic link through Cornelia his mother. That link may not have been present to the mind of Tacitus, and though by his reference to the repair of the Basilica Paulli he certifies the lineage of Marcus Lepidus, he has not bothered to mention his father Paullus (*suff.* 34 B.C.), the last senator to hold the censorship. As for Arruntius, whom he designates as

(*cos.* 33), cf. Suetonius, *Otho* I. 3. The date of his marriage to Aemilia Lepida is not directly attested; and she could be a younger sister of M. Lepidus' 'nubilis filia' referred to in 21 (III. 35. 2).

[1] VI. 5. I.

[2] He had been arrested in 30 (Dio LVIII. 3. 3 f., cf. *Ann.* VI. 23. I).

[3] VI. 23. I.

[4] VI. 27. 4: 'obiit eodem anno M. Lepidus de cuius moderatione atque sapientia in prioribus libris satis conlocavi. neque nobilitas diutius demonstranda est: quippe Aemilium genus fecundum bonorum civium, et qui eadem familia corruptis moribus inlustri tamen fortuna egere'.

[5] VI. 48. 3: 'documento sequentia erunt bene Arruntium morte usum'. The sentence has been condemned as an interpolation by a recent editor.

'divitem, promptum, artibus egregiis et pari fama publice',[1] the decisive factor that puts him in such exalted company is not perhaps those excellent qualities but his aristocratic connections—and they were no doubt adverted upon later, when the rising of Arruntius Scribonianus came to be narrated. In Asinius Gallus there stood out the 'ferocia' of his father Pollio, oratorical talent as well, and an inordinate ambition.[2] Suspect on those grounds, he incurred the resentment of Tiberius because he had married Vipsania, whom Tiberius for reasons of high policy had been compelled to divorce. The allegation of an affair with the widowed princess Agrippina was to come later.

Introduced in high relief at the outset in the *Annales*, the three consulars Arruntius, Lepidus, and Gallus seem to provide a leading theme in the complicated, tightly packed, and all but intractable record of Tiberius' principate. In what follows Tacitus has marred his effect by a slightly incongruous addition. He goes on to say that some versions put Cn. Piso in the place of Arruntius—and the ruin of all those men, except Lepidus, was subsequently contrived by Tiberius.

A felicitous invention like the story of the three *principes* ought not perhaps to be scrutinized with too anxious or too hopeful a gaze. Who can tell how soon it arose after the death of Augustus—and in how many variants?[3] What Tacitus reports reveals more traces than one of subsequent events. It can be said with some confidence that the insertion of Cn. Piso is due, not to his rank and importance in A.D. 14, but to what came later—the episode of Germanicus Caesar. Of a truculent character, it is true, and Republican in his family tradition, Piso did not approach the public distinction or the dynastic connections of Marcus Lepidus. Nor could he compete, though of ancient nobility, with the personal attainments of L. Arruntius; and in Arruntius were concentrated the Sullan and Pompeian claims to power (for Manius Lepidus, 'socors, inops,' carried no weight).

The third consular, Asinius Gallus, might seem barely to qualify. Like Arruntius, he was the son of a *novus homo*. Yet ambition, eloquence, and prestige in the Senate counted; those advantages were reinforced by the marriage with Agrippa's daughter, and Gallus' numerous sons were cousins of the offspring of Germanicus Caesar and Agrippina. His dangerous prominence, however, came later, after the death of Germani-

---

[1] I. 13. 1. He was an orator of distinction (XI. 7. 2): not mentioned by the elder Seneca, presumably because still among the living.

[2] I. 13. 1.

[3] The younger Agrippina would be eager to demonstrate in her memoirs that Tiberius was not at all the necessary and inevitable successor to Augustus.

cus, when a chance to marry the widow would offer prospect of a role such as must have tempted Iullus Antonius during Tiberius' exile at Rhodes—namely to become guardian of the heirs presumptive and consort of their mother: the disgrace of Julia in 2 B.C. involved the destruction of Antonius.

The malignity in Tacitus' assertion that Tiberius encompassed the destruction of these consulars (with the exception of Lepidus) has not escaped the notice of commentators. His insertion of Cn. Piso deserves attention. It weakens his case. The whole point of the anecdote is that the men in question were considered worthy of empire or likely to make a bid for power, hence suspect to Tiberius and subsequently destroyed. But the story of the Pisonian affair as Tacitus tells it, with all the insinuations, is the ruin of a loyal agent whom the Princeps disowned and so drove to suicide. All in all, the narrative fails to bear out the anecdote.[1]

V. Of the ostensible or potential pretenders, Marcus Lepidus is by far the most remarkable. Tacitus pays him a handsome tribute for virtue. But his full stature only emerges from two particulars not mentioned by Tacitus—his Scipionic blood and his previous military distinction. Without the latter, he might seem, as he seems in the *Annales*, no more than an aristocrat of abnormal sagacity and discretion—and there were plenty of aristocrats about, wise or foolish, who had never commanded an army even in peace-time, still less earned the *ornamenta triumphalia*. Cn. Piso, it is true, had been legate of Tarraconensis;[2] Arruntius, appointed rather late to Tarraconensis, was not allowed to go there;[3] and there is no evidence that Gallus ever governed a military province.

Though it may be counted as a dereliction against Tacitus that he has failed to reveal the fact that Lepidus was a 'vir triumphalis', there criticism can stop. Without Tacitus, Lepidus could scarcely be built up as a historical character. Velleius, it is true, is effusive in laudation; and, though Velleius is an adulatory and dishonest writer, he yet turns out to have told the truth—'vir nomini ac fortunae Caesarum proximus'.[4] Cassius Dio,

---

[1] How explain the inconsistency? Tacitus, penning I. 13. 2, did not know much about the subsequent history of Tiberius' reign (R. Reitzenstein, *Neue Wege zur Antike* IV (1926), 30); or he forgot what he had there written (E. Löfstedt, *JRS* xxxviii (1948), 6). A different explanation offers—the passage is a later addition by the author. Inserted between the first pair of speakers (Gallus and Arruntius) and the second (Haterius and Scaurus), it interrupts the debate. (The insertion probably begins, not with 'quippe Augustus', but with the preceding sentence describing Arruntius—'sed divitem promptum', etc.)

[2] III. 13. I.

[3] VI. 27. 3 (under 33), cf. Dio LVIII. 8. 3. He was probably appointed in 23 or 24.

[4] Velleius II. 114. 5.

who has noted Lepidus' service in Illyricum, has nothing to tell about him in his account of the reign of Tiberius. Nor does any significant detail emerge from any other source.

Lepidus had several children. A daughter, married to Drusus, the son of Germanicus, turned out badly.[1] She had brought damaging charges against her husband. As long as her father lived, she enjoyed impunity. Subsequently, when accused of relations with a slave (and the evidence was held to be convincing), she committed suicide. Another daughter may be that Aemilia Lepida who married a noble of illustrious and patrician lineage, Ser. Sulpicius Galba (*cos.* 33).[2] Of this Galba, Tiberius Caesar, skilled as he was in the learning of the Chaldaeans, made the prophecy that he would have a taste one day of the supreme power.[3]

If Lepidus by lineage and dynastic connections stood near to the throne, his son came close to occupying it. Intimate in the friendship of Caligula, who gave him his sister Drusilla for wife, the young M. Aemilius Lepidus was promised the succession by that ruler. He came to grief in the conspiracy of Lentulus Gaetulicus.[4]

That was the end of the patrician Aemilii Lepidi. The one branch, that of M'. Lepidus (*cos.* 66 B.C.), showing no distinction at all, produced a consul under Augustus, Q. Lepidus (*cos.* 21 B.C.), and then no more. The descendants of the other branch, from the turbulent and revolutionary consul of 78 B.C. down to Caligula's friend, are a large part of history. Among them are the Triumvir, and his grandson Manius, whose sole notoriety seems to be a family tree that flaunted Sulla Felix and Pompeius Magnus; also Paullus the censor, Cornelia's husband, and his sons Lucius and Marcus. By the paradox of Roman dynastic politics, the aristocratic monarchy of the Julii was continued by a Claudius, passed to descendants of M. Antonius, and ended with the last of the Domitii Ahenobarbi. Artful men who studied pedigree and astrologers in their science might have been tempted to predict that an Aemilius would emerge among the rulers of Rome.

There were men of power and crime among the Aemilii. Though the historian Tacitus delights in violence and drama, his predilection goes to a safe Aemilius who survived when his brother, Julia's husband, fell and who

[1] vi. 40. 3, cf. above, p. 44, n. 5.

[2] Suetonius, *Galba* 5. 1. Perhaps the daughter who was 'nubilis' in 21 (iii. 35. 2). There is no point in adducing an unattested daughter of M'. Lepidus.

[3] vi. 20. 2: 'et tu, Galba, quandoque degustabis imperium'.

[4] The parentage of this Lepidus (*PIR²*, A 371) is nowhere explicitly attested. A year or two younger than Caligula (born in 12), he could easily be one of the children of M. Lepidus referred to in 21 (iii. 35. 2).

escaped damage when the factions of Germanicus and of Seianus divided and decimated the aristocracy. In fact, Tacitus creates Marcus Lepidus as a historical character; for the role of this illustrious consular in the principate of Tiberius is, if not wholly passive, at least nowhere decisive. Lepidus in the *Annales* is a bright serene character to be set against the vice or sloth, the corruption or the subservience of so many *nobiles*. But he is not merely that. He is Tacitus' hero. The character of Marcus Lepidus and his conduct inspire the historian to pause for a moment and conceive doubts about fatalism. Here was the middle path. As it was the ideal of the Principate to avoid the extremes of anarchy and despotism, so the good senator might eschew both truculence and servility, maintaining personal honour and the dignity of his station. The days of Tiberius Caesar are still close enough to the Republic for the exemplar of civic virtue to be a noble and a patrician.

When Tacitus wrote, the great days and the great men were only a memory. Though the aristocracy had been transformed, with new families dominant, the central problem remained: how might a senator serve the *res publica* with dignity and honour in evil days, under an evil ruler. Agricola provides the answer. There could still be great men. Glory would attend, not on fractious or fanatical opposition, but on duty and discretion.[1] Marcus Lepidus as depicted by Tacitus in the *Annales* is a proto-type of his Agricola. And Agricola is much more than the historian's father-in-law, posthumously commemorated.

If the *Histories* of Tacitus had survived in their entirety, one might have expected to discover in them some hint of the future, some omen perhaps in the eastern lands where the young Trajan served as a military tribune, some significant prediction uttered by popular rumour (or by an elder statesman's sagacity) when he led the legion from Spain to suppress the rising of Antonius Saturninus. The loss of the later books of the *Histories* need not, however, impair or exclude all speculation about Trajan's pre-destination to empire—at least as reported after the event. Agricola him-self foretold the rule of Trajan, so his biographer avers;[2] and the pamphlet itself is an exposition of the theme 'capax imperii'.[3]

[1] *Agr.* 42. 5.

[2] *Agr.* 44. 5: 'durare in hanc beatissimi saeculi lucem ac principem Traianum videre, quod augurio votisque apud nostras auris ominabatur'.

[3] Let it be added in postscript that 'capaces imperii' acquired sensational value twenty years later when, in the first year of Hadrian, four eminent consulars were executed for con-spiracy. The incident may have impelled Tacitus to insert the (highly questionable) anecdote about Augustus' assessment of the three *principes* (cf. above, p. 47, n. 1). I deal with this matter elsewhere.

V

SOME PISONES IN TACITUS*

AT THIS late date there is not much prospect of producing new and cogent emendations in Tacitus. 'Hoc artificium periit.' Past excesses counsel sobriety, and there has been a strong revulsion. Among the items which scholars unjustly impugned and prematurely corrected were a number of proper names, their sole offence often being rarity or an unusual shape. However strange a name may look, it should not lightly be altered. The vast and vivid nomenclature of ancient Italy invades the lower orders of the Roman Senate well before the Republic ends, and proliferates under the Caesars.[1]

Names of a more familiar contour can still be a source of perplexity. The senatorial annals of Tiberius' principate carry a plethora of persons, among them the recurrent and aristocratic members of a few families. The consular historian, however, was adequately equipped for his task. He knew the methods of documentary enquiry, he was ferociously accurate, and he was interested in all the characters of his narrative, down to the most obscure—'originem non repperi' (VI. 7. 4). That being so, two Aemilii Lepidi, a Marcus and a Manius (the consuls of 6 and of 11), gave him no trouble.[2] That he could avoid error everywhere, too much to hope. There are slips.[3] And he might be held guilty of inadvertence. For example, it is an annoyance that the same person should appear as 'Cotta Messallinus' in the year 16 (II. 32. 1), as 'Aurelius Cotta consul' in 20 (III. 17. 4).

Homonyms are a plague and a nuisance. The Romans had various devices for dealing with them: marks of parentage or paternity, rank and seniority, the holding of one of the superior priesthoods.[4] Frequent

* Reprinted from *JRS* XLVI (1956), 17–21.

[1] For examples of premature correction, *JRS* XXXIX (1949), 6 ff. [below, pp. 58 ff.].

[2] cf. the argument developed in *JRS* XLV (1955), 22 ff. [above, pp. 30 ff.].

[3] Thus 'Latinius Latiaris' (IV. 68. 2) and 'Latinius' (71. 1), but 'Lucanius Latiaris' (VI. 4. 1). The correct *gentilicium* is probably 'Lucanius', but the discrepancy ought to be retained in the text, for the historian himself may be responsible, cf. *JRS* XXXIX (1949), 13 [below, p. 70]. Different sources, perhaps.

[4] *JRS* XLV (1955), 157 (discussing the homonymous Messallae, the consuls of 61 and 53 B.C.).

recourse to labels of identity did not appeal to the composer of taut and finished prose. He preferred to operate unobtrusively, by significant allusion. Cornelius Tacitus wrote for the alert as well as the exacting. Posterity has not always repaid the compliment.

Calpurnii Pisones are abundant in the last age of the Republic, and the early Empire had a fair share. Three Pisones of consular standing find a place in the narrative of *Annales* I–VI. First comes Cn. Piso Cn. f. (*cos.* 7 B.C.), the truculent legate of Syria, son of the consul of 23 B.C. Then his brother, L. Piso the *augur* (*cos.* I B.C.), likewise an intractable fellow. Third and last, L. Piso the *pontifex* (*cos.* 15 B.C.), mild and bibulous: the son of L. Piso Caesoninus (*cos.* 58 B.C.). The parentage of L. Piso the *pontifex* was registered by Tacitus somewhere in Book V, for he states 'patrem ei censorium fuisse memoravi' (VI. 10. 3). The three passages here to be discussed all concern the consular Pisones in one way or another.

(1) A debate in the year 15 about measures to restrain the flooding of the Tiber issued in a negative result—'ut in sententiam Pisonis concederetur, qui nil mutandum censuerat' (I. 79. 4). Which Piso? Nipperdey had the answer. He inserted the *praenomen* 'Cn.'. That improvement found some favour.[1] However, the three most recent editors prefer to discard it;[2] and a scholar of great authority hesitates to assume that Cn. Piso is meant.[3] Yet that ought to be clear enough. Cn. Piso had been mentioned shortly before in the annalistic record of the year (I. 74. 5).[4] Therefore the *praenomen* is not in fact required. On the other hand, if the author wrote 'L. Pisonis', he was grossly incompetent. The incident offered no clue for identification (the *pontifex* or the *augur*), and no Lucius Piso had so far cropped up.

(2) After the suicide of Libo Drusus in 16, the historian puts on record the 'sententiae' advocated by seven men of rank. The documentation is deliberate and deadly. He wished to show that subservience and conformism had an early origin—'quorum auctoritates adulationesque rettuli ut sciretur vetus id in re publica malum' (II. 32. 2). The list is not without

[1] Thus H. Furneaux (ed. 2, Oxford, 1896); Halm-Andresen (ed. 5, Teubner, 1913); E. Koestermann (Teubner, 1934).
[2] viz., M. Lenchantin de Gubernatis (*Regia Academia Italica*, 1940); H. Fuchs (*Editiones Helveticae*, 1946); E. Koestermann (Teubner, 1952).
[3] E. Groag in *PIR²*, C 287: 'incertum num etiam Tac. I. 79 *Piso* hic significetur (in cod. praenomen excidit)'.
[4] He occurs, to be sure, among the 'capaces imperii' (I. 13. 3). That passage is patently an accretion on Tacitus' main source—and might even be a subsequent insertion by the author, cf. *JRS* XLV (1955), 32 [above, p. 47, n. 1].

its problems. Cotta Messallinus leads off, which is enigmatic—and an
encouragement to those who, doubting whether he is the same person
as M. Aurelius Cotta, the consul of 20, suppose that he might have held
the *fasces* in some year prior to 16.[1] However, an easy solution could be
devised, that the man spoke as *praetor designatus*; and the *Fasti Arvalium*
can be persuaded to disclose a Cotta, *praetor peregrinus* in 17.[2] Next, a
senior consular, Cn. Lentulus (*cos.* 14 B.C.), then Pomponius Flaccus
(who was consul designate for 17). So far three 'sententiae'. The fourth
and last was backed by no fewer than four men—'L. ⟨Piso⟩ et Gallus
Asinius et Papius Mutilus et L. Apronius'. The first of these names depends on the supplement admitted by J. F. Gronovius in 1672. It has
been reproduced by almost all editors of any consequence since then.[3]
As for rank, Gallus was consul in 8 B.C., Papius and Apronius *suffecti* in
A.D. 9 and 8 respectively.

If 'L. P⟨iso⟩' be accepted, which of the two, the *pontifex* or the *augur*?
Scholars are in difficulties, or ought to be.[4] On Tacitus' showing neither
Piso will do. The *pontifex* on his decease in 32 at the age of eighty receives
a handsome commendation for dignity and discretion—'nullius servilis
sententiae sponte auctor et, quotiens necessitas ingrueret, sapienter
moderans' (VI. 10. 3). More, it is true, than is justified by the narrative
as extant, but not contradicted by anything else. Most of Book v being
lost (he was mentioned there once at least), a solitary action stands on
record of L. Piso the *pontifex*, and that not due to his own initiative.
Asked by Tiberius to pronounce an opinion when the proceedings
against a delinquent proconsul of Asia were drawing to an end, he complied, 'multum de clementia principis praefatus' (III. 68. 2).[5] There is no
sign that the author is imputing servility to L. Piso—it is the next speaker,
P. Dolabella, who indulges in 'adulatio' (69. 1). Nor is Piso's behaviour

---

[1] Groag voiced grave misgivings, among which 'neque probabile mihi videtur Cottam
Messalinum a. 16 sententiam dixisse inter praetorios' (*PIR²*, A 1488). He lists the consul of
20 separately (A 1487). Against, and for identity, S. J. de Laet, *Ant. Class.* VI (1937), 137 ff.;
A. Degrassi, *Epigraphica* VIII (1946), 38.

[2] *Inscr. It.* XIII. 1, p. 297, where Degrassi reads ']s [. . .]a per.' One might speculate with
the *cognomina* 'Cotta', 'Galba', 'Nerva'. But recourse to Degrassi's drawing (the photograph
does not help) would justify 'Cot[t]a'.

[3] The encouraging exception is G. H. Walther (Halle, 1831), the scholar who refused
to alter the *praenomen* of M. Lepidus in *Ann.* I. 13. 2. Obdurate against 'L. P⟨iso⟩' and
against other names, he firmly printed 'L. P.' in his text. The exact *lectio* of the *Codex
Mediceus* is 'L. p.' (with the stops after each letter).

[4] For the *augur*, Nipperdey; Ph. Fabia in his *Onomasticon Taciteum* (1900); *PIR¹*, C 233
(with no warning). For the *pontifex*, Furneaux; Groag in *PIR²*, C 289.

[5] For the *augur*, Nipperdey; Fabia; *PIR¹*, C 233. For the *pontifex*, Furneaux; Groag in
PIR², C 289.

in discrepancy with the terms of the obituary notice. He was not in fact a strong and independent character. Tacitus admits as much—'quotiens necessitas ingrueret'. But no necessity compelled the venerable *pontifex* to sponsor a proposal that the anniversary of Libo's suicide should be celebrated thereafter as a public holiday—for such was the 'sententia' of the four consulars.

Still less was the *augur* likely to be found in such company. The next episode but one after the Libo business introduces a Lucius Piso raising fierce protest about the condition of justice at Rome and threatening to go away for good—'ambitum fori, corrupta iudicia, saevitiam oratorum accusationes minitantium increpans', etc. (II. 34. I). Tacitus adds a detail to illustrate his temper, 'haud minus liberi doloris documentum' (34. 2). Piso took a firm stand against the powerful Urgulania who so ruthlessly exploited the favour and friendship of the old Augusta. Referring later to that transaction, the historian styles him 'nobilis ac ferox vir' (IV. 21. I). Now Tacitus nowhere calls him 'L. Piso augur', or states plainly that he was the brother of Cn. Piso. The technique is instructive, on two counts. First, Cn. Piso (we are told) was just such a man of recalcitrant temper, 'insita ferocia a patre Pisone' (II. 43. 2). Second, a Lucius Piso is registered among the advocates who agreed to defend the legate of Syria—'M. Lepidus et L. Piso et Livineius Regulus' (III. II. 2). The identity emerges from the Emperor's speech where, in injunction to the defence, he says 'si quos propinquus sanguis aut fides sua patronos dedit' (12. 6). Tacitus was in no danger of confusing homonymous Pisones.

Some other name is needed. Perhaps the *cognomen* 'Gallus' fell out of the manuscript, expelled by the 'Gallus Asinius' which follows 'L. P⟨.....⟩'. There was extant a senior consular, L. Caninius Gallus (*suff.* 2 B.C.), who had not been mentioned hitherto in the *Annales*. He occurs once, much later, as one of the *quindecimviri sacris faciundis*, and is shown to be elderly by the Emperor's rebuke, 'scientiae caerimoniarumque vetus' (VI. 12. 2). The form 'L. Gallus' is not perhaps very attractive, for 'Gallus' is not a distinctive *cognomen* adhering to a single family or to one notable individual, and easily recognized. Observe, for example, that Tacitus never refers to C. Asinius Gallus as 'C. Gallus'.

On the other hand, there is nothing against 'L. P⟨lancus⟩'.[1] That is, the consul of A.D. 13, and leader of a mission of appeasement, whom mutinous troops on the Rhine incriminated—'Munatium Plancum

---

[1] It can be noted, as of antiquarian relevance, that Freinsheim suggested 'Publius', 'Paullus', or 'Plancus' (in that order): see his note cited in the edition of J. F. Gronovius (Amsterdam, 1672). The first two are ruled out.

consulatu functum, principem legationis' (I. 39. 3). He is the son (or perhaps rather the grandson) of the consul of 42 B.C., that smooth, pliant and
eloquent man who, betraying various causes in turn for the good of the
Commonwealth, survived to sponsor the name 'Augustus' for Caesar's
heir. Now the great Munatius Plancus affected the aristocratic style of
nomenclature, dropping the *gentilicium* (compare 'L. Sulla', 'M. Metellus',
etc.). He is 'L. Plancus' on his own dedicatory inscription at Rome.[1]
The 'Munatius' tends to be squeezed out. Contemporaries (as the correspondence of Cicero shows) generally call him 'L. Plancus' or 'Plancus'.
That being so, the style 'L. Plancus' is appropriate to the next consul of
the family, who happens to be the last—and so is the behaviour documented in the year 16. The name of Plancus was synonymous with
adulation.[2]

L. Plancus (*cos.* A.D. 13) is named first in the series of four consulars.
That violates seniority—which in any case has been disregarded by
putting Apronius before Papius. Tacitus decided to abandon the order
of the protocol, for his own good reasons. Thus, in the whole transaction,
the first 'sententia' he registers is that of a praetor designate, preceding
those of a senior consular and a consul designate. The device is patent.
The historian intends to rise to a climax of shameful enormity, the day
of public rejoicing solemnly enjoined by the authority of four men of
consular station to perpetuate the unplausible conspiracy of the silly
Libo, 'tam stolidus quam nobilis'.[3]

To sum up this item. There seem to be no objections to 'L. P⟨lancus⟩'.
If any refuse assent, clinging to the belief which has now become 'traditional', namely that a Lucius Piso must be intended, they would none the
less do well to leave a lacuna and print 'L. P⟨.....⟩', for the corruption
might be deeper.[4]

(3) Under the year 24 Tacitus, mentioning a Calpurnius Piso, recapitu-
lates what he had related earlier about Piso's public and angry resolve to
quit Rome, his pertinacious quarrel with Urgulania (IV. 21. 1; cf. II. 34).
He goes on to observe that Tiberius betrayed no resentment, but did
not forget—'sed in animo revolvente iras, etiam si impetus offensionis
languerat, memoria valebat'. The next sentence proceeds to enumerate

---

[1] *ILS* 41: 'L. Plancus L. f. cos./imp. iter. de manib.'

[2] Seneca, *NQ* IV, praef. 5: 'Plancus, artifex ante Villeium (*Vitellium*, O. Hirschfeld)
maximus, aiebat non esse occulte nec ex dissimulato blandiendum: "perit," inquit, "pro-
cari, si latet." ' The Plancus of Seneca is registered as *PIR*[1], P 335: no reference under
M 534 f., or in P-W XVI. 545 ff. He is assumed to be the great Plancus in *Rom. Rev.* (1939),
501, worthy to be named with L. Vitellius (*cos.* III. 47).

[3] Seneca, *Epp.* 70. 10.   [4] That is, having swallowed up another consular as well.

charges brought against Piso, not all of them held valid. But there were others. Piso was therefore indicted, but died opportunely before the trial could take its course.

The accepted modern text reads 'Pisonem Q. Granius secreti sermonis incusavit adversus maiestatem habiti', etc. (21. 2). Hence a new character altogether, unexplained and undefined: Q. Granius, apparently a senator, for the whole context is one of transactions in the Senate, and the next item is 'relatum et de Cassio Severo exule' (21. 3). Two Granii occur in the *Annales*, namely (M.) Granius Marcellus, proconsul of Bithynia (I. 74. 1), and another, defined by status, 'Granius Marcianus senator' (VI. 38. 4). No senator of the time called Q. Granius stands on attestation anywhere.

The name derives from an emendation. Justus Lipsius produced it and all modern editors concur, with no hesitations expressed.[1] What the *Codex Mediceus* offers is 'pisonemque gravius'. A doubt arises. Might it not be better to supply the name of a person known in the *Annales* and recognizable at sight, needing no label? Read therefore 'Pisonem Q. Veranius'; or 'Pisonemque Veranius', if a link be thought desirable with the previous sentence which ended on Tiberius' resentment—'memoria valebat'.[2]

Q. Veranius, the first senator of the name (and it is a rare *gentilicium*), was one of the 'comites' of Germanicus Caesar in the eastern lands. Eager for vengeance, he took a part in the prosecution of Cn. Piso, with a priesthood for his recompense. The indictment was laid by L. Fulcinius Trio, but Germanicus' friends and members of his staff were very active— P. Vitellius, Q. Veranius and Q. Servaeus. Of the three, Servaeus is the least prominent. The historian has been careful to name Q. Veranius no fewer than five times in association with P. Vitellius (II. 74. 2; III. 10. 1; 13. 2; 17. 2; 19. 1). He would not fail to be curious about what happened to all those characters in the aftermath.

P. Vitellius, implicated with Seianus, took his own life (v. 8. 2). Q. Servaeus also came to grief, though not seriously compromised— 'modeste habita Seiani amicitia' (VI. 7. 2). Condemned, he furnished information against others (7. 4). Descendants will have been known to Tacitus, namely the '[Servaeus In]noc(ens)' revealed by a fragment of the *Fasti Ostienses* as consul suffect in 82, and Q. Servaeus Innocens,

[1] *PIR*[1], G 133 adds 'e coniectura Lipsi non certa', but there is no adequate warning in *PIR*[2], G 206. That entry also fails to indicate the source of the 'Q.', or allow for the man's being a senator.

[2] Observe that Ritter had suggested the desirability of reading 'Pisonemque ⟨.⟩ Granius', supposing a *praenomen* to have fallen out.

consul suffect in 101 (was that remarkable *cognomen* a protest and defence of the ancestor?). As for Veranius, his next action (if the emendation be approved) was in keeping with his début as a prosecutor—he is found attacking the brother of Cn. Piso, with allegation of *maiestas*.

Vitellius and Servaeus ended miserably, but the Vitellii could not be kept down—a *consul suffectus* in 32, an *ordinarius* in 34. Veranius may have managed to escape retribution. His son, loyal to Claudius the brother of Germanicus, had a resplendent fortune: *consul ordinarius* in 49, adlected among the patricians, and subsequently legate of Britain where he died, still in the prime of life.[1] Tacitus alludes with distaste to the terms of the testament he left, 'multa in Neronem adulatione' (XIV. 29. 1). This man will have been mentioned more than once in the lost books (VII–X).[2]

To avoid confusing the argument, two other Lucii Pisones have been held back. The one, consul in 27, is only a date in the *Annales*, but a notable person, being the elder son of Cn. Piso (previously Gnaeus, he changed his *praenomen*), destined to a long life, but not happy, and re-membered as a paradoxical relic of history.[3] More difficult the other. Tacitus under the year 25 records a crime in Hispania Citerior. A native assassinated the governor—'praetorem provinciae L. Pisonem' (IV. 45. 1). The author uses an old-fashioned designation for a provincial governor, 'praetor'. It can pass muster when applied to a proconsul (as for Bithynia in I. 74. 1), but it is perhaps going too far to style thus a *legatus Augusti pro praetore*. Piso was governing Hispania Citerior, a consular province. Hence another consular L. Piso has been assumed.[4] Not easy to find a place for him on the *Fasti*.[5] Doubts can be conceived, and more than doubts. Piso must be a praetorian legate.

---

[1] For his career see now *AE* 1953, 251, the remarkable inscr. detected at Rome by A. E. Gordon and published with full commentary, *Univ. of Cal. Pub. in Class. Arch.* II. 5 (1952), 231 ff. For his age and promotions, E. Birley, *Roman Britain and the Roman Army* (1953), 1 ff.

[2] Tribune of the plebs in 41, Veranius carried messages between the Senate and the candidate of the Praetorian Guard (Josephus, *AJ* XIX. 229 ff.). When legate of Lycia-Pam-phylia (? 43–7) he conducted operations against mountain tribes in Cilicia, to the east of his province: Tacitus in the extant books did not neglect the recalcitrant Cietae (VI. 41. 1; XII. 55. 1 f.).

[3] *PIR*², C 293, cf. especially Pliny, *Epp.* III. 7. 12.

[4] *PIR*², C 292: 'ante legationem fasces gesserit necesse est.' Cf. A 1130 (on the date of the governorship of L. Arruntius).

[5] Degrassi stated 'è altresi poco probabile che non sia stato console' (*Epigraphica* VIII (1946), 39); but in *I Fasti consolari* (1952), Piso is entered below the line with a note of doubt 'se fu governatore della Spagna citeriore'. The expulsion of Piso will ease some of the problems inherent in the *Fasti* of the years 13, 21, and 22.

Both Hispania Citerior and Syria had been accorded a paradoxical treatment. Tacitus, registering under 33 the decease of the *praefectus urbi*, L. Aelius Lamia, alludes to his absentee governorship of Syria, and, reporting the death of another governor of that province (Pomponius Flaccus), which elicited a dispatch from Tiberius with criticism of consulars for their reluctance to undertake provinces, turns the edge against the Emperor, who seemed to have forgotten that L. Arruntius, appointed to Spain ten years since, had not been allowed to go there—'decimum iam annum attineri' (VI. 27. 3). The approximate date of the appointment thus emerges as 23 or 24 (allowing for the round number). But perhaps 23, perhaps just before the death of Drusus Caesar, which occurred in October of that year. Hence a fact of no small consequence in the political history of the reign. The parallel instance, L. Aelius Lamia (*cos.* 3), legate of Syria *in absentia* may be closely contemporaneous. Tacitus says nothing about these matters in Book IV; but he was aware, when composing Book I, of governors not permitted to go to their provinces (I. 80. 3). He was proposing to furnish some elucidation (it can easily be divined) in Book V.[1]

L. Piso, governing Hispania Citerior in 25, is clearly a subordinate legate, acting as deputy in the absence of the consular.[2] As for identity, presumably a son of the old *pontifex*. It may be recalled in conclusion that these Pisones have no right to the *cognomen* 'Frugi'. Asconius (the normally impeccable), expounding the *In Pisonem* of Cicero, has misled himself, and others in the sequel.[3] Furthermore, an inscription from Lepcis records 'Frugi' as part of the nomenclature of M. Licinius Crassus (*cos.* 14 B.C.).[4] That discovery renders obsolete at some point or other the *stemmata* that have been devised to exhibit the descent of those Pisones who carry the lineage of the dynasts Pompeius and Crassus, and a melancholy doom: the victims of Claudius and Nero, the ill-starred heir of Sulpicius Galba, and the Calpurnius Crassus who was put to death when Hadrian came to the power.[5]

---

[1] Lamia's governership must have been mentioned, for Tacitus writes 'administrandae Suriae imagine tandem exsolutus' (VI. 27. 1). And Arruntius came into the story of the year 31, cf. *PIR*[1], A 1130: Dio has the incident, but not the name (LVIII. 8. 3).

[2] Three legates under the consular, cf. Strabo III. 166 f. One of them had no legionary command. In Syria Pacuvius, one of the legionary legates, was deputy for Aelius Lamia (Seneca, *Epp.* 12. 8, cf. *Ann.* II. 79. 2).

[3] Asconius 2: 'tamen non puto vos ignorare hunc Pisonem ex ea familia esse quae Frugi appellata sit.' Groag in P-W III. 1396, attached 'Frugi' to the name of the *pontifex*; also R. Syme, *Rom. Rev.* (1939), Index. See, however, Groag in *PIR*[2], C 289. (Cassius Dio is also apparently an offender, cf. the Φούρτιος after the name of the *pontifex* in the Index to Book LIV.)

[4] *IRT* 319.   [5] Thus the table in *PIR*[2], vol. II (facing p. 54), or Table V in *Rom. Rev.*

5—T.S.I.T.

VI

PERSONAL NAMES IN *ANNALES* I–VI*

AMES of persons in the *Codex Mediceus prior* exhibit familiar corruptions, and many of the necessary corrections were easily made.[1] The cogent evidence was often external—the same character appeared elsewhere in Tacitus, or in some other writer, and inscriptions might certify the orthography of a name or even permit the identification of an individual. None the less, there were, and there are, traps and uncertainties. First, an inoffensive or unimpeachable name need not be correct. Nobody would have suspected 'Livius' (*Ann.* II. 30. 1—twice): only later passages (IV. 13. 2; 28. 1) showed that the person referred to was in fact Vibius Serenus. And 'Vescularius Atticus' (*Ann.* VI. 10. 2) would stand but for 'Vescularius Flaccus' (II. 28. 1). Second, the rarity (genuine or only fancied) of a name has often been allowed to impugn it. On the contrary, if a *gentilicium* is uncommon, or even unique, that is no ground for discomfort. The nomenclature of Italy is startling, fantastic and myriad in its manifestations. The *Annales* of Tacitus display names which, deceptively familiar from their occurrence in a classical text, are yet of a rarity to adorn an onomatological aviary.

Again, an error here and there, of a kind not obviously to be explained by a copyist's confusion of forms and letters, might be due to the author's own inadvertence. A Roman senator or a Roman historian carried in his head an enormous collection of names and personalities, for that was a necessary equipment in either profession if a man were not to incur the deadly reproach of ignorance about the *res publica* in one at least of its aspects, namely knowing who was who in politics. Prosopography is not a modern invention. Though Tacitus was a scrupulous investigator, as witness his note on an obscure fellow—'originem non repperi' (*Ann.* VI. 7. 4)—the very variety and complexity of the material might cause a senator or a historian to make a slip about a name, in speech or in writing. For example, it was peculiarly easy to confuse Latinii and Lucanii (see below,

---

* Reprinted from *JRS* xxxix (1949), 6–18.

[1] The common types of corruption were neatly classified and discussed by G. Andresen, 'Korrumpierte Eigennamen bei Tacitus,' *Woch. für cl. Phil.* 1915, 1097 ff.; 1121 ff.

p. 70). Modern scholars have the index and the lexicon. Those aids do not always preserve them from errors about names when they edit the text of Tacitus.[1]

Fourth and last, orthography. It is not enough to establish, on the basis of epigraphic usage, the commonest, or even the best, spelling of a name. What is in fact the same *gentilicium* may show variations between writer and writer, period and period—and according to the social status of its owner. Some forms are archaic (which often means respectable), or regional, others careless, vulgar—or just innovatory. For example, there are consonants doubled or not doubled. And, most remarkable perhaps, there are the variations between '-iedius', '-edius', and '-idius'. Those terminations are non-Latin in type and origin. Their incidence has been properly and thoroughly investigated in statistics of the inscriptions of central Italy: they are found to be characteristic of the region of the Abruzzi, being thickest among the peoples of the Marsi and Paeligni.[2] Several of these names occurring in Tacitus demand attention, for orthography and for other reasons.

Names ending in '-enus' and '-ienus' have not been studied in the same systematic fashion.[3] Yet it can be said that their area of greatest frequency seems to lie in the northern zone of the Osco-Umbrian dialects; Etruscan influence has been plausibly surmised. Here, too, variations occur in the ending of fundamentally identical family names, as between '-enus', '-ienus', and '-enius'. One may observe, for example, numerous 'Passenii' on the inscriptions from the sepulchre of the Passieni on the Via Latina (*CIL* VI. 7257–7280). At the same time, however, it is not at all to be believed that any of the senatorial Passieni of the early Principate ever chose to be styled 'Passenius'. And though variants in the spelling of the same *gentilicium*, even a senator's *gentilicium*, might occur at different periods and in different authors, it is not likely that a historian deliberately allowed

---

[1] Thus Fisher, 'Latinus' (*Ann.* IV. 71. 1); Koestermann, 'Curtius' (IV. 27. 2) and 'Publicum' (*Hist.* IV. 10. 1).

[2] A. Schulten, 'Italische Namen und Stämme', *Klio* II (1902), 167 ff. and 440 ff.; III (1903), 235 ff.

[3] W. Schulze in his monumental work ('Zur Geschichte lateinischer Eigennamen', *Gött. Abh., phil.-hist. Klasse*, N.F.V., 5, 1904: referred to in the following observations as *LE*) did not realize until it was too late the importance of establishing the regional distribution of names in '-ienus'. He was therefore compelled to employ the material as published by Conway—whose methods he describes as 'crude and superficial'. Compare his remarks, 'Conway's Gedanke, das Namenmaterial in die Stoffsammlung für die italischen Dialekte aufzunehmen, ist ausgezeichnet, aber seine Ausführung ist doch allzu roh und äusserlich. Leider habe ich versäumt, rechtzeitig die Frage nach der Verbreitung des Suffixes *-ienus* in meine Untersuchung einzubeziehen und muss nun das Material benutzen, wie es bei Conway dargeboten wird' (*LE* 104).

himself the licence of writing now 'Trebellenus', now 'Trebellienus'. Some editors would argue that such variants should be retained in the text.

To constitute a legitimate text is indeed a tricky business. Many valid corrections of proper names in the *Codex Mediceus prior* have been made since the year 1515, Lipsius' operations being especially notable and decisive, though some had to wait until the nineteenth century (for example, it was Borghesi who first interpreted 'Fulnicium' as 'P. Vinicium', *Ann.* III. 11. 2). Yet it turned out that a number of the alterations were questionable and even erroneous. It thus became necessary to go back and purge the received texts.[1] The conservative reaction has been maintained in recent years. Even so, the latest editions of *Annales* I–VI contain personal names that derive from premature and superfluous emendation.

The appended list, while taking its origin from names that have been questioned or altered, is not confined to that class. It also includes several that were never remotely suspected. The justification for their appearance is a simple one: they exemplify rarities of nomenclature or variations in orthography, and so provide guidance or parallel in disputed instances. And there is one name, that of the *delator* Romanius Hispo (*Ann.* I. 74. 1) which stands in all the modern texts as it stood in the *Codex*, in a flagrantly incorrect form. Here a change is unavoidable.

Two *cruces*, unmanageable in the scope of the present paper, have been deliberately omitted. As for the one, it is enough to cite it—'†que tedii et Vedii Pollionis luxus' (*Ann.* I. 10. 5). The other is 'M. Lepidum', whom Augustus in his latest conversations reckoned among the 'capaces imperii' (*Ann.* I. 13. 2). Lipsius altered the *praenomen*, reading 'M'. Lepidum', and all editors of any consequence since Lipsius (with the solitary exception of G. H. Walther) follow his procedure, and some have investigated for themselves. Marcus Lepidus or Manius, this is no place to state the problem in all its complications or even adumbrate the case for M. Aemilius Lepidus (*cos.* A.D. 6), of Scipionic ancestry, the son of Paullus (*cos.* 34 B.C.), and of Cornelia.[2]

To conclude this preface. Though most of the items discussed seem to be little more than questions of orthography, in some an identity is at stake, as when an emendation reveals a new Atia (a member of the family of Augustus on the maternal side), or a lady of the Sextii Africani. The

---

[1] Andresen's new edition (1913) of Halm's Teubner text of the *Annales* registered many improvements on the previous edition of Halm (1883), among them rectifications of proper names; cf. also his article referred to above, p. 58, n. 2. Of some three hundred changes of all kinds, about one-half were a return to the readings of the *Codex*.

[2] [Above, pp. 30 ff.] For a brief hint about M. Lepidus, see *Rom. Rev.* (1939), 433.

more important benefit accrues from the less prepossessing specimens of nomenclature. Rare and peculiar *gentilicia*, confined for the most part to one district of Italy or to one family of senatorial rank, illustrate the origin and the vicissitudes of *novi homines* under the early Principate, especially persons from the central highland zone, and fill out with colour and relief the social and political history of the age.[1]

Some of the names are so uncommon that it has been possible to record all the known instances.[2] For others it is enough to concentrate on the significant details in the evidence, that is to say the marked preponderance of a name in some region of Italy or its attestation in local families of magisterial rank. In the search for origins the inscriptions of the capital and of the suburban towns of Latium are naturally of little use; yet even here the data about freedmen may help to show the rarity of certain *gentilicia*.

Nor will it be necessary at this late date to recall all the emendations of proper names, whether convincing or superfluous, that have been offered by scholars ever since the *editio princeps*. It would make a curious record, not without a certain melancholy instruction. For brevity and for convenience, references will be confined almost exclusively to the treatment of the names in the latest three editions of *Annales* I-VI.[3] Each item is prefixed with the form that occurs in the *Codex*.

M. ALETVS, 11.47.4: a senator of praetorian rank. The accepted remedy 'M. Ateius', sponsored by Borghesi and by Mommsen, is printed in all modern texts. 'Ateius' is a name rendered familiar by the tribune of 55 B.C., C. Ateius Capito, who called down curses on M. Crassus, and by the illustrious, and obsequious, jurist, C. Ateius L. f. L. n. Capito (*suff.* A.D. 5), who was the grandson of a Sullan centurion, son of a senator of praetorian rank (*Ann.* III. 75. 1): the latter may be identified as the 'L. Ateius L. f. An. Capito' attested in 50 B.C. (Cicero, *Ad fam.* VIII. 8. 5). Their local origin is unknown—perhaps Castrum Novum in south Etruria, cf. the inscription (late Republican or early Imperial) recording a magistrate there, L. Ateius M. f. Capito (*CIL* XI. 3583 = *ILS* 5515). The tribe of Castrum Novum has not been established: the collocation of this evidence might suggest the 'Aniensis'. Apart from the three Ateii Capitones, no Ateius is known as a

---

[1] cf. *Rom. Rev.* (1939), 360 ff.; 456.

[2] If some have been overlooked, the scattered and unsystematic publication of epigraphic material can take a part of the blame.

[3] Namely those of E. Koestermann (Teubner, 1934, replacing Halm-Andresen,[5] 1913); M. Lenchantin de Gubernatis (*Regia Academia Italica*, 1940); H. Fuchs (*Editiones Helveticae*, 1946). For observations on the last of these, cf. *JRS* XXXVIII (1948), 122 ff. Lenchantin's text is provided with a complete and admirable *apparatus*. The present enquiry has been conducted independently of Fabia's *Onomasticon Taciteum* (1900), and, for the sake of brevity, makes no reference to that work.

senator, and there is no strong reason for producing another. Alternatives become equally plausible. Orelli conjectured 'Aletius', for which name cf. *TLL* s.v. 'Allius' and Schulze, *LE* 90 f. Also to be thought of is 'Aleius' (on which name, cf. *LE* 345). The smallest change of all, the common reading of 't' for 'i', will explain how 'Aleius' could pass into 'Aletus', cf. 'eiusque' giving 'et usque' (I. 13. 6). At the same time, however, one should ask whether 'Aletus' might not come from 'Aietius', with an eye on the senator Aietius Pastor (Seneca, *Controv.* I. 3. 11). The corruption 'l' for 'i' is easy, cf. 'se lustrabo' for 'Seius Strabo' (I. 7. 2)—and perhaps the 'L. Alenus' of Cicero, *De natura deorum* III. 74, where the *Codex Vindobonensis* in fact has 'L. Aienus'. The name 'Alenus' is rare. The only epigraphical instance cited by the *TLL* is 'Ulpius Alenus v.p.' of *c.* A.D. 306 (*CIL* IX. 687, Herdoniae); but 'Alenus', 'Alenius', and 'Alennius' are very much the same thing, observe 'L. Aleni C. f. Clu. Capitoni(s)' (*CIL* XI. 4577, Carsulae), clearly of the same family as 'C. Alennius L. f. Clu.' (*CIL* VI. 11383 = *ILS* 8325). On the other hand, 'Aienus' is rendered singularly attractive by the two Republican inscriptions of *magistri vicorum* in the land of the Vestini, 'T. Aienus V. f. Med.' (*CIL* I². 1804) and 'L. Aienus L. f.' (*CIL* I². 756 = *ILS* 4906).

A case could thus be made for 'Aietius' in Tacitus. But Seneca's 'Aietius Pastor' is unique—or at least it should be noted that the only epigraphically attested form of the name is 'Aiedius' (cf. *TLL*, a dozen instances). And he might really be 'Aletius Pastor'. However, to conclude, there are no adequate grounds for preferring 'Ateius' in *Ann.* II. 47. 4. The claims of 'Aletius', 'Aleius', and 'Aietius' must be considered.

ALIA, III. 68. 2: mother of C. Junius Silanus (*cos.* A.D. 10). Various suggestions have been made. For example, Grotius' 'Manlia' (preferred by Borghesi), which would produce the last known survivor, after Horace's friend Torquatus (*Epp.* I. 5. 3; *Odes* IV. 7. 23), of the patrician Manlii—and might seem at first sight to explain the emergence of the *cognomen* Torquatus among the Junii Silani of the early Empire. But that *cognomen* goes back a long way, deriving from the son of T. Manlius Torquatus (*cos.* 165 B.C.), adopted by D. Silanus (Cicero, *De finibus* I. 24); hence the *imagines* of the Manlii were displayed at the funeral of M. Brutus' half-sister, Cassius' widow (*Ann.* III. 76. 2). As this justification for 'Manlia' is superfluous, 'Allia' might seem to suffice. But this is ruled out by the context, which assigns the distinction and identity of Silanus' mother as the reason for exempting the maternal property from confiscation, and therefore supports Madvig's 'Atia'—'eadem ceteri, nisi quod Cn. Lentulus separanda Silani materna bona, quippe Atia parente geniti, reddendaque filio dixit, adnuente Tiberio'. The emendation is accepted by the recent editors of Tacitus, but the historical consequences seem to have been overlooked, save by E. Hohl (P-W x. 1088); and the lady does not find a place in *PIR²*. She must be no less than a descendant of Augustus' maternal grandfather M. Atius Balbus, a senator of praetorian rank from Aricia.

There were two women called Atia. The one, the mother of Augustus, took for her second husband L. Marcius Philippus (*cos.* 56 B.C.). The other, her younger sister, passed also into this house, being married to the consul's son L. Philippus (*suff.* 38 B.C.). Who then is the third Atia? Conceivably the same as the younger sister. Of her husband Philippus nothing is recorded subsequent to his triumph in 33 B.C. and construction of the Porticus Philippi from the proceeds of the booty. He might have died soon after, and his widow might have married a Junius Silanus, the otherwise unrecorded parent of C. Junius C. f. M. n. Silanus (*cos.* A.D. 10). The latter would then be half-brother of Marcia, the wife of Paullus Fabius Maximus (*cos.* 11 B.C.), and, like her, first cousin to the Princeps, which is paradoxical but not impossible. Despite his lineage Silanus need not have reached the consulate at the earliest permissible age (thirty-two), but might have suffered some retardation, like other *nobiles* in this period, especially those whose fathers had missed the supreme magistracy.

Conjecture for conjecture, it might be preferable to produce a third Atia. It could be done. Certain arguments tell for the existence of a younger M. Atius Balbus, maternal uncle of Augustus and governor of Sardinia in the triumviral period, cf. M. Grant, *From* Imperium *to* Auctoritas (1946), 150 ff. Atia might be identified as his daughter.

Speculation about these relatives of the Princeps should not neglect Sex. Pompeius, the consul of A.D. 14, described by Cassius Dio as his συγγενής (LVI. 29. 5. cf. Seneca, *De tranquillitate animi* II. 10). Borghesi suggested that the link might be a second Marcia (*Oeuvres* v (1869), 141). Unfortunately the inscriptions he relied on were spurious (*CIL* VI. *977ᵃ⁻ᶜ), and the problem subsists. The second Marcia may still excite hopes—she occurs in Drumann-Groebe, *Geschichte Roms* IV² (1908), 325.

The kinship of Sex. Pompeius with the dynasty happened to be recorded in the literary evidence. That an Atia was the mother of C. Silanus (*cos.* A.D. 10) is a casual fact, emerging from an emendation in Tacitus. It helps to explain the remarkable prominence of the Silani in the early Empire. The Silani were numerous as well as successful—it was another branch of them that rose highest, with M. Silanus (*cos.* A.D. 19), who married Aemilia Lepida the great-granddaughter of Augustus (cf. the stemma, *PIR¹*, J 550).

ANTEIVS, II. 6. 1: a legate of Germanicus Caesar in A.D. 16. Urlichs bracketed this name, supposing it wrongly inserted, because of 'C. Antio' in the preceding phrase; and of the recent editors Fuchs concurs. Yet it would not be a surprise to discover an earlier member of the family of the consular P. Anteius (*PIR²*, A 731) whom Agrippina the daughter of Germanicus is said to have favoured (*Ann.* XVI. 14. 2). The only other senatorial Anteii are a father and a son, the one killed by Caligula, the other by his German bodyguard after the assassination of the tyrant (Josephus, *AJ* XIX. 125 f.). The local origin of the Anteii cannot be ascertained—but observe Anteia L. f. Procula, married to one of the Voluseni of Sestinum in Umbria (*CIL* XI. 6019), perhaps more significant than the Anteia wife of the younger Helvidius Priscus (Pliny, *Epp.* IX. 13. 4).

ARVSEIVS, VI. 7. 1: a *delator*, the accuser of L. Arruntius, perhaps but not necessarily the same person as L. Aruseius (VI. 40. 1). Reinesius proposed to read 'Aruleius' in both places, but the grounds are seen to be inadequate, for, though 'Aruleius' (cf. the not very frequent 'Arulenus') occurs, it occurs only on three inscriptions, all at Rome (*CIL* VI. 12490; 33540; 26466—two persons, each with the *praenomen* 'Lucius'). Now 'Aruseius' does in fact exist. The unique instance is *CIL* VI. 12492—a freedman of P. Aruseius. No modern editor has been frivolous enough to substitute 'Aruleius' for 'Aruseius'.

ATIDIVM GEMINVM, IV. 43. 3: proconsul of Achaia, presumably in the time of Augustus. This *gentilicium* exhibits the predictable variants 'Atiedius', 'Atedius', 'Atidius', also the forms with the doubled 't'. The archaic form 'Atiedius' is discovered as the name of a religious confraternity at Iguvium, e.g. 'fratrus atiersier' (*Tab. Iguv.* VII b 1 Devoto), and on early inscriptions from the Marsian country, 'Paapia Atiedi l.' (*CIL* I². 1817= *ILS* 3817) and 'V. A[t]iedius' (I². 392= *ILS* 4023). There are further examples to be found in central Italy and in Umbria, e.g. *CIL* XI. 4795 (Spoletium, a magistrate). And, as a curiosity, may be noted a group of Atiedii in Africa, all at or near Thugga (*CIL* VIII. 26726 f.; 27361; 27368). The form 'Atedius', familiar from Statius' friend Atedius Melior (*PIR²*, A 1277) is very rare; likewise 'Atidius', though attested in literature for an agent of Verres (*In Verrem* II. 3. 75). The only epigraphic instances in Italy are suburban (*CIL* XIV. 2532, 4090³⁰ f., a pair of tiles, all from the territory of Tusculum). The forms with the doubled 't' are not so instructive: 'Attidius' becomes rather common.

There is no call to alter the name 'Atidius' in Tacitus, even though a person called M. Ἀττήδιος Κόγνιτορ be attested (*Inschr. v. Olympia* 86. 11), whose family may be assumed to have derived its *gentilicium* from the proconsul of Achaia.

'Atiedius' and its derivatives will find parallel in these notes: compare the remarks on 'Bruttedius', 'Carsidius', 'Titedius', 'Vibidius', all Tacitean characters. It is a temptation to add 'Murredius', a *rhetor* much disliked by the elder Seneca (*Controv.* I. 2. 21, etc.). The *gentilicium* is not elsewhere attested in this form. There is only 'Murridius', and rare at that (*CIL* VI. 22723; 23075, mentioning the same woman as IX. 5571, Tolentinum in Picenum).

AVFIDIENVM RVFVM, I. 20. I: *praefectus castrorum*, a common soldier to begin with. The name is rare—*CIL* V. 5575 (territory of Comum); XI. 4670 (Tuder); IX. 4242 (Amiternum); 4396 (between Amiternum and Reate, a *tribunus militum*). Compare the alternative form 'Aufidenus', significantly only in Umbria (*CIL* XI. 4676, Tuder; and XIV. 4500—a Tudertine soldier in the *Vigiles* in A.D. 168) and in Picenum (IX. 5015, Hadria; 5092, Interamnia), apart from the capital (VI. 12810; 20385; 22239), and its remarkable emergence in the nomenclature of a philosopher at Sparta, cf. the inscription published by A. M. Woodward, *BSA* XXIX (1927/8), 55=*AE* 1931, 5. The equation 'Aufidenus'—'Aufidienus' may be supported by the fact that instances of each occur at Tuder.

The local habitat of the name seems to be the northern part of central Italy, and its social standing is not high. 'Salvidienus', rendered notorious by Octavianus' plebeian marshal, along with 'Salvidenus', will repay study. Of the regional and indigenous character of such *gentilicia*, a palmary example is 'Sibidienus', only found in Umbria (cf. *LE* 232), and in Umbria only in the north-east, at Tuficum (*CIL* XI. 5703–8; 8056; 8058 f.), and at Attidium close by (XI. 5673)—apart from a centurion at Carnuntum (III. 14348[21a]), no doubt an Umbrian. As for 'Sibidenus', there are only *CIL* VI. 1057 and 33183.

BRVTTEDIVS NIGER, III. 66. I: a senator and noted prosecutor whose ambition brought him to a bad end. Also 'Bruttedium' (ib. 4), which form is certified by the elder Seneca (*Controv.* II. 1. 35 f.), while Juvenal (X. 83) calls him Bruttidius and shortens the vowel into the bargain. Of the same family presumably is the *rhetor* Bruttedius Brutus (Seneca, *Controv.* VII. 5. 9; IX. 1. 11), also the official 'C. Bru[tt]idi(us) Brutus' (M. Rostowzew, 'Römische Bleitesserae' *Klio*, Beiheft III (1905), 49, nr. 521).

Epigraphically the name 'Bruttedius' is so rare as to give no hint whatsoever of local provenance. On the inscriptions of Italy, even including the capital, there is no 'Bruttedius', only one Brutedius (*CIL* VI. 28776). Even 'Bruttidius' registers only two examples (VI. 13646; V. 5446, near Comum), apart from the tiles stamped with the name of 'L. Bruttidius Augustalis' at Rome (xv. 373-9) and elsewhere (e.g. x. 8042²⁵, v. 8110⁷³, in Istria; viii. 22632⁷ and 22632⁴⁶, Carthage).

CAESILIANVS, vi. 7. 1: a senator. All recent editors endorse and perpetuate Lipsius' emendation 'Caecilianus', presumably because of Magius Caecilianus, praetor in A.D. 21 (iii. 37. 1). The reading of *M* is kept in *PIR*², C 187 —rightly. Though the *gentilicium* 'Caesilius' occurs only once in senatorial nomenclature (*CIL* x. 7287, Panormus, of the Antonine period), it is quite reputable. To the instances cited in *TLL* add a magistrate at Ocriculum, of early date, without *cognomen* (*Epigraphica* iii (1941), 149), and a *duumvir* at Ostia in A.D. 94 (*Inscr. It.* xiii. 1. 5, p. 94). That would suffice. 'Caesilianus' happens to be found once at least, namely Λ. Ἀνείλιος Καισειλιανός (*IG* xiv. 1584, Rome).

CARSIVS SACERDOS, iv. 13. 2; GRASIDIVS SACERDOS, vi. 48. 4: a senator. Reinesius' emendation 'Carsidius' is unanimously accepted. The man was *praetor urbanus* in A.D. 27, '[Cars]idius Sa[cerdos]' (*CIL* i², p. 71 = *Inscr. It.* xiii. 1. 24, p. 297). One would like to know where he was when he supplied corn to the Numidian insurgent Tacfarinas, or so it was alleged, in A.D. 21: the same charge was brought against a Roman residing and trading in Africa, the son of the exile Sempronius Gracchus (*Ann.* iv. 13. 2 f., cf. i. 53. 3 ff.). For a man (Surdinius Gallus) who transferred his domicile to Carthage in A.D. 47 in an attempt to escape the burdens of the senatorial career, see Dio lx. 29. 2. The rarity of this *gentilicium* deserves comment—six instances only, three of them at Rome (*CIL* vi. 14440; 34697; 38638), one at Ostia (*CIL* xiv. 4838), one at Burnum in Dalmatia, a soldier 'P. Carsidius P. f. Calvus' from Lugdunum (*CIL* iii. 14995), and one at Ephesus, a *grammateus*, Ποπλίου Καρσιδίου Ἐπίφ[ρονος] (*OGIS* 493). But observe 'Carsedius' which may be regarded as an alternative form, attested once only in 'Maxuma Carsedia T. f.' (*CIL* ix. 5058, near Hadria in Picenum): the style of nomenclature admitting a woman's *praenomen* is not orthodox Roman usage. For the origin of the name 'Carsidius' Schulze (*LE* 147) points to Etruscan 'carsna' (*CIE* 1963, Clusium), and 'Carso' used either as *nomen* (*CIL* xi. 3060, Horta) or as *cognomen* (*CIL* xi. 4387, Ameria); and of course there is the place Carsulae in Umbria, to say nothing of the *vicus* of Carso at Iguvium, 'carsome hoier' (*Tab. Iguv.* vi a 14 Devoto). But the incidence of 'Carsius' may arouse disquiet (*CIL* v. 7603, Alba Pompeia; xii. 679, Arelate; 993, Glanum), and, combined with the place-names Carsium (or Carsum) in Moesia Inferior, Carsidava in Dacia, it suggests rather a Celtic origin ultimately. Names of a Celtic type in Umbria and Picenum are a topic that still awaits investigation.

CETHECIO LABEONI, IV. 73. 3: legate of the Fifth Legion. All modern editors accept, and print, 'Cethego Labeoni.' Groag, however, hesitates, asterisks the entry 'Cethecius Labeo' (*PIR²*, C 698), and observes: 'quod nomen lateat in *cethecio* parum liquet; *Cethego* corr. Lipsius nescio num recte.' There is nothing to criticize in the name-form produced by Lipsius' emendation, 'Cethegus Labeo.' The ancient aristocratic *cognomen* of a branch of the patrician Cornelii can be used as the equivalent of a *nomen*. That is normal enough. What deserves notice is the fact that 'Cethegus' as a *cognomen* is never vulgarized—it is only used by Cornelii of the *nobilitas*, whether Republican or their ostensible descendants under the Empire (see the evidence collected in *TLL*). No direct link can be established between Republican and Imperial Cethegi—the first of the latter is Ser. Cornelius Cethegus (*cos.* A.D. 24), and he may really be a Cornelius Lentulus (cf. E. Groag, *PIR²*, C 1336). So far, therefore, a 'Cornelius Cethegus Labeo' would be unobjectionable, though the *cognomen* Labeo is not attested among the Cethegi of the imperial age. Furthermore, one should at least call attention to the enigmatic writer on antiquarian topics Cornelius Labeo, much drawn upon for his learning by Macrobius, Servius, and other authors (*PIR²*, C 1373): the date of Cornelius Labeo is a matter of deep and wide controversy. For all that, 'Cethegus' is not proved. Are there any alternatives? From 'Cethegus' was formed the *gentilicium* 'Cethegius', borne by three persons of low degree in the city of Rome (*CIL* VI. 14712 (two people); 19807); and there is 'Cethecius Pelagius v.p.' about A.D. 350 (*CIL* VI. 37123). 'Cethecius' is not impossible at an earlier date. Compare the Etruscan 'ceti' (*CIE* 1997, Clusium), 'A. Caitho C. f. Faber' (*CIE* 4278= *CIL* XI. 2037, Perusia), and the forms 'Caetennius', 'Caetrius', 'Cetrius', etc. (Schulze, *LE* 137; 337). Nor is the termination '-ecius' without parallel in the nomenclature of Italy, for example, 'Titecius', an early *primus pilus* and *tribunus militum* in the Marsian territory (*CIL* IX. 3851 f., Supinum), and 'Venecia' one of the names borne by the wife of the Umbrian senator Q. Camurius Numisius (*CIL* XI. 5672, Attidium: presumably Trajanic). All in all, it might be expedient to print the text according to *M*.

COMICIO POLLIONI, II. 86. 1: the parent of a Vestal Virgin. Ever since Lipsius' emendation of the *nomen*, the senator Domitius Pollio has stood as an undisputed character, e.g. *PIR²*, D 159. It may be noted that the unprepossessing *gentilicium* 'Comicius' in fact exists. To the instances cited by Schulze (*LE* 42, viz. *CIL* X. 5984, Signia; XIV. 3749, Tibur) add *CIL* IV. 1321 (Pompeii); VIII. 2405 (Thamugadi) and 3544 (Lambaesis).

T. CVRTISIVS, IV. 27. 1: a former soldier of the Guard. Reinesius' conjecture

'Curtilius' is adopted by Fuchs but not by Koestermann and Lenchan-
tin. The *nomen* 'Curtisius' happens not to be attested. It did not trouble
Wilhelm Schulze (*LE* 236); and observe that 'Curisius' (*CIL* v. 5033,
Tridentum, noted in *LE* 156) appears to be unique, likewise 'Curidius'
(Cicero, *In Verrem* II. 4. 44: not in *LE*). On the other hand, though 'Curtil-
ius' is familiar from the Neronian consular T. Curtilius Mancia (*PIR²*,
C 1605), there is no other senator, and the name is not really very com-
mon (see *LE* 78a and *TLL*, s.v.).

EXITIA, VI. 29. 4: wife of Mam. Aemilius Scaurus (*suff.* A.D. 21). Lipsius
disengaged 'Sextia' from the 'hortantes exitia uxore' of *M*, and the
moderns concur, with the exception of Lenchantin, who prints in his text
'hortante exitium uxore'. Yet Tacitus would not defraud of name and
fame the noble wife who urged and shared Scaurus' end, 'dignum veteri-
bus Aemiliis.' Compare, in the same paragraph the suicide of Pomponius
Labeo—'aemulataque est coniunx Paxaea.' Not that argument is needed.
'Sextia' is certain. The inscription *CIL* VI. 23073 (duly noted in *PIR²*, A
404) reveals Nostus, freedman of Mam. Scaurus, married to Helice, freedwoman of Sextia. The name of Scaurus' wife (his second, at the least) is of
some importance in bridging a gap in family history between T. Sextius,
legate of Caesar in Gaul and governor of Africa Nova through vicissitudes
of war and politics in 44-40 B.C. (P-W II A, 2041 ff.), and T. Sextius
Africanus (*suff.* A.D. 59). Another member has recently emerged,
clearly the parent of the consul, as honorary *duumvir* at Ostia in A.D. 36
(*Inscr. It.* XIII. 1. 5, p. 188). The Sextii, having the tribe 'Voturia', are an
old Ostian family (cf. E. Groag, P-W II A, 2039). Their womenfolk explain—or at least attest—their resurgence after temporary eclipse under
Augustus, namely this Sextia, married to the illustrious Mam. Scaurus,
and another (*Ann.* XVI. 10. 1), mother-in-law of L. Antistius Vetus (*cos.*
A.D. 55). They were presumably aunts of the consul T. Sextius Africanus;
and both ended by suicide.

FALANIVS, I. 73. 1, and FAIANIVS, ib. 2: a Roman knight. The most peculiar problem of names in all Tacitus: the scribe who wrote the *Codex
Mediceus* wrote 'Faianius', and then altered it to 'Falanius', but did nothing
to 'Faianius' in the next sentence. The palaeographical facts are clear,
though unfortunately neglected by Fisher, who printed 'Falanius' without
comment in both instances. They are properly stated by the recent editors.
But here concord ends. Koestermann and Fuchs have 'Falanius' while
Lenchantin opts for 'Faianius'. The onomatological evidence should be
considered and assessed, though it cannot intervene decisively. The *gentilicium* 'Falanius' has not turned up. That did not disturb Schulze, who cited

the ancient Roman god 'Divus pater Falacer' (Varro, *LL* v. 84) and the Sabine village Falacrinae where a Roman emperor was born (Suetonius, *Divus Vesp.* 2. 1), also names like the Etruscan 'falasial' (*CIE* 3413, Perusia) and 'Falius'—which occurs only in the remarkable 'L. Falius L. f. Tinia' a magistrate with a celestial *cognomen* at Hispellum in Umbria (*CIL* XI. 5281). Tinia is the Etruscan Juppiter. One may add a reference to the word 'fala' meaning 'a wooden tower' (Servius on *Aen.* IX. 705), and the Etruscan 'falado'—'falae dictae ab altitudine, a falado, quod apud Etruscos significat caelum' (Festus, p. 78 L). Further, to support 'Falanius', may be adduced the facts about 'Velanius'. The equestrian officer Q. Velanius (Caesar, *BG* III. 7. 4) was impugned by Hübner—'nomen nullum' (*Eph. Ep.* II. 73); and 'Veianius' must have seemed the obvious correction, compare for example the Veianii, comfortable farmers from Falerii who served as soldiers under Varro in Spain (*RR* III. 16. 10), or Veianius Niger, tribune in the Guard (*Ann.* XVI. 67. 4). But Schulze (*LE* 377) rehabilitated 'Velanius' with Etruscan 'velanial' (e.g. *CIE* 52, Volaterrae) and other forms, and with the Latin inscription that providentially turned up mentioning a 'Q. Vela[…]' (*N. Sc.* 1893, 380, Cascia in the Sabine country)—who might, however, be a 'Velatius': for that name, not cited in *LE*, see *CIL* VI. 1970; 32314 f.

On the other side, 'Faianius' though unusual in appearance, ought not to be regarded as a rarity. To the examples cited in *LE* 185 add a freedman of P. Faianius (*CIL* VI. 35220), L. Faianius Olympus from Ostia (*CIL* XIV. 4382), and Q. Faianius Clemens, a soldier of the legion III Augusta (*AE* 1927, 41 = *I. l. Tun.* 464, Ammaedara). And, indeed, a municipal Faianius would fit very well the 'modicus eques Romanus' in Tacitus, cf. *CIL* XI. 838 (Mutina): 'L. Faianio/L. f. Sabino/aed. flam. patr. col./trib. coh. prim. Ligurum.' To conclude, let it be noted that Stein, who always preferred 'Faianius' (P-W VI. 1967), now prints that name without comment in *PIR*², F 107.

A postscript on 'Faianius' may allude to the possibility of its occurrence at an earlier date, on the list of the *consilium* of Cn. Pompeius Strabo in the camp before Asculum (*CIL* I². 709 + p. 714 = VI. 37045: all the names are not printed in *ILS* 8888). Cichorius, from a personal examination of the bronze tablet, concluded that one of the missing names (no. 22 on his list) was a *gentilicium*, the second and the fourth letters of which were 'a', and proposed '[M]aia[ni]' (*Römische Studien* (1922), 130 ff., at 154 f.). There had been a Maianius, moneyer in the second century B.C. (*BMC, R. Rep.* II. 243 f.). Cichorius noted and rejected certain alternatives—but 'Faianius' was not among them. That is not the end of the matter. Bang produced a slightly different reading, namely 'Fab[i]': indeed, he suggested a supplement to fill the whole gap, viz. 'M. Fab. [i] M. f. [Se]r.'—or '[Te]r.' On this reading, 'Fai[ani]' is not wholly excluded.

LATINIVS LATIARIS, IV. 68. 2, and LATINIVS, IV. 71. 1: a senator. Cassius Dio calls him Λατιάριος (LVIII. 1. 1b). Tacitus later refers to the man and the incident, calling him 'Lucanius Latiaris' (VI. 4. 1). Beroaldus here replaced 'Lucanius' by 'Latinius'. Andresen, however, observing that the collocation of 'Lucanius' and 'Latiaris' is supported by the tile of L. Lucanius Latiaris (*CIL* XV. 1245), corrected the first two instances, and 'Lucanius' now appears in the texts of Koestermann and Fuchs. A pretty problem is raised. It has not always been dealt with properly, or even understood, see for example the article 'Latinius Latiaris', P-W XII. 925 f.; and in 'Lucanius', P-W XIII. 1552 f. this Lucanius, like others of the name, will not be found. What should be done is clear—nothing. Lenchantin therefore prints the text according to *M*. Rather than assume a scribe's error, identically repeated, it would be preferable to suppose that the historian himself may have made a mistake in nomenclature. On the margin of this problem, but supporting 'Lucanius' will be noted Q. Lucanius Latinus, who was *praetor aerarii* in A.D. 19 (*CIL* I², p. 74= *Inscr. It.* XIII. 1 p. 305).

The first known Lucanius is 'M. Lucanius M. f. Hor.' in the *consilium* of Cn. Pompeius Strabo (*CIL* I². 709+ p. 714= VI. 37045), compare the observations of Cichorius (*Römische Studien* (1922), 171f.). His tribe should be taken into account—it is the tribe of Aricia. Now as shown above, the *cognomina* 'Latiaris' and 'Latinus' are attested for Lucanii in the early Empire—and are singularly appropriate if these men came from a town so prominent in Latin history and religion. The *gentilicium* 'Latinius' also occurs there, as witness 'Ti. Latinius Ti. f. Hor. Pandusa' (*CIL* XIV. 2166), identical with or related to the Latinius Pandusa who was praetorian legate in Moesia (*Ann.* II. 66. 1). A historian might have something to plead in extenuation if he mixed up his Lucanii and Latinii.

OLENNIVS, IV. 72. 1: a *primipilaris*. The name is unique, but unimpeachable, cf. Schulze, *LE* 73, who cites, *inter alia*, 'Q. Aulinna Sex. f. Sab.' (*CIL* XI. 1758, Volaterrae), 'Aulenus' (*CIL* X. 4926 f., Venafrum, etc.) and the Etruscan soothsayer in a famous story, Aulenus Calenus (Pliny, *NH* XXVIII. 15). Add 'L. Olienus L. f.' a *magister* at Capua in 110 B.C. (*CIL* I². 674= *ILS* 3770).

PONTIVS FREGELLANVS, VI. 48. 4: a senator. Koestermann and Lenchantin make no change, but Fuchs reads 'Pontilius'. The justification for the proposal deserves to be known. It is an inscription from Salonae: 'C. Pontilio/ Fregellano/cos., patrono/d.d./publice' (*CIL* III. 8715= *ILS* 960). This may, or may not, be the same man. For Pontilii see *LE* 212. No other senators are known.

The *gentilicium* 'Pontius' is so common in the Oscan regions that it is no surprise to find Pontii designated for convenience by a distinctive *cognomen*, thus the famous Pontii Telesini, the senator C. Pontius Paelignus (*CIL* v. 4348 = *ILS* 942, Brixia), or Pliny's friend Pontius Allifanus (on the address of *Epp.* v. 14 in the *Codex Ashburnhamensis*). Pontilii are much rarer. Where the family of the consular C. Pontilius Fregellanus was established, there is no means of telling: the Latin colony of Fregellae had been razed to the ground and abolished for ever because of its recalcitrance in the year 125 B.C. The survivors dispersed. One of them, an Ovius, went to Ariminum, cf. A. Degrassi, 'Il monumento riminese di Q. Ovius Fregellanus,' *Athenaeum* XXIX (1941), 133 ff.

ROMANO HISPONE, I. 74. 1: a *delator* regarded as archetypal by Tacitus. By a strange inadvertence all recent editors let this pass without compunction or comment, and are satisfied that 'Romanus Hispo' was the fellow's name; also Groag, in *PIR²*, C 149 (discussing A. Caepio Crispinus). In *PIR¹*, R 57/58, however, and in P–W I A, 1063, he appears properly designated as 'Romanius Hispo'. Hispo is familiar from the elder Seneca, e.g. 'Hispo Romanius' (*Controv.* IX. 1. 11, where one MS. has 'Romanus') with inversion of *cognomen*, as in 'Silo Pompeius' and 'Brutus Bruttedius' (ib.). Now a *cognomen* of the type of 'Hispo' can actually be used strictly and officially as a *gentilicium*, cf. the 'Caepio' of 'Caepio Crispinus' in the same sentence in Tacitus, and so in theory 'Hispo Romanus' could stand as *nomen* and *cognomen*, and as such be subject to inversion, giving the order 'Romanus Hispo'; but such an explanation neglects the evidence for the *gentilicium* 'Romanius'. Again, in noble families with several *cognomina*, the *gentilicium* is frequently dropped and one of the *cognomina* functions in its place, for example 'Messalla Corvinus' or 'Cethegus Labeo' (*Ann.* IV. 7. 3), if 'Cethegus' is right, see above (p. 67). The *delator* cannot claim this aristocratic privilege.

The name 'Romanius' concerns controversy about the nature and origin of the name 'Roma'. The contribution of Schulze (*LE* 579 ff.) was notable: he invoked 'Romilius' as an Etruscan name. But Schulze was reluctant to have anything to do with 'Romanius' (*LE* 368); at the same time he did not commit himself (*LE* 524) to the view that it derives from 'servi publici' (cf. Varro, *LL* VIII. 83 and Livy IV. 61. 10). It is unfortunate that he did not provide and interpret the evidence for the distribution of the name 'Romanius' throughout Italy. The following brief indications may be instructive. No examples in *CIL* IX, in X only one (8059[342], on an object in the Naples Museum); and of the five inscriptions in *CIL* XI (Etruria, Umbria, and the Aemilia), most belong to persons of freedman status, none appears indigenous—and there is none at all in Etruria proper (*CIL* XI. 140; 208 (Ravenna); 3847 (Saxa Rubra); 3761 (Careiae); 5895 (Iguvium)). Cisalpine Gaul is another matter—over a dozen inscriptions, the majority at Brixia, which was not a colony but a native capital in origin. Note, for example, 'Q. Romanius Camburonis f.' (Pais, *Supp. It.* 1275, Brixia). And, appropriately enough, the name occurs in Noricum, e.g. *CIL* III. 5362 (Solva), 5078 (Iuenna), and the early cavalryman from Celeia, C. Romanius Capito, buried near Moguntiacum (*CIL* XIII. 7029). Cognate and confirmatory is 'Romatius', the evidence for which is furnished by Schulze, *LE* 368. It includes Pliny's friend and schoolfellow Romatius Firmus from Comum (*Epp.* I. 19; IV. 29), and other Romatii from that town (*CIL* V. 5286; 5305; Pais, *Supp. It.* 784; 1287, a magistrate).

The data point strongly to Cisalpine Gaul, and precisely to the Transpadane zone, as the place where 'Romanius' is prevalent. Its adoption by natives there and in Noricum suggests that 'Romanius' and 'Romatius' are Illyrio-Celtic, or whatever term be preferred, in origin. It is likely enough that the low-born *delator* Romanius Hispo comes from this region—perhaps from Ateste. It is worth while mentioning an inscription from the capital, of approximately Augustan date: 'P. Romanius C. f. Rom./ C. Romanius P. f. Rom./tr. mil. II/Manlia P. f.' (*CIL* VI. 3534). These people have the tribe 'Romulia', in which only two communities were enrolled, Sora and Ateste; they may be members of Hispo's family, in the previous generation.

The *cognomen* 'Hispo' is uncommon, apparently attested only for Cicero's friend the *publicanus* P. Terentius Hispo (*Ad fam.* XIII. 65. 1 and *Ad Att.* XI. 10. 1, cf. *Inschr. v. Magnesia* 140), for a magistrate at Caelium in Lucania (*AE* 1926, 141), and for the Trajanic senator M. Eppuleius Proculus Ti. Caepio Hispo (*PIR*[2], E 83), whose origin has not been ascertained, but may be northern, cf. the dedications to him at Mediolanum and at Ravenna (*CIL* V. 5813; XI. 14= *ILS* 1027): Juvenal, however, utilizes the name for a disgusting character (II. 50). To complete the evidence about 'Hispo', note *liberti* of the 'Hispones' near Comum (*CIL* V. 5496) and the tile from the vicinity of Rome with the stamp of a Caecilius Hispo (*CIL* XV. 895, corrected, and supported by another specimen from Tarracina, cf. P. Groebe, 'Ein neuer Ziegel aus Terracina,' *Klio* V (1905), 284 f.). Caecilii are not unknown at Comum—the younger Pliny was born a Caecilius.

The feminine of this *cognomen*, 'Hispulla', also appealed to Juvenal, being used for an unchaste woman and for a fat woman (VI. 74; XII, 11). The other instances point to Transpadane Italy and make quite a good showing—Terentia Hispulla Cn. f., mother of L. Valerius Catullus (*IG* II/III. 4159), and presumably of the family of the *publicanus*; Hispulla, wife of the consular Q. Corellius Rufus (Pliny, *Epp.* I. 12. 10), patently mother of Corellia Hispulla (to whom III. 3, is addressed); and, suggesting a link of kinship in this Transpadane circle, Calpurnia Hispulla, the aunt of Pliny's second wife (IV.19 and VIII.11 are addressed to her). The origin of Corellius Rufus is not discussed in *PIR*², C 1294 or by G. E. F. Chilver, *Cisalpine Gaul* (1940); but Momigliano (*JRS* XXXII (1942), 137) draws attention to Corellius, the *eques Romanus* born at Ateste (Pliny, *NH* XVII. 122), and to freedmen there (*N. Scav.* 1930, 280).

SANCIA, VI. 18. 1: the sister of Considius Proculus. Hirschfeld's 'Sancta' was accepted in *PIR*¹, S 130, but Groag (P-W IV. 914) pointed out that 'Sancius' exists, adducing *CIL* VI. 25859a (a freedwoman), and the latest editors stick to *M.* Schulze (*LE* 473) cites no other instance of the name, and there does not appear to be one.

SANGVNNIVM, VI. 7. 1: accuser, along with Aruseius, of L. Arruntius. The name is corrected in *M* by the *manus posterior* which writes 'qui' over it. Hence the generally accepted 'Sanquinium'. That name occurred in fact two chapters earlier, 'Sanquinius Maximus e consularibus' (VI. 5. 3). A wholly different person: the correction might not be right. The name 'Sanquinius' attracted the notice of Schulze, who, referring to Semo Sancus, argued that it is a 'theophoric' name (*LE* 467). Its preternatural rarity deserves to be emphasized. There are three members of a senatorial house, the enigmatic Q. Sanquinius Maximus, *praefectus urbi* and consul suffect for the second time in A.D. 39, legate of Germania Inferior in A.D. 45 (*PIR*¹, S 136); earlier, the Augustan moneyer M. Sanquinius Q. f. (*BMC, R. Emp.* I, 13 and 38); and, presumably brother or parent of the moneyer, the senator of praetorian rank Q. Sanquinius Q. f. Stel. (*CIL* XI. 3755, cf. I². 837= *ILS* 905, Lorium, between Rome and Caere). By paradox this successful but soon extinct senatorial family has left behind not even a freedman anywhere to perpetuate its *gentilicium*, still less a provincial client. The only other Sanquinius in the epigraphical record seems to be Sanquinia C. f. (*CIL* XI. 2613= I². 2613, Caere). If Caere be the home of the Sanquinii, then the tribe of Caere, not so far established, may be the 'Stellatina', not the 'Voturia' (*CIL* XI. 3615).

The rarity of 'Sanquinius' is not in itself an argument of any validity against a second instance of it in *Annales* VI. Nipperdey's brilliant 'Sangurium' produced a name attested once only in the form 'Sanguri C. f.':

this Sangurius along with another local magistrate called L. Gargonius erected a small shrine near Hadria in Picenum (*CIL* IX. 5019= I². 1894). Schulze (*LE* 369) compares the *cognomen* 'Sanga' in the name of Q. Fabius Sanga, *patronus* of the Allobroges (Sallust, *Cat.* 41. 4, etc.), but perhaps not one of the patrician Fabii (cf. Münzer, P-W VI. 1867 f.). Münzer notes the slave name 'Sanga' (Terence, *Eun.* 776; 814). Add 'L. Licinius L. f. Sanga', soldier in the legion II *Adiutrix*, early Flavian in date (*CIL* VII. 186, Lindum). Nipperdey's conjecture might be right.

SIRPICVS, I. 23. 5: a centurion. One might have wondered whether the better form was not 'Serpicus', in view of the *cognomen* 'Serpicanus' found at Saepinum in Samnium (*CIL* IX. 2465; *N. Scav.* 1929, 218) and the apparently unique 'Serpoleius' (*BCH* XXXVI (1912), 77, Delos). But observe the place Sirpium in Samnium (*Geogr. Rav.* IV. 34 and *Tab. Peut.*); and Stein (P-W III A, 360) discovered a Sirpicus, in Numidia: 'L. Sirpicus/ vixsit a. IX/h.e.' (*CIL* VIII. 6167, Arsacal in the territory of Cirta). For *gentilicia* of this Illyrian termination, such as 'Paeticus', 'Patalicus', see especially W. Schulze, *LE* 36. A new example is 'Saulicus', a man from Ateste (*CIL* VI. 37567).

TITIDIVS LABEO, II. 85. 3: a senator, husband of the shameless Vistilia. Identified with the senator of praetorian rank Titedius Labeo (Pliny, *NH* 35. 20—the *Codex Bambergensis* certifies 'Titedius'). Of the recent editors of Tacitus, Fuchs chooses to print 'Titedius'. The change is not justifiable. 'Titedius', 'Titidius' and 'Titiedius' are merely different spellings of the same name, cf. above under 'Atidius'. The *gentilicium* looks very ordinary and undistinguished. Nor are other senators known. In fact, it is not at all common. Instances in *CIL* IX are confined to the territory of the Aequi and Marsi, viz. 'Titidius', *CIL* IX. 3654= I². 1767 (Marruvium); 'Titedius,' 3877 (Supinum); 3948 (Alba); 'Titiedius,' 4035, 4054, and 4059 (Carseoli); 3950 (Alba). Somewhere in these hills and valleys lies the home of the senator Titidius Labeo.

TREBELLENVS RVFVS, II. 67. 2: a senator of praetorian rank, put in charge of the Thracian royal family. Elsewhere in the *Annales* this *gentilicium* appears as 'Trebellienus' (III. 38. 3, twice, and VI. 39. 1, twice). Now two dedications to T. Trebellenus Rufus in the town of Concordia, which is his domicile (he bears its tribe, the 'Claudia'), should surely put the spelling of the name beyond doubt (*CIL* V. 1878= *ILS* 931; *AE* 1888, 24= *ILS* 931a). Hence modern editors duly correct the four instances of 'Trebellienus'—except Lenchantin. And, indeed, it might seem desirable to retain the evidence for this variant: 'Trebellenus' and 'Trebellienus' may be regarded as alternative forms of the same name, compare above, on 'Aufidenus' and 'Aufidienus'. Yet is might be doubted whether a writer deliberately chose to spell the same senator's name in two different ways: a different source might be the explanation of the variant in orthography.

The name is remarkably rare. Schulze has one other instance (*LE* 246), namely, 'Trebelliena Nereis' (*CIL* VI. 27577); and the Italian volumes of the *Corpus* yield only 'Trebelliena Felicitas' (*CIL* IX. 2306, Telesia in Samnium). Nor is it found in the provinces of the West. As for the East, three persons called Τρεβελληνός, all at Sparta, no doubt derive the name from the senator, cf. H. Box, 'Roman Citizenship in Laconia,' *JRS* XXII (1932), 172.

The attempt to analyse the ethnic structure of northern Italy on the basis of nomenclature is baffled at almost every step (cf. G. E. F. Chilver, *Cisalpine Gaul* (1940), 80 ff.). Not only do the natives assume common Latin *gentilicia*. They modify their original names so as to simulate *gentilicia* of Etruscan or Oscan origin. Yet now and then it may be possible to detect immigrant families, at least in the early period and among the 'honestiores'. The name 'Trebellenus' is reassuring, likewise the *cognomen* of the senator C. Pontius Paelignus, presumably a citizen of Brixia (*CIL* v. 4348= *ILS* 942).

VESCVLARIVS ATTICVS, VI. 10. 2: a Roman knight, familiar friend of Tiberius. The correction of the *cognomen* from 'Atticus' to 'Flaccus' is universally accepted, because of the reference in the context to the affair of Libo Drusus, where one finds him designated as 'Flaccum Vescularium' (II. 28. 1). And a plausible explanation of the reading 'Atticus' is to hand— 'librarii oculis ad *Curtium Atticum* paulo inferius memoratum aberrantibus' (Lenchantin). The mistake 'Atticus' for 'Flaccus' could have originated not only in the eye of a copyist but in the mind of the historian, preoccupied with the name of Curtius Atticus which he was going to mention later in the same sentence.

The *nomen* 'Vescularius' might not look reassuring at first sight. There is no need, however, to dally with 'Vesiculanus' (found apparently only at Teanum Sidicinum, *CIL* x. 4797= *ILS* 6298; 4819; *Eph. Ep.* VIII. 145, n. 579) or 'Versiculanus' (*CIL* x. 4397, Capua). Schulze points to the Umbrian word 'veskla', and two instances of 'Vesclarius' (*LE* 333; 417), one at Rome, the other at Corfinium (*CIL* VI. 5044; IX. 3188). To be added are three freedmen of a P. Vesclarius at Rome (*CIL* VI. 17154 (two men); 17154 *bis*).

SEX. VESTILIVM, VI. 9. 2: an elderly senator of praetorian standing, personal friend first of Drusus, then of Tiberius. Clearly a 'Vistilius', compare 'Vistilio' in the next sentence. Yet Lenchantin by an excess of scruple prints 'Vestilium' in his text. In Pliny, *NH* VII. 39, some *codices* have 'Vestilia' for 'Vistilia', it is true; and Schulze (*LE* 256) states that the Vestilii and the Vistilii belong to the same *gens*—this is based on the fact that, whereas two inscriptions of Rome mention freedmen of a Sex. Vistilius (*CIL* VI. 29051 f.), persons called 'Sex. Vestilius' are attested as well (*CIL* X. 628, Salernum; XIV. 1751, Ostia: the sole epigraphic instances of 'Vestilius').

The family is presumably Umbrian, compare the name 'Veistinius' in magisterial inscriptions at Asisium (*CIL* XI. 5389, in the Umbrian dialect; 8021, two members of the family; 5426; 5442= *ILS* 6619). The distribution of 'Vistilius' throughout Italy is instructive. It does not occur in *CIL* V, or IX, or in X (except for the 'Vestilius' mentioned above). On the other hand, four instances in *CIL* XI, all in Umbria, at Interamna (4317), Ameria (4511; 4539), and at Iguvium (5825)—the last of these is in fact a *libertus* of a Sex. Vistilius.

It may be presumed that the Vistilii in the senatorial order of society are members of a single family of local, and Umbrian, origin. Sex. Vistilius took his own life, having incurred the displeasure of Tiberius, 'seu composuerat quaedam in C. Caesarem ut impudicum, sive ficto habita fides' (*Ann.* VI. 9. 2). No doubt he was the parent of Vistilia, wife of Titedius Labeo—her father was of praetorian standing. This lady went so far as to seek official sanction for an irregular life—'licentiam stupri apud aedilis vulgaverat more inter veteres recepto, qui satis poenarum adversum impudicas in ipsa professione flagitii credebant' (*Ann.* II. 85. 3). This exercise of 'Romana simplicitas' was not appreciated. Perhaps it was a comment on the conduct of that other Vistilia, who was married at least six times and who produced a string of children, among them Domitius Corbulo, and Caesonia, whom Caligula espoused (Pliny, *NH* VII. 39). Husbands and offspring were investigated by C. Cichorius, *Römische Studien* (1922), 429 ff. He might have spared a word for the rest of the family.

VIBIDIVM VARRONEM, II. 48. 3: expelled from the Senate in A.D. 17. It is certain that the true form of the *cognomen* is 'Virro'. The evidence, cited and utilized in *PIR*[1], V 373 f., reveals a Sex. Vibidius Virro (perhaps the same person) as father of a Vestal Virgin (*IG* II/III[2]. 3532; 4161), and she is obviously the one whom Tacitus calls 'Vibidiam virginum Vestalium vetustissimam' (*Ann.* XI. 32. 2); and there is also 'Sex. Virro L. f.' (the *gentilicium* has fallen out) of the tribe 'Sergia' attested in 9 B.C. (Frontinus, *De aquae ductibus* 129). Whether there is one Vibidius, or two, or three, need not matter: they belong to the same family. The corrected *cognomen* is printed by Koestermann and Fuchs, but not by Lenchantin. There is a case for letting it stand—Tacitus might have made a slip.

Elsewhere the *cognomen* 'Virro' appears to occur only in Juvenal (v. 39 ff., etc.), denoting a luxurious wastrel. Appropriately enough: the resentment of Tiberius Caesar in A.D. 17 was visited upon 'prodigos et ob flagitia egenos' (*Ann.* II. 48. 3). Previous items in this catalogue have disclosed the unsatisfactory conduct proved or alleged against Italian *novi homines* of rare and distinctive nomenclature—Bruttedius, Carsidius and Titedius. Now Vibidius Virro joins the collection. Observe the tribe 'Sergia' and the distribution of the name 'Veibedius' in *CIL* IX, viz. 3228 and 3274 (Corfinium); 3828 (Ortona). Also from Corfinium is the dialect epitaph 'N. Vibedis N.' (Conway, *The Italic Dialects*, nr. 223). Vibidius Virro was probably a Paelignian. Perhaps one should not omit the 'scurra' Vibidius whom Maecenas brought to the banquet of Nasidienus (Horace, *Sat.* II. 8. 22).

VIBVLENVS AGRIPPA, VI. 40. 1: an *eques Romanus* who took poison during his trial before the Senate. Perhaps he was really 'Vibullius Agrippa': Dio calls him Οὐιβούλιός τε ᾿Αγρίππας ἱππεύς (LVIII. 21. 4). There are no Vibuleni of any consequence at any time (the other Vibulenus in Tacitus is a common soldier, *Ann.* I. 22. 1, etc.), and the local distribution of 'Vibulenus' and 'Vibullius' in Italy furnishes no criterion of preference.

The *nomen* 'Vibullius', however, deserves attention. It first crops up in historical record with L. Vibullius Rufus, an agent of Pompeius Magnus in 56 B.C. (Cicero, *Ad. fam.* I. 9. 10) and his *praefectus fabrum* in 49 B.C. (Caesar, *BC* I. 15. 1, etc.). Then there is a Vibullius praetor in A.D. 56 (*Ann.* XIII. 28. 1). But the notable thing is its occurrence in the nomenclature of great families in the Antonine age, Greek in origin or with Greek connections. First the family of the consular sophist Herodes Atticus: his mother was Vibullia Alcia Agrippina, daughter of a Vibullius Rufus (*Inschr. v. Olympia* 621, cf. P. Graindor, *Un milliardaire antique: Hérode Atticus et sa famille* (1930), 28 f.). The *cognomina* 'Agrippina' and 'Rufus' might tempt speculation. Secondly, 'L. Vibullius Pius' belongs to the name of the Hadrianic senator of the Spartan Euryclid line, C. Julius Eurycles Herclanus L. Vibullius Pius (*IG* v. 1, 1172, Gythium); it is assumed by Q. Pompeius Falco (*suff.* A.D. 108), along with the Euryclid name, at some time subsequent to A.D. 116, so it appears (cf. *ILS* 1035, and his grandson's inscription, *ILS* 1104); and it recurs with P. Coelius Balbinus Vibullius Pius, *cos. ord.* A.D. 137.

How the name 'Vibullius' was originally disseminated in Greece, it is impossible to say. Vibullii are frequent at Corinth, cf. L. Robert, *Hellenica* II (1946), 9 f. Observe especially the agonothete L. Vibullius Pius (*Corinth* VIII. 2. 95). It must suffice in this place to indicate the problems as briefly as possible.

VITIA, VI. 10. 1: the mother of C. Fufius Geminus, *cos.* A.D. 29. Nipperdey's 'Vibia' has not won acceptance. The *gentilicium* 'Vitius' occurs four times—all women of libertine class or nomenclature. Schulze has *CIL* III. 7912 (Sarmizegethusa) and VI. 29095: add VI. 2853 and 34259.

VVLCATIVS MOSCHVS, IV. 43. 5: the rhetorician who had been exiled to Massilia. The *nomen* should be given a better orthography, likewise 'Vulgacium Araricum' (*Ann.* XV. 50. 1) and 'Vulcacius Tertullinus' (*Hist.* IV. 9. 2)—the latter is the same person as 'Volcacius Tullinus' (*Ann.* XVI. 8. 2), whichever *cognomen* be correct. Koestermann is satisfied with 'Vulcacius' in all four instances (*Annales* and *Histories*), and Fuchs prints 'Vulcacius' in *Ann.* IV. 43. 5, but Lenchantin here insists on 'Volcacius'. Classical epigraphic usage is uniform, at least in its earliest instances, in support of 'Volcacius', for example, the *Fasti Venusini* with L. Volcacius Tullus, *cos.* 33 B.C. (*CIL* I², p. 66= *Inscr. It.* XIII. 1. 7, p. 254), and the inscription from Priene mentioning apparently his nephew—Λευκίου Οὐολκακίου [Τ]ύλλου (*OGIS* 458. 11, l. 42): to say nothing of Volcacius the *haruspex* (*CIL* I². 990= *ILS* 3038, Insula Tiberina) and 'C. Volcacius C. f. Varus Antigonae gnatus' (*CIL* XI. 2084= *ILS* 7836), at Perusia, which city was no doubt the home of the consular Volcacii (cf. Propertius I. 22. 3). Furthermore, the index of *CIL* VI reveals fifteen Volcacii but only two Volcatii at Rome, one Vulcacius—the latter is Vulcacius Rufinus (*CIL* VI. 3205= *ILS* 1237, of A.D. 347).

The Etruscan house of the consular Volcacii, showing two consuls (66 B.C. and 33 B.C.), not to mention an officer under Caesar in the Gallic and the Civil Wars, and a friend of Propertius, deserves study. Even the minor Volcacii here cited on a point of orthography are a temptation. Moschus, according to Porphyrio (on Horace, *Epp.* I. 5. 9) was a man of Pergamum, and Kiessling conjectured that he got his *nomen* along with the Roman citizenship from L. Volcacius Tullus, the consul of 33 B.C. ('Tacitus, *Ann.* IV. 43', *Hermes* XXVI (1891), 634 f., noted in *PIR*¹, V 621). Now the *cognomen* of the Roman knight Volcacius Araricus, which is unique and surely derives from the river Arar, suggests either an ancestor's exploit in Gaul or, as is much more likely, an origin thence; and, for that matter, the senator Volcacius Tullinus (or Tertullinus) might be a provincial rather than a descendant of the aristocratic Volcacii—none of them is known subsequent to Propertius' friend Tullus, nephew of the consul of 33 B.C. But this is not the place to speculate how and when one or other of the Volcacii—and one will not omit 'C. Volcacium Tullum adulescentem' (Caesar, *BG* VI. 29. 4)—came to make a grant of the citizenship to a native of Gaul. On the inscriptions of the Gallic provinces there is only one Volcacius, namely Volkacius Dioscorus (*CIL* XII. 3508, Nemausus).

VII

OBITUARIES IN TACITUS*

NOTHING could touch the pomp and splendour of a Roman funeral: the portraits of ancestors carried on parade, the emblems of magistracy, and the ultimate laudation. The thing was pageant, and history, and the material for history.

When by decree of the Senate it was ordained that the obsequies of some person of mark should be celebrated as act and homage of the community, at public expense and with a selected speaker, the item passed into the record and archives of the high assembly. Often no doubt there to be buried and forgotten (if there were no curious and competent enquirer), but the occasion might be retained in memory, the oration preserved by the author or by the family. Apart from that, a long tradition in literature enjoined the appraisement of a man's actions and virtues at the end. Among the Roman historians not often in Sallust, but Livy was amicable and generous, subsequent historians quite lavish.[1]

The two streams of derivation meet and mix in Cornelius Tacitus, with the senatorial and documentary in preponderance. His procedure will prove instructive, for more reasons than one.

On a surface view, the recording of events in strict order of time, year by year, constrained and hampered a historian. The author of the *Annales* himself bears witness, several times. It does not appear that he was unduly incommoded. Various devices offered. He might discover where he pleased some subject for an oration, he could turn aside and digress. Those portions of the work confirm his autonomy, reveal his predilections, and permit an approach to his character and opinions.

The obituary notices are likewise the product of will and choice. The *Annales* present twelve entries of this type, embracing twenty men.[2]

* Reprinted from *American Journal of Philology*, LXXIX (1958), 18–31.

[1] Seneca, *Suas.* VI. 21: 'hoc semel aut iterum a Thucydide factum, item in paucissimis personis usurpatum a Sallustio, T. Livius benignius omnibus magnis viris praestitit: sequentes historici multo id effusius fecerunt'.

[2] *Ann.* III. 30; 48; 75; IV. 15; 44; 61; VI. 10; 27; 39; XIII. 30; XIV. 19; 47. Not taking into account the remarks on Tiberius (VI. 51), Livia (V. 1), Julia (I. 53), the younger Julia (IV. 71),

They tend to be put at the end of the annual chronicle. Four are registered explicitly as the last events of a year, two are in fact the last items, four penultimate. Hence only two in the body of the narrative.[1] A certain artifice might be suspected. Of the men commemorated, five stand alone, one entry groups three persons, the rest are disposed in pairs.[2]

In four instances the vote of a public funeral is specified, and in two of them that ceremony is styled 'censorium funus'.[3] Some of the other personages may in fact have been accorded that supreme honour. For example, the *nobiles* Cn. Cornelius Lentulus (*cos.* 14 B.C.) and L. Domitius Ahenobarbus (*cos.* 16 B.C.) whose decease is recorded (conjointly and in that order) under the year 25.[4] Each had earned the *ornamenta triumphalia*, and Ahenobarbus was close kin to the dynasty, having married Antonia, the niece of Caesar Augustus.

Not all *viri triumphales* of the Empire can be deemed to have a claim. The award, which Augustus invented as substitute and consolation for a triumph, was granted quite frequently. With Claudius, it became cheap and was vulgarized. However that may be, persons of high public station like the Prefects of the City and the holders of a second consulship cannot easily have been denied a public funeral.

Of the twenty characters singled out by the historian, all but three are senators of consular rank. Tacitus has quietly and artfully extended the category to take in these three anomalies. Namely, Asinius Saloninus (otherwise unknown), who was betrothed to a daughter of Germanicus Caesar;[5] the Roman knight Sallustius Crispus, the minister of Augustus and Tiberius;[6] and L. Antonius (son of the ill-starred Iullus), who died in reclusion at the university city of Massilia.[7]

The emergence and distribution of these necrological notices demands attention: nine of the twelve in the first hexad of the *Annales*, but none in the second (as extant), while the third has only three (registering five persons).

The earliest of them is peculiar and significant. It comes nearly half-way

and the funeral of Cassius' widow (III. 76); or, for that matter, comment on sundry deaths that belong to the narration.

[1] IV. 15 (Lucilius Longus); VI. 10 (L. Piso). Each had a public funeral.

[2] Standing alone, III. 48 (Sulpicius Quirinius); IV. 15 (Lucilius Longus); VI. 10 (L. Piso); VI. 39 (Poppaeus Sabinus); XIV. 47 (Memmius Regulus). A group of three, IV. 44 (Cn. Lentulus, Domitius Ahenobarbus, L. Antonius).

[3] Public funerals, III. 48 (Sulpicius Quirinius); VI. 11 (L. Piso); 'funus censorium', IV. 15 (Lucilius Longus); VI. 27 (Aelius Lamia). For that phrase, cf. XIII. 2 (the obsequies of Claudius Caesar); *Hist.* IV. 47 (Flavius Sabinus).

[4] IV. 44.   [5] III. 75.   [6] III. 30.   [7] IV. 44.

through Book III. Had no person of due consequence in the Roman State passed away in the course of the six years preceding? Notable *viri triumphales* such as M. Vinicius (*suff.* 19 B.C.) or M. Plautius Silvanus (*cos.* 2 B.C.), it may well be, outlived Augustus.[1] Of them, or of certain others, no record. Perhaps the historian was slow to see the value of the device. Once aware, he exploits it to the full. The occasion is the decease of a consular, L. Volusius Saturninus (*suff.* 12 B.C.).[2] It is not only, or mainly, for his sake that Tacitus operates. A few words for Volusius, and he goes on to Sallustius Crispus, recounting his parentage (he was adopted by the historian, his great-uncle), the paradox of great ability under the show of indolence, the parallel with Maecenas; and he concludes with general reflections on princes and their favourites, on the transience of power and influence.

The next entry comes soon after, in the next year. It is devoted to P. Sulpicius Quirinius (*cos.* 12 B.C.).[3] That the great majority should congregate in the Tiberian books is no surprise. The author had a purpose. He wanted to show that the matter of Roman history was not yet as dynastic and monarchic as it later became, that there still subsisted 'quaedam imago rei publicae'. And (it can be contended in face of confident doctrines) Tacitus paid little attention to the written authorities for the period, doubting their veracity and insight, but preferred to build up his narrative mainly on the basis of the *acta senatus*. Further, as he went on he discovered more and more transactions that evoked the previous reign (or ran continuous from its main themes, domestic or foreign), until before long he was impelled to announce that, if life was vouchsafed, he would turn back and narrate the times of Caesar Augustus.[4] The episode in question (the return to Rome of D. Junius Silanus) called up to renewed notoriety one of the scandals of the dynasty: the affair of Julia, the granddaughter of the Princeps. The decease of illustrious survivors (among them relatives of the reigning house, or involved in its vicissitudes) will have contributed to sharpen the historian's curiosity about that earlier and obscure epoch which (it appears) he had not studied with sufficient care when he decided to begin his imperial annals with the accession of Tiberius.

The second hexad of the *Annales* (as extant) is truncated, Caligula being lost, and also Claudius down to a point in the year 47 (subsequent to the beginning of Book XI). The missing books must be allowed for.

[1] *PIR*[1], v 444 (to whom should be assigned the anonymous *elogium* at Tusculum, *ILS* 8965); P 361.
[2] III. 30. [3] III. 48. [4] III. 24.

Two men are known whom other sources credit with a public funeral, namely M. Vinicius and Passienus Crispus.[1] Each has a place in the sequence of second consulates with which Claudius Caesar embellished the early years of his reign, from 43 to 46, and both stand close to the dynasty. M. Vinicius (*cos.* 30, *II ord.* 45) had been married to a princess, Julia Livilla, the daughter of Germanicus.[2] Passienus (*suff.* 27, *II ord.* 44), who inherited the name and the wealth of Sallustius Crispus, was a wit and an orator of high celebrity. He must have been mentioned more than once in those books—and he was the husband of two princesses in succession, Nero's aunt Domitia and Nero's mother.[3] Nor would it have passed the knowledge and ingenuity of the historian to discover other persons fit for commemoration (if he needed them).

As for Books XI and XII, to palliate their apparent void, it can be pointed out that they contain two concealed obituaries, which happen to furnish sharply contrasted portraits of two successive legates of Germania Superior. Recording the *ornamenta triumphalia* of Curtius Rufus (*suff. c.* 43)— not for any action in the field but for opening a mine in the territory of the Mattiaci—the historian subjoins an anecdote about the surprising career of that person (humble beginnings, a miraculous prophecy of future greatness, and the Emperor Tiberius' support and testimonial), and terminates with a damning character sketch of the detestable parvenu —subservient though surly towards superiors, oppressive to those beneath, and not easy with equals.[4] Pomponius Secundus, however (*suff.* 44), is accorded a handsome farewell after his campaign against the Chatti: the *ornamenta triumphalia* are but a small portion of his renown, for posterity remembers Pomponius as a poet.[5] It can be taken that the consular dramatist died not long after—and nothing more was going to be said about Curtius Rufus.

Finally, Books XIII–XVI. Two pairs and one single entry: all persons who had not found mention hitherto in this section of the work. They exhibit sundry peculiarities. The first chronicles the decease of C. Caninius Rebilus (*suff.* 37) and L. Volusius Saturninus (*suff.* 3), the latter dying

---

[1] Dio LX. 27, 4; *Schol.* on Juvenal IV. 81. It would take too long to discuss the opulent Pompeius, starved to death by his kinsman Caligula—'fame ac siti periit in palatio cognati dum illi heres publicum funus esurienti locat' (Seneca, *De tranquillitate animi* II. 10). Generally (but I suspect wrongly) identified as Sex. Pompeius, the consul of 14 (*PIR*[1], P 450). The recent treatment in P-W XXI. 2265 ff. is not satisfactory.

[2] VI. 30, cf. *PIR*[1], V. 445.

[3] *Schol.* on Juvenal IV. 18, with the allegation 'periit per fraudem Agrippinae'. The previous wife is *PIR*[2], D 171.

[4] XI. 21.   [5] XII. 28.

at the age of 90.[1] Caninius is here described as outstanding in the science of law. No other source knows him as a jurist, and it is not clear that he was a notable personage. Further, the kind of treatment he gets. The necrology is normally benevolent, though Tacitus is ready with derogatory comment (social or moral) on several persons, such as Sulpicius Quirinius, Ateius Capito, and Domitius Afer.[2] Of Caninius, who committed suicide (unique among these entries), he says that nobody thought he had the courage for it, such was his vicious effeminacy.[3] Adventitious and undisclosed reasons (it can be divined) go to explain the introduction of Caninius (see below). As for Volusius, a strange omission. Tacitus neglects to put on record the important fact that he was *praefectus urbi*. He was appointed under Caligula, presumably in succession to the mysterious Q. Sanquinius Maximus (*suff. II* 39); and he held that post to the day of his death.[4]

The next pair briefly couples two orators, Cn. Domitius Afer (*suff.* 39), and M. Servilius Nonianus (*cos.* 35)—but Nonianus was also a historian, and he comes off best in the confrontation.[5] Afer, whom Quintilian reckoned the greatest orator he had heard and worthy to take rank with the classic performers, had no doubt earned a mention several times in the missing books; and Tacitus, presenting Afer for the first time (in 26), went on to allude to the decline of his oratorical powers in old age.[6] That was early in the *Annales*. Some recapitulatory remarks would have been pertinent and helpful. By various devices and annotation Tacitus in the exordium of Book XIII indicates that he is making a fresh start and beginning a new section. Thus Annaeus Seneca and Afranius Burrus are introduced as though for the first time, their personalities and functions being deftly characterized.[7] Tacitus on Afer and Nonianus seems cursory or unduly concise: a revision might have expanded.

Nor is everything plain and easy about the last item of all, the death of P. Memmius Regulus (*suff.* 31) in 61.[8] Tacitus appends an anecdote. Nero fell ill, the courtiers were full of alarm and foreboding for Rome, but Nero reassured them. The *res publica*, he said, could look for stay and support to Memmius Regulus. If Nero's illness is the 'anceps valetudo' described in the previous year,[9] there is not much point in the comment added by Tacitus: 'vixit tamen post haec Regulus quiete defensus'. Now

---

[1] XIII. 30.   [2] III. 48; 75; XIV. 19.

[3] III. 30: 'haud creditus sufficere ad constantiam sumendae mortis ob libidines muliebriter infamis'.

[4] Pliny, *NH* VII. 62. For the date of his appointment, *PIR*[1], v 661.

[5] XIV. 19.   [6] IV. 52.   [7] XIII. 2.   [8] XIV. 47.   [9] XIV. 22.

Regulus since his consulship had not been named in the *Annales* (as extant), apart from a piece of annotation on Lollia Paullina (he had been one of her husbands).[1] Tacitus pays generous tribute to the virtues and public renown of Memmius Regulus. To make things clear to the reader, ought he not perhaps to have stated that Regulus was the loyal and exemplary *novus homo* who as consul had managed the destruction of Seianus?

Various phenomena in the latest books of the *Annales* provoke reflection. On the lowest count they inspire a doubt whether the author revised those books. One might also be impelled to wonder whether he lived to complete the work, down to Book XVIII (for that is clearly the design and structure, three hexads).

Not that the relative poverty of the necrological rubric in the third hexad need in itself be a cause for surprise. The texture of history had changed since the days of Tiberius (less for the Senate and more for the Palace), and with it the historian's method (and in great part his sources also). He is far less preoccupied with the annalistic schema. Further, a number of the men commemorated in the Tiberian books were relics of an earlier age, whereas the consulars in prominence under Caligula, Claudius, and Nero (few of them comparable in fame) could be adequately depicted through the actions and performances of their prime.

The author may (it is true) have been guilty of inadvertence here or there throughout the work. In conformity with his keen interest in the history of Roman oratory, Tacitus allots not less than their due to the descendants of Asinius Pollio and Messalla Corvinus, the dominant speakers in the time of Augustus.[2] Messallinus (*cos.* 3 B.C.), the elder son of Corvinus, delivers an oration marked by grace, candour, and tolerance, reflecting (it may be surmised) the manner of his parent.[3] The historian does not report his death—perhaps the oration was honour enough. The younger son, Cotta Messallinus (*cos.* 20), may have survived Tiberius.[4] A speaker of great promise was heralded in the person of M. Claudius Marcellus Aeserninus, one of the five men (the others ex-consuls) whom Cn. Piso the legate of Syria asked to undertake his defence.[5] He does not recur in the narrative. Praetor in 19, Aeserninus should have had quick

---

[1] XII. 22.

[2] For the descendants of Pollio, who present sundry problems, cf. J. H. Oliver, *AJP* LXVIII (1947), 147 ff.

[3] III. 34.

[4] Last mentioned in 32 (VI. 5 and 7), but his proconsulate of Asia should fall in 35/6. By his full name M. Aurelius Cotta Maximus Messallinus (*PIR²*, A 1488), to be identified with M. Aurelius Cotta the consul of 20 (A 1487). [For a fresh proof, above, p. 52.]

[5] III. 11. For his fame, cf. XI. 6 f., where he is named in the company of consular orators.

access to the consulate. It will therefore be inferred that he died not long after 19.[1] Aeserninus was a grandson of Pollio on the maternal side: also the last of the Claudii Marcelli.

Again, Cossus Cornelius Lentulus (*cos.* A.D. 1), *praefectus urbi* after L. Aelius Lamia (*cos.* 3): Lamia's decease at the end of 32 is registered by the historian, and another prefect was in office in 37.[2] Cossus is not only known to fame as the general who terminated the Gaetulian War in A.D. 6.[3] Somnolent though he seemed and bibulous, he had the trust of Tiberius Caesar, and he never let out a secret: like L. Piso the Pontifex (*cos.* 15 B.C.), a rebuke and a warning to superficial moralists, as Seneca is careful to point out.[4]

As for the reigns of Claudius and Nero, three or four men can be named who might be thought to deserve an entry. Last heard of in 51,[5] the great L. Vitellius, consul three times (as had been nobody since M. Agrippa), fades from the pages of the *Annales*: yet he was not defrauded of a public funeral.[6] Perhaps his activities (abundantly chronicled) had said enough— and the portrait at his first presentation in Book VI could not have been improved upon.[7] L. Salvius Otho (*suff.* 33), a close and loyal friend of the dynasty (Tiberius liked him, and their physical resemblance excited surmise and suspicion), had rendered unusual services to Claudius, among them a conspiracy unmasked, in recognition of which his statue was set up on the Palatine.[8] Legates of Britain naturally attract the attention of the man who married the daughter of Julius Agricola. A. Plautius (*suff.* 29), who led the invasion of Britain for Claudius Caesar, returning to Rome in 47, was allowed to celebrate an ovation (a distinction without parallel under the Empire). But Tacitus in a remark about Plautius under the year 57 had already referred to that ovation.[9]

A Messalla consul with Nero in 58 put old men in mind of Corvinus, colleague of Augustus (i.e. in 31 B.C.), so Tacitus affirms.[10] The family was in decay—this man took financial subsidy from Nero (without, however, incurring censure from Tacitus). He was also (it appears) the last consul in the direct line of the patrician Valerii. Again, ought not Tacitus to have set on prominent record the demise of that Paullus Fabius

---

[1] Groag, invoking XI. 6, argues that he reached the consulate (*PIR*², C 928). Against, A. Degrassi, *Epigraphica*, VIII (1946), 38. Nor does Degrassi allow him to appear 'below the line' in his *Fasti consolari* (1952).

[2] VI. 27 (Aelius Lamia). The prefect in 36/7 was L. Calpurnius Piso (*cos.* 27), cf. *PIR*², C 293.

[3] Dio LV. 28. 3 f., cf. *AE* 1940, 68 = *IRT* 301.

[4] *Epp.* 83. 14 f.   [5] XII. 42.   [6] Suetonius, *Vit.* 3.   [7] VI. 32.

[8] Suetonius, *Otho* 1.   [9] XIII. 32.   [10] XIII. 34.

Persicus (*cos.* 34), whom Claudius Caesar (irony rather than amity) styled
'nobilissimum virum, amicum meum'?[1] He was a man of evil living,
and, along with Caninius Rebilus, comes into the family history of the
historian's wife. They offered to contribute towards the cost of games
which her grandfather, L. Julius Graecinus, had to celebrate. That excellent man rejected help from the infamous pair.[2] Persicus was the last
consul of the *gens Fabia*. The decline and fall of the *nobilitas* is one of the
main themes of the *Annales*—brought down by and with the aristocratic
dynasty of Julii and Claudii, but perishing through its own vices
also.

The obituary satisfied various needs and aspirations in the historian.
The longer a man went on living, the more he was struck by the para-
doxes of fame and survival, the operations of fate or hazard, the 'ludibria
rerum mortalium cunctis in negotiis'.[3] Tacitus is preoccupied with the
vicissitudes of the governing order, and he insists on making it clear that
he writes according to the manner and categories of the Roman past.
The obituaries reinforce his design, and they proclaim his employment
of the Senate's archives (not that all the items are thence derived).

Tradition and the Republic can be suggested in diverse fashions.
Dying in 32 at the age of eighty, L. Piso the Pontifex is in his own person
a memorial of history: the son of Caesoninus, consul in 58 B.C. and
censor. Choice language contributes to the effect: Piso's titles to renown
stand in a sequence of bare disconnected phrases, reproducing the old
annalistic manner.[4] Similarly, the death of the excellent M. Lepidus
(*cos.* 6) is adorned with comments archaic and Sallustian on the Aemilii
of ancient days.[5]

Furthermore, Tacitus is able to bring in episodes of Augustan history,
as when the aristocratic generals Cn. Lentulus the Augur and L. Domitius
Ahenobarbus, victorious beyond the great rivers, echo back to a more
expansive epoch, evoking nostalgia and pointing the contrast with the
deep peace of Tiberius' reign. Not only that. Ahenobarbus' father will
be named, the admiral of the Republic and partisan of Marcus Antonius.
By a felicitous coincidence the historian can go on to chronicle the death

---

[1] *ILS* 212, col. II. 1. 25 (Lugdunum).

[2] Seneca, *De ben.* II. 21. 5 f. For the vices of Persicus, ib. IV. 30. 2.

[3] III. 18.

[4] VI. 10: 'patrem ei censorium fuisse memoravi; aetas ad octogesimum annum processit;
decus triumphale in Thracia meruerat'.

[5] VI. 27: 'quippe Aemilium genus fecundum bonorum civium, et qui eadem familia
corruptis moribus, inlustri tamen fortuna egere'.

of L. Antonius at Massilia—hence a mention of his father Iullus, the paramour of Julia, the daughter of the Princeps.[1]

It was the scandal of the younger Julia, brought to notice a number of years later, that prompted Tacitus to announce the project of a future history (above). A connected theme was Tiberius Caesar in his earlier discomforts and vicissitudes—friction with the daughter of Caesar Augustus, the clash with the Princeps, the wilful retreat to an island.

The significance of Tiberius' sojourn on Rhodes was not properly estimated by Tacitus (it can be argued) when he began to compose the *Annales*: a passage alluding to it in Book I may not have been there inserted until the historian had come to speculate about the reasons that induced the Emperor to go away to Capreae.[2] Two of the necrological notices cannot have failed to stimulate his curiosity. In the year 21 Tiberius requested that the Senate vote a public funeral for P. Sulpicius Quirinius (*cos.* 12 B.C.).[3] Among the reasons he adduced was the loyalty and good sense of Quirinius. When in official employment in the eastern lands, Quirinius had not neglected to show respect to Tiberius in reclusion at Rhodes—and Tiberius, reminded of those painful years, deviated into a bitter attack on another man, M. Lollius, the author of feud and discord.[4] Then, in 23, came the death of Lucilius Longus (*suff.* 7). No superior public offices or provincial commands explain this man (who, but for Tacitus, is only a name and date on the consular *Fasti*). But Lucilius Longus had been a personal friend of Tiberius all through—in fact the only senator who went with him to Rhodes. Wherefore a public funeral and a statue in the Forum of Augustus. The abnormal honour caught the attention of Tacitus.[5]

Scepticism, experience of affairs, and hostility to consecrated opinions predisposed the historian to take an unfavourable view of Augustus, which was reinforced by pieces of forgotten knowledge that came to his notice when he studied the reign of Tiberius. Too late, however, to subvert the standard historical tradition or play Tiberius against Augustus.

The facts emerging about certain consular worthies cast a dubious light on patronage and honours in the Republic of Caesar Augustus.

---

[1] IV. 44.

[2] The reference to Rhodes in IV. 57, itself not well fitted in its near context, may have prompted the similar piece of annotation in I. 4.

[3] III. 48.

[4] Ib.: 'incusato M. Lollio, quem auctorem Gaio Caesari pravitatis et discordiarum arguebat'.

[5] IV. 15: 'ita quamquam novo homini censorium funus'.

For the senator lacking benefit of birth, advancement accrued (as before) from military merit, from oratory, or from science of the law.[1] The standard and colourless paragon of the *novus homo* was C. Poppaeus Sabinus (*cos.* 9), enjoying the confidence of the government and kept in a provincial command for twenty-four years on end: the obituary quietly and suitably hits him off as 'par negotiis neque supra'.[2] The historian, however, goes deeper in his revelations. Three detestable *novi homines*, characterized in the ultimate verdict, exemplify the three types of pro-motion, soldier, orator, and jurist: P. Sulpicius Quirinius (*cos.* 12 B.C.), grasping and much disliked in his old age, Q. Haterius (*suff.* 5 B.C.), voluble and adulatory, and C. Ateius Capito (*suff.* 5), the lawyer sub-servient to power.[3] The obituaries have their own validity. But the author was in a fortunate position—he had been able to display two of these three consulars in action, performing to character.[4]

But not all was evil and sinister. Men whom Tacitus approves for sagacity, moderation, and civic wisdom can stand as testimony. Thus L. Piso the Pontifex, 'nullius servilis sententiae sponte auctor';[5] M. Lepidus, whose virtues the narrative had adequately attested;[6] and old Volusius Saturninus, unharmed and unimpaired by the friendship and favour of a whole sequence of rulers.[7]

Good and bad stand in contrasted pairs. On the unsavoury Caninius Rebilus follows the venerable Volusius Saturninus;[8] and Domitius Afer is matched and mastered by Servilius Nonianus.[9]

Further, the selection of entries for the necrological rubric indicates a preoccupation with families whose members were known to Cornelius Tacitus. The descendants of Messalla and Pollio concerned not past history and the annals of Roman eloquence only. The direct line of the patrician Valerii had lapsed—but Vipstanus Messalla carried their blood through descent on the female side, the friend of Tacitus' youth, and one of the four interlocutors of the *Dialogus*.[10] The Asinii show several consuls more or less contemporaneous with the historian,[11] and Asinii in the obituaries ought to be closely scrutinized. One is there though only a name and a prospect frustrated—Saloninus who was betrothed to a

---

[1] IV. 6 (Tiberius' principles in the award of *honores*).

[2] VI. 39.   [3] III. 48; IV. 61; III. 75.

[4] I. 13 and III. 57 (Haterius); III. 70 (Ateius).   [5] VI. 10.

[6] VI. 27: 'M. Lepidus, de cuius moderatione atque sapientia in prioribus libris satis con-locavi.' Marcus (*cos.* 6), not Manius (*cos.* 11), [cf. above, pp. 30 ff.].

[7] XIII. 30.   [8] XIII. 30.   [9] XIV. 19.   [10] *PIR*[1], *v* 468.

[11] Asinius Pollio Verrucosus (*cos.* 81), '[Po]llio filius' (*suff.* 85), M. Asinius Marcellus (*cos.* 104), Q. Asinius Marcellus (*suff. anno incerto*, cf. *PIR*[2], A 1235).

princess.[1] Another, M. Asinius Agrippa (*cos.* 25), earns a generous laudation for virtue as well as pedigree—'claris maioribus quam vetustis vitaque
non degener'.[2] No word or act of his had been found worth a mention
by the author of the *Annales*. As for the Volusii, the consul suffect of 12
B.C. hardly seems distinctive enough to inaugurate the first of the obituaries (and, as has been shown, he serves to bring in Sallustius Crispus).
But Tacitus betrays some interest in the family, and in its opulence. This
Volusius was the 'primus adcumulator', as he observes in a striking
phrase.[3] There were two Volusii close coevals of Tacitus, the consuls of
87 and of 92:[4] quiet men, it may be presumed, and, like their old grandfather, not involved in politics or molested by a despot.

And, to conclude. Like the speeches and the digressions, the obituaries
may convey personal disclosures about Cornelius Tacitus, consul, orator,
and historian. What he has to say about Q. Haterius shows up the fluent
facile speaker who enjoyed an enormous vogue in his lifetime, and left
nothing behind: it is style that matters, and the effort of style.[5] Matched
with the great Domitius Afer, Servilius Nonianus earns the primacy, an
orator who passed on from eloquence to the writing of history: equal
in talent to Afer, but a better man, and commended for grace of living.[6]

Not that the literary and structural value of the obituary should be
neglected. Like the historical excursus, it can supply variety, tighten a
link, or permit a transition most elegant and insidious. Reporting the
decease of Ateius Capito, Tacitus inserts a reference to his rival in mastery
of the law, the highly respectable Antistius Labeo, who was Republican
by family, sentiment and doctrine—and not liked by the government.
The pliant Capito won preferment and the consulate.[7] The next item
is the funeral of Cassius' widow, the sister of Marcus Brutus, concluding
Book III in splendour and power and evoking the Republic. The *imagines*
of twenty-four noble families adorned that ceremony, but not those of
the Liberators: 'sed praefulgebant Cassius atque Brutus eo ipso quod
effigies eorum non visebantur'.[8]

[1] III. 75.   [2] IV. 61.

[3] III. 30. Observe that Nero in his reply to Seneca is made to adduce a Volusius—'quantum Volusio longa parsimonia quaesivit' (XIV. 56). Presumably the long-lived *suffectus* of
A.D. 3.

[4] *PIR*[2], v 663; 665.

[5] IV. 61: 'utque aliorum meditatio et labor in posterum valescit, sic Haterii canorum.
illud et profluens cum ipso simul exstinctum est'. [See below, pp. 87 ff.]

[6] XIV. 19: 'mox tradendis rebus Romanis celebris et elegantia vitae quam clariorem effecit,
ut par ingenio ita morum diversus'.

[7] III. 75.   [8] III. 76.

7—T.S.I.T.

During his apprenticeship to public life in the reign of Vespasian Tacitus may have attended the obsequies of illustrious survivors, not neglecting the matter and quality of the laudation or the informed commentary of old men there present. L. Piso wound up his life at last (*cos.* 27), the son of Germanicus' enemy and *praefectus urbi* in the last year of Tiberius;[1] also C. Cassius Longinus (*suff.* 30), the great jurist, who had come back from exile.[2]

Consul himself in the year 97, Tacitus was chosen to deliver the laudation on Verginius Rufus, within reach of the purple in the crisis that brought down Nero, and surviving the emperors who feared and suspected him: Verginius was born in the year of Augustus' death.[3]

Tacitus had witnessed the obsequies of several rulers. When he came to chronicle the end of Caesar Augustus, no word of all the elaborate ceremonial, no oration. Instead, malice or a subversive equity. The spectacle of soldiers on guard excites derision—how superfluous and anachronistic! An age had lapsed since the tumultuous funeral of Caesar the Dictator.[4] And abundant comment is served up from the bystanders. That earlier historian, whom Cassius Dio copied and followed, and whose traces can be intermittently detected in the opening chapters of Book I, duly equipped the spectators with eulogistic reflections on their dead ruler.[5] Tacitus took over those reflections, modifying and abbreviating.[6] But Tacitus goes further. He makes the men of understanding, the 'prudentes', diverge into another track. They add the other side, detrimentally. More of it, and with more relish.[7]

[1] *PIR*², C 293. For his survival, Pliny, *Epp.* III. 7. 12.
[2] *Dig.* I. 2. 2. 52.   [3] Pliny, *Epp.* II. I.   [4] I. 8.   [5] Dio LVI. 43 f.
[6] I. 9.   [7] I. 10: 'dicebatur contra', etc.

VIII

THE HISTORIAN SERVILIUS NONIANUS*

O F THE Roman annalists in the long interval between Livy and Tacitus, the record is sparse and casual. For the most part, little more than names. And the incidence of their mention can be instructive. Apart from an anecdote in the younger Pliny, only Tacitus attests the fact that Cluvius Rufus, senator and consul, wrote history; and only Tacitus certifies Fabius Rusticus by name. That being so, it is expedient as well as legitimate that learned enquiry should admit here and there an *Ignotus* of some merit and consequence.

Quintilian furnishes a select list of the historians worthy to be prescribed for the aspirant to public eloquence (x. 1. 101–4). It was axiomatic that the two styles tended to be incompatible, and the list is short indeed. After the classic and inevitable glories of Sallust and Livy the professor registers Servilius Nonianus and Aufidius Bassus. The next name has fallen out of the text (Cremutius Cordus is to be supplied), and the count is closed with a eulogistic and anonymous reference to a writer still among the living, i.e. Fabius Rusticus.

The author of the *Dialogus* adduces Aufidius and Servilius as historians of the imperial age noteworthy for their 'eloquentia' (23. 2). Aufidius is an isolated figure. An Epicurean, serene and confident in the face of extinction, so is he portrayed by Seneca (*Epp.* 30). No hint in Seneca that this man had written history, and no sign anywhere that he might have belonged to the governing class. Nor are friends, family and connections to be discovered. In contrast stands the illustrious M. Servilius Nonianus, consul in 35. That contrast comes out in various ways. An attempt can be made to build up Servilius, on heterogeneous evidence, and give him substance.

I. The elder Pliny won early entrance to high society in the days of Caligula. Sundry notices in his encyclopedia disclose familiarity with an eminent personage, P. Pomponius Secundus (*suff.* 44), the famous

* Reprinted from *Hermes* XCII (1964), 408–14.

dramatist. Pliny later saw service as an officer under Pomponius in Germania Superior, and he wrote his biography.[1] Pliny also knew Servilius Nonianus. Three items bear witness.[2] First, Servilius used to wear an amulet round his neck to protect him from an affliction of the eyes, 'lippitudo' (*NH* xxviii. 29). Second, his daughter was cured of an ailment by goats' milk, as enjoined by the family doctor Servilius Democrates (xxiv. 43).[3] Third, reporting the precious gem which caused the senator Nonius to be put on the proscription lists by M. Antonius, Pliny adds personal detail: Nonius was not only the son of the Nonius Struma derided by the poet Catullus, he was 'avus Servili Noniani quem consulem vidimus' (xxxvii. 81).

The parent of the historian, so it appears, married a Nonia, daughter of the proscribed senator. And that parent (nobody doubts it) is M. Servilius M.f., consul with L. Aelius Lamia in A.D. 3. He comes twice into the pages of Tacitus (*Ann.* ii. 48. 1; iii. 22. 2). The first entry has an exceptional value. The careful Tacitus specifies his *nobilitas*.

It is worth the effort to look for his ancestry, which standard manuals ignore or evade.[4] The line goes back (one can conjecture) to a patrician Servilius who renounced his status, namely C. Servilius Geminus, praetor *c.* 220. He had two sons, consuls in 203 and in 202.[5] They were ambitious and exorbitant in their public actions, and it is no surprise that a long period elapsed before a plebeian Servilius was again allowed to reach the consulate. Their resurgence begins with C. Servilius Vatia, who married a daughter of Q. Metellus Macedonicus: hence P. Servilius C. f. M. n. Vatia (*pr.* 90, *cos.* 79) who as proconsul in Cilicia earned the triumphal *cognomen* 'Isauricus'.

The ancestor of Isauricus (it is presumed) was M. Servilius Pulex Geminus (*cos.* 202), to whom the M. Servilius attested as *pontifex* in 170 is assigned as a son.[6] At some time in the course of the second century a collateral line branched off, which ultimately produced the Augustan consul M. Servilius M. f. Its members are not easy to trace and verify.

---

[1] As his nephew states (*Epp.* iii. 5. 3). Cf. F. Münzer, *Bonner Jahrbücher* civ (1899), 80; C. Cichorius, *Römische Studien* (1922), 423 ff.

[2] F. Münzer, *Beiträge zur Quellenkritik der Naturgeschichte des Plinius* (1897), 404 f.

[3] For this notable doctor, see M. Wellmann, P-W iv. 2069 f.

[4] By grave inadvertence the consul of A.D. 3 was omitted from the context of the Servilii in P-W ii A. The article of E. Westermeyer was a brief, tardy and inadequate compensation (Supp. vi. 818 f., published in 1931).

[5] For the detailed evidence about these and other Servilii of the Republican age see F. Münzer, P-W ii A, 1759 ff.; T. R. S. Broughton, *MRR* (1952).

[6] Livy xliii. 11. 13. To be identified with the *tribunus militum* in 181 (xl, 27, 4), cf. Münzer, P-W ii A, 1765.

There are gaps and uncertainties, the *praenomen* 'Marcus' providing a clue, albeit imperfect.

Sundry *monetales* give trouble—as was to be expected. Thus three who by their types assert descent from the Servilii Gemini, viz. C. Servilius, C. Servilius M. f., M. Servilius C. f. Datings have exhibited a wide range, respectively 124–94, 134–108, 104–84.[1] According to the latest catalogue, they should be put in 125–120, 110–108, 100–95.[2] These allocations, like some others in the period, must be viewed with extreme caution.[3]

Again, the Servilii who turn up during the ten years of tribulation: Q. Servilius, praetor or ex-praetor in 91, who was assassinated at Asculum in Picenum (the *praenomen* is not secure, he might have been a C. Servilius); Servilius the praetor of 88; a Servilius defeated in battle near Ariminum in 87; the 'duo Servilii' victorious for Sulla at Clusium in 82. These might be sorted out in more ways than one, except that the 'duo Servilii' are clearly P. Servilius Vatia (*pr.* 90, *cos.* 79), and one of his brothers. The brother has been claimed identical with the *monetalis* M. Servilius C. f.[4]

Enquiry is not only arduous but baffled. In passing a brief word can go to P. Servilius Rullus (*tr. pl.* 63). His parent can be identified as the *monetalis* P. Servilius M. f. Rullus.[5] Of the tribune Cicero says 'temptavit, ut opinor, patientiam vestram, cum se nobilem esse diceret' (*De leg. agr.* 2. 19). It follows that he claimed consular ancestry, remote though it was. Then one comes down to a certain M. Servilius, attested in 51: he was involved in the aftermath of the prosecution of C. Claudius Pulcher (*Ad fam.* VII. 8. 2 f.). This man may, or may not, be identical with M. Servilius, the tribune of the plebs who was active for the cause of the Republic on the first day of January 43:[6] he also comes on record as a legate of Cassius.[7] Despite which, he appears to have survived. A *senatus consultum* of 39 registers the name of M. Servilius C. f.[8] It is good to have the filiation, but not of much practical use, unless (and there is no objection) he be regarded as the son of the *monetalis* C. Servilius C. f., who is assigned *c.* 63 (perhaps a little too late).[9] This *monetalis* by his type recalls the Servilii Gemini.

[1] For a useful conspectus of dates and authorities see *MRR* II. 452.

[2] E. A. Sydenham, *The Coinage of the Roman Republic* (1952), 57 f.; 66; 84.

[3] Few will favour the assignment of the quaestors Piso and Caepio to *c.* 96–1 (Sydenham, 85).

[4] Sydenham, 84, cf. Münzer, P-W II A, 1766; 1812.

[5] Sydenham, 84, cf. Pliny, *NH* VIII. 210.

[6] *Phil.* IV. 16; *Ad M. Brutum* II. 5. 3.   [7] Sydenham, 204 f.

[8] P. Viereck, *Sermo Graecus* (1883) no. 20. The father's *praenomen* is not registered in *MRR*.

[9] Sydenham, 147.

Therefore, let M. Servilius, tribune of the plebs in 43, be assumed the parent of the Augustan consul. These Servilii, it is clear, belong to a depressed stratum in the *nobilitas*—compare Cicero's remark about P. Servilius Rullus. None the less, they perpetuated their line through two centuries and manifold hazards. There had perhaps been a praetor or two among them; but no curule office happens to stand on direct attestation since M. Servilius Pulex Geminus, consul in 202.

II. The vicissitudes of noble families afford instruction and entertainment. The Servilii are a patrician *gens* that went back to the nobility of Alba Longa. Their last consul is Q. Servilius Caepio (*cos.* 106), defeated at the Battle of Arausio, their last member on clear record the Servilius Caepio who adopted by his testament M. Junius Brutus, transmitting the name in the style 'Q. Caepio Brutus'. The plebeian branch was now in the ascendant—the excellent P. Servilius Vatia Isauricus and his opportunistic son. After beginning as an ally of Cato, the son secured a consulship from Caesar and a second from the Triumvirs. Married to a sister of Brutus, he was the brother-in-law of Cassius and of M. Lepidus. Might not this man be suitably reckoned among those whom the historian Sallust castigates for surrendering honour and liberty in abasement before despotism (*Jug.* 3. 4)?

In 43 the alert Isauricus managed to get his daughter betrothed to the heir of Caesar.[1] That arrangement quickly lapsed, and Servilia was given to the eldest son of Lepidus the Triumvir, in fact to her cousin. Her husband became a victim, indirectly, of the victory at Actium. Treason and a plot was alleged in 30, and Servilia shared his end by heroic suicide (Velleius II. 88. 3).

The last in this line has a deplorable commemoration. Seneca mentions Servilius Vatia, an opulent old senator of praetorian rank who lived for long years in his villa by the sea at Baiae (*Epp.* 55. 2 ff.). None of the calamities before and after the destruction of Aelius Seianus impinged on his tranquillity. The man became a proverb—'O Vatia, solus scis vivere'. On another interpretation, however, a living corpse. When Seneca passed by the mansion he was wont to exclaim 'Vatia hic situs est'.

Meanwhile the neglected branch of the plebeian Servilii, damaged perhaps but not destroyed by civil war and proscriptions, came to flower under the Caesars with two consuls, the second of them a paragon of 'bonae artes' lacking precedent in that family.

---

[1] Suetonius, *Divus Aug.* 62. 1(the sole evidence).

In the year 17 Tiberius Caesar furnished two examples of disinterested virtue. The estate of Aemilia Musa, a wealthy freedwoman intestate, was assigned to an Aemilius Lepidus; and the Emperor enjoined that M. Servilius should take the fortune of a Roman knight Pantuleius, who in fact had named him heir in an earlier will. Tiberius announced his reasons—'nobilitatem utriusque pecunia iuvandam' (*Ann.* II. 48. 1). The Lepidus in question is patently M. Lepidus (*cos.* A.D. 6), of Scipionic descent: the man deemed 'capax imperii' (I. 13. 2), for whose integrity and sagacity the historian avows a fervent admiration (IV. 20. 2 f.).[1] Not all of the *nobiles* who enjoyed the bounty of the Caesars deserved aid and emolument.

The other notice in Tacitus shows Servilius a friend of the successful and much-disliked *novus homo* P. Sulpicius Quirinius (*cos.* 12 B.C.). Tiberius persuaded him to produce testimony in favour of Quirinius against his divorced wife (III. 22. 2).

Nothing else was known about M. Servilius apart from his consular date, his filiation and his marriage to a Nonia. Epigraphy brings a welcome supplement. Two inscriptions at Pisidian Antioch disclose as honorary *duoviri* P. Sulpicius Quirinius and M. Servilius—not as colleagues, but in that order of time.[2] Quirinius had been Caesar's legate governing the province Galatia–Pamphylia.[3] What then was the rank and function that explains the honouring of Servilius? Perhaps a legate under Quirinius in his war against the Homonadenses. Perhaps rather governor of Galatia—either before or after his consulship.[4]

III. So far the facts about M. Servilius, consul in A.D. 3. His son, it might be supposed, was born *c.* 3–1 B.C., a close coeval of the patrician Ser. Sulpicius Galba (*cos.* 33), and of Seneca. If that is so, he entered the Senate as quaestor about A.D. 24.

About this marriage, a guess could be hazarded. Since he had a daughter called Considia (*NH* XXIV. 43), that might have been the name of his wife; and she might be kin to L. Considius Gallus, *praetor* and *XVvir sacris faciundis*.[5] It would follow that neither of the Servilii, though

---

[1] Marcus Lepidus (*cos.* A.D. 6), not Manius (A.D. 11), [cf. above pp. 30 ff.].

[2] *ILS* 9502 f. Not noted in P-W Supp. VI. 818f.

[3] As argued in *JRS* XXIII (1933), 24; 27.

[4] *Klio* XXVII (1934), 147. He may in due course have become proconsul of Asia or of Africa. And he might be identical with the consular Servilius who reached the age of ninety (Suidas, s.v. M. Apicius).

[5] *CIL* VI. 31705. In annotation on this man (*PIR*², C 1280), Groag, suggests that he may be identical with Considius, the senator of praetorian rank who attacked P. Pomponius Secundus (*Ann.* v. 8. 1).

acquiring favour with the dynasty, had sought to strengthen their claims through marriage into groups of notable political influence. No Considius reached the consulship.

Not but that the *nomen* might reflect some earlier link. One lot of Nonii in the late Republic were connected with Considii, observe M. Considius Nonianus (*pr.* 52 B.C.) and the *monetalis* C. Considius Nonianus.

Apart from Considia, no offspring of the historian is on record anywhere. Conjecture is excited by another consular whose daughter had a *gentilicium* different from his own, namely (Q. ?) Marcius Barea Soranus (*suff.* 52). In 66, in the aftermath of the Pisonian conspiracy, Nero resolved to destroy a whole group and party. Close upon the doom of Thrasea Paetus and linked to it, came the prosecution of Soranus and his young daughter Servilia (*Ann.* XVI. 23; 30 ff.). Soranus when proconsul of Asia had behaved with conspicuous 'iustitia atque industria'. He was impugned for his friendship with Rubellius Plautus, and for treasonable designs. Now Rubellius was notorious for his addiction to the doctrines of the Stoics (XIV. 57. 3); and one of the principal witnesses against Soranus was his own client, the Stoic philosopher Egnatius Celer, whose detestable character is delineated by the historian Tacitus as a solemn warning against hypocrisy and perfidy (XVI. 32. 3). There is a danger, it is true, to make too much of the doctrines avowed in the group hostile to Nero. Primarily, their attitude can be defined in terms of 'dignitas' and of 'libertas'. Terms had changed their meaning with the course of time—and these men were not politically Republicans. None the less, their creed is indicative. More so, perhaps, the personal loyalties and attachments.[1]

Servilia, the daughter of Barea Soranus, may carry the maternal nomenclature. That is to say, her father married a daughter of Servilius Nonianus —Considia or another. Servilii abound under the Republic, but no other senatorial Servilii can be detected in this epoch.

IV. That dearth of Servilii prompts a further conjecture. An inscription at Rome, bearing the consular date of 51 and showing the Claudian archaism and the innovatory Claudian digamma, records gratitude expressed to Isis Invicta and Serapis by the freedman 'M. Aidius Serviliai Aviol[ai]/lib. Amerimnus' (*CIL* VI. 353 = *ILS* 4375). It discloses a lady of some consequence, Servilia, wife of Aviola—that is, wife of a highly aristocratic senator, M.' Acilius Aviola (*cos.* 54).

Might this Servilia be a daughter of the consular historian? Not so, it

[1] *Tacitus* (1958), 561.

appears. Freedmen of a woman commonly take the *praenomen* of her father as well as the *gentilicium*. Now inscriptions at Allifae in Samnium produce a pair of Aedii, described as freedmen of Servilia (IX. 2363; 2365). Also a slave of Aedia Servilia (2424). Therefore Servilia is the daughter of an Aedius who had 'Marcus' for *praenomen* (cf. VI. 353). She is properly styled 'Aedia Servilia' (cf. *PIR²*, A 114), not 'Servilia Aedia'.

Not a daughter of M. Servilius Nonianus—but the nomenclature can still be put to good employ. It implies, one generation back, the marriage of a Servilia to M. Aedius of Allifae. That Servilia, mother of Aedia Servilia, can be supposed a sister of the historian. Ties of matrimony between the Roman aristocracy and the men of substance and repute in the *municipia* are a theme of no small significance in any age. M. Servilius (*cos.* 3), who had little in the way of inherited wealth (cf. *Ann.* II. 48. 1), may have been able to lodge his daughter with a family of local opulence. The occurrence of the *nomen* 'Aedius' is restricted—three inscriptions at Rome, one at Ostia, one each at Forum Novum and at Alba Fucens, but no fewer than five at Allifae.[1]

'Aidius', 'Aedius' or 'Aiedius' it is much the same thing. That *nomen* comes into debate through a notorious crux in the text of Tacitus. In the year 17, after the great earthquake, a special commissioner was despatched to Asia 'delectus est M. Aletus e praetoriis, ne consulari obtinente Asiam aemulatio inter pares et ex eo impedimentum oreretur' (*Ann.* II. 47. 4). The *nomen* is corrupt. The standard remedy, adopted in all modern texts, is to read 'M. Ateius'. No such person is known or plausible. Other *gentilicia* must be canvassed, among them 'Aiedius' or 'Aietius'.[2]

Now 'Aedius' is indigenous at Allifae. There is a temptation to adduce two fragments of inscriptions patently referring to senators at that town. First, ']dius M. f. Ba[......]/[......]i Caesaris Augusti' (IX. 2341). Next, the piece which shows the beginnings of four lines (perhaps long lines), namely 'M.A[......]/aedium[......]/desti[......]/Ti.C[......]' (2344). Both, it is an easy supposition, belong to the reign of Tiberius. Speculation, prompted by the word 'desti[', should not fail to move on to an acephalous inscription from the same place, which comes into

---

[1] W. Schulze, *LE* 116. The instances at Allifae are *CIL* IX. 2363 f. (=*ILS* 6514 f.); 2365; 2370; 2424. Outside Italy perhaps only one occurrence, viz. VIII. 3321 (Lambaesis).

[2] [Above, p. 61]. There was an Augustan senator called Aietius Pastor (Seneca, *Controv.* I. 3. 11). 'Aietius' is not attested epigraphically, but there are a dozen instances of 'Aiedius' (cf. *TLL*).

discussions about the consular elections under Tiberius. The person in question was 'per commendation./Ti. Caesaris Augusti/ab senatu cos. dest.' (2342= *ILS* 944).[1] This person, it should appear (though other explanations have been advanced), had been selected for the consulship but died before he could be elected ('designatus'), still less assume the *fasces*—otherwise, why should he be signalized as 'cos. dest.'? Perhaps therefore the senator of praetorian rank who went out to Asia in 17, a meritorious appointment deserving promotion if normally successful or not impugned.[2] Apart from Drusus Caesar, this may not have been the only senator who succumbed to a natural decease in 23 (for the death of Drusus an unhealthy season or an epidemic disease can be invoked in preference to poisoning).[3]

To resume. From the evidence of inscriptions a Servilia can be deduced, married to M. Aedius of Allifae (the further speculation about the identity and career of this man can be waived). The daughter of this match is therefore to be styled 'Aedia M. f. Servilia'. She married M'. Acilius Aviola, the consul of 54—who managed to escape all vexation and survive to a melancholy old age, his son or grandson being M'. Acilius Glabrio, the consul of 91, exiled and put to death.[4]

More important, for the argument here conducted, is the conjecture that a daughter of Servilius Nonianus married Barea Soranus (*suff.* 52)—whence Servilia, the bride of Annius Pollio (*Ann.* XVI. 30. 3).

V. How far is that conjecture useful or relevant? It takes a daughter of the historian into the ambiance of Nero's enemies—and among adepts of Stoic doctrines.

The poet Persius (it happens to be recorded) revered Servilius Nonianus like a father.[5] If anybody was a Stoic (vague or incriminated label) it was

---

[1] The words 'per commendation.' also 'Augusti' and 'cos. dest.' had perished before Mommsen. They were seen by Antonius Augustinus, the Archbishop of Tarragona—unimpeachable on epigraphy.

[2] It is not expedient to invoke the word *aedium* on the fragment (IX. 2344) as referring to a restoration of temples and public buildings in Asia. Praetorian curators at Rome are attested in this period, e.g. Q. Varius Geminus—'curatori aedium sacr. monumentor.que public. tuendorum' (*ILS* 932: Superaequum).

[3] Observe the disappearance, *inter alios*, of M. Claudius Marcellus Aeserninus (*pr.* 19), already on show as an orator along with consular advocates (*Ann.* III. 11. 2), and a grandson of Asinius Pollio. He ought to have had quick access to the consulate [above, p. 81].

[4] Groag inclines to identify the aged Acilius in Juvenal IV. 91 with Aviola, the consul of 54 (*PIR²*, A 62, cf. 49). As for M'. Acilius Glabrio (*cos.* 91), he points out that later Glabriones kept up the link with Allifae (*CIL* IX. 2333 f.).

[5] *Vita Persi* (OCT, 1959), l. 17.

Persius. He was cherished by Thrasea Paetus. Further, he was a relative of Thrasea's wife Arria, the daughter of A. Caecina Paetus.

The name of Caecina Paetus (*suff.* 37) evokes family loyalty, a dramatic incident never forgotten—and armed treason in the second year of Claudius Caesar. Arruntius Camillus, legate of Dalmatia and a descendant of Pompeius Magnus, cast off his allegiance and proclaimed the Republic. The episode, briefly reported and abortive, is of vital importance for the understanding of imperial history.

It tends to be passed over rather lightly in modern narrations. Illumination is needed wherever it can be got. Certain allies of the pretender must be noted and assessed. One of them is Caecina Paetus, who went to Dalmatia, was there arrested, and was brought back to Rome. Encouraged by the heroic example of his wife Arria, he too took his own life. The younger Pliny furnishes the classic account of this transaction (*Epp.* III. 16).

Two other eminent partisans are on record: Q. Pomponius Secundus (elder brother of the consular dramatist) and L. Annius Vinicianus. They stand in direct relation to the events of the previous year—Caligula assassinated and the brief interlude of 'Libertas' before Claudius Caesar was installed in the power. Pomponius supported the other consul, Cn. Sentius Saturninus, who made an oration and advocated the restoration of Republican government. As for Annius Vinicianus, he was not only prominent among the conspirators: he tried to put up his kinsman M. Vinicius as a candidate for the power.[1] Further, according to Cassius Dio, his fears in the sequel moved him to instigate Arruntius Camillus, who already had ambitious thoughts in that direction (LX. 15. 1 f.).

The children of the rebels were spared—at least for the moment. Vinicianus had a son, Annius Pollio.[2] It is not without significance that Barea Soranus chose him as bridegroom for his daughter Servilia. The approximate date for their marriage emerges from the fact that in 66 Servilia was not twenty (XVI. 30. 3). Annius Pollio, though guiltless, was incriminated in the Pisonian conspiracy and sent into exile (XV. 56. 4; 71. 3).

---

[1] Josephus, *AJ* XIX. 49; 52; 251. For his kinship with M. Vinicius, cf. *PIR²*, A 677; 701: perhaps his father had married a Vinicia. There might be another potent link concerning the transactions of this year and the next. The wife of Arruntius Camillus is assumed a Vibia—'adnectebatur crimini Vibia' (*Ann.* XII. 52. 1). The *Codex Mediceus* has 'vivia', but the *Leidensis* 'vina'. Should one read 'crimini Vin⟨ici⟩a'?

[2] *PIR²*, A 678. In passing should be noted the other son, Annius Vinicianus (A 700): son-in-law of Corbulo (*Ann.* XV. 28. 3) and perishing in 66 on the charge of a conspiracy hatched at Beneventum (Suetonius, *Nero* 36. 1). Important—but another story, namely Corbulo in relation to the prosecutions of 66.

Thrasea, for his part, was not only married to the younger Arria, the daughter of Caecina Paetus. He took over into his own nomenclature the *cognomen* of her father. That was a more than normal declaration of 'pietas'.

On these facts, the enemies of Thrasea Paetus and of Barea Soranus might have alleged that each nourished an allegiance or an attitude that was tantamount to a feud with the dynasty. In fact, that notion crops up in the Tacitean narrative, but only in relation to a minor character whose father had been a victim of Tiberius. The historian registers 'Paconium Agrippinum, paterni in principes odii heredem' (XVI. 28. 1). The nearest he comes to it is the brief recall of a known story and a family tradition towards the end, when Thrasea adjures his daughter not to follow her mother's example (XVI. 34. 2). That is all.

As Tacitus sets the scene, the prosecutor Cossutianus Capito makes direct appeal to Nero (XVI. 22). He works on the emperor's vanity, fears and resentments; he launches a diatribe against Thrasea and the Stoics, he brings up Cato, Cassius, Brutus. That is to say, ancient history and conventional themes. No word of Arruntius Camillus or Caecina Paetus.

The historian's procedure might invite speculation on various counts. One thing is clear. He was eager to indulge his art and to produce, exaggerated to parody, the violent and dishonest oratory of the 'delatores'.[1] Cornelius Tacitus proposed, here as elsewhere, to damn a speaker through the speaker's own words.

For the rest, Tacitus was familiar with certain facts (damaging facts) in the family and group now under attack. So far, in the hexad, nothing had been said about the events of 42. Indeed, the only reference anywhere concerned the wife and the son of Arruntius Camillus (XII. 52. 1). Not a word about Caecina Paetus or the parent of Annius Pollio. This historian is a master in the art of structure and of timing, often withholding facts deliberately until they emerge with proper effect. He may have been proposing to introduce, at a later stage in the *Annales*, an allusion to the transactions he had narrated some time before, in Book IX.

VI. To resume. Two things are relevant to Servilius Nonianus—a fact and a conjecture. The fact is the notice about the poet Persius, the conjecture adduces Servilia, the daughter of Barea Soranus. They bring Servilius Nonianus into the ambit of the Stoics, and perhaps under their influence.[2] That may not have mattered much for a historian, unless to

[1] *Tacitus* (1958), 537, cf. 332 f. (the invective of Suillius Rufus).
[2] The notice about Servilius in the *Vita Persi* is accorded especial significance by F. Klingner, *Mus. Helv.* XV (1958), 200 = R. *Geisteswelt*[4] (1961), 479.

confirm and enhance a senator's normal distaste for tyranny. Nor need it affect his political behaviour or his official career. To be sure, some of his friends may have been involved in the proclamation of Camillus Scribonianus. That affair is obscure and mysterious. And it was not until the twelfth year of Nero's reign that the group of which Thrasea and Soranus stood as the head and symbol, 'Virtus ipsa', so Tacitus designates them (XVI. 21. 1), was arraigned as a menace to the imperial government —with what justice, it is a question. And, if Servilius comes into the account, it is only through his putative grand-daughter, Servilia the daughter of Barea Soranus. Servilius died in 59.

Servilius had been consul in 35. In that season L. Vitellius (*cos.* 34) was a power, trusted by Tiberius Caesar and influential with Antonia, his brother's long-lived widow, who had a court of her own, and perhaps a policy. Signs are not lacking. The first consul from Narbonensis now emerges, the highly presentable D. Valerius Asiaticus (*suff.* 35). He was an old friend of Vitellius, together they had cultivated Antonia (XI. 3. 1).

VII. In the *Annales* as extant, Servilius is only a consular date until the year of his decease. The persons whom Tacitus singles out for necro-logical commemoration invite inspection, on various counts.[1] They will be found to illumine not only his standards of value and historical rele-vance, but also certain of his personal interests, such as the annals of Roman eloquence or the ancestry of coeval consuls and aristocrats.[2]

He concludes the year 59 with Domitius Afer and Servilius Nonianus, set in contrast. Both of them orators, but the latter was also a historian and he has the advantage—'ut par ingenio ita morum diversus' (XIV. 19, quoted in full below).

Domitius Afer was a worthy rival of the great masters of the Republican and Augustan prime, so Quintilian asseverates, who had heard him (X. 1. 18). Afer had been mentioned in the *Annales* at his début, not for praise—'modicus dignationis et quoquo facinore properus clarescere' (IV. 52. 1). In epilogue on that incident, the historian subjoins comment about his character ('prosperiore eloquentiae quam morum fama fuit'), his eloquence and its decline in his old age: comment which anticipates, or renders superfluous, an obituary notice. Afer, in fact, must have occurred in the lost books, more than once. Also Servilius Nonianus, perhaps not often.

[1] [Above, pp. 79 ff.]   [2] *Tacitus* (1958), 302; 313; 478.

The notice itself is brief. Tacitus might have expected the reader to be aware of a further contrast between the two: Servilius a *nobilis*, Afer a new man from Narbonensis (the second consul after Valerius Asiaticus). Nor was there any call to adduce a small fact from the career of Servilius, his proconsulate of Africa. That is revealed by an inscription.[1]

After long practice at the bar, Servilius went on to the writing of history—'diu foro, mox tradendis rebus Romanis celebris' (xiv. 19). As the younger Pliny reports, Claudius Caesar one day, hearing a great volume of applause, entered a hall and found himself at a recitation party where Servilius was holding forth (*Epp.* i. 13. 3). Servilius' choice of a new vocation may (or may not) have come in immediate sequel to his attaining the peak of a consul's career, the proconsulate (perhaps 46/7). Cornelius Tacitus, it is not fanciful to assume, embarked on his second historical work after he came back from the proconsulate in Asia.

VIII. Some historians, modest, or at least cautious, chose to start with monographs. Thus Sallust, reticent about any ulterior and greater project, such as a history of his own times. Aufidius Bassus wrote a *Bellum Germanicum*, and he may also have tried his hand with a study of the last year of Cicero's life, glorious and ruinous.[2] About Servilius, speculation is vain, almost everything about his *Historia* being obscure, and at the best a solitary fragment on show. Speaking of Sallust and Livy, he said 'pares eos magis quam similes'. Perhaps from the preface.[3] But even that is not certain. It might be a *dictum* only of the orator. Quintilian, who cites the phrase, had heard Servilius plead in the courts or declaim—'qui et ipse a nobis auditus est'. Quintilian goes on to furnish his own assessment of the historian—'clari vir ingenii et sententiis creber sed minus pressus quam historiae auctoritas postulat'. That is valuable. The style of Servilius was a little too copious—as may well happen when a public speaker turns historian. The *Historiae* of Tacitus betray a certain Livian flow and eloquence. He curbed those habits. The later manner, as exhibited to perfection in the first hexad of the *Annales*, draws heavily on Sallust. That writer had forged a style all of his own, startling in its originality. It is easy to exaggerate the rapidity with which his influence percolated.[4] If

[1] Namely the two fragments on record as *CIL* viii. 24585a (Carthage, really from Utica), rearranged by Carcopino. Hence *AE* 1932, 24=*ILT* 1170. The document shows him 'VII vir epulonum', also 'patron. mun.' (i.e. of Utica).

[2] The elder Seneca cites Aufidius on the death of Cicero (*Suas.* vi. 18; 23. Perhaps from a monograph, not the full-length history, cf. the arguments adduced in *Tacitus* (1958), 698.

[3] Indubitably, according to A. Klotz, P-W ii A, 1802.

[4] As in *Tacitus* (1958), 135.

any one among the annalistic predecessors of Cornelius Tacitus was a strong Sallustian (which might be doubted) it was certainly not Servilius Nonianus.

Servilius and Aufidius were the principal historians who dealt with the reign of Tiberius. The space of time each covered is a problem. A standard assumption takes the inception of Aufidius' work back to 44 or 43 B.C.[1] Yet he may have begun where Livy left off, exactly half-way between the Battle of Actium and the decease of Caesar Augustus. More important, at least for sundry scholarly investigations, his point of termination: some take him well into Claudius' reign, even to the end (which is not in any way probable). Indeed, he might have ended in 31, with the catastrophe of Aelius Seianus.[2]

Let that matter pass. For Servilius, no clue avails. He may have begun with the death of Augustus. If so, Tacitus was not an innovator when he elected A.D. 14 as his point of departure. Yet, although this writer's own time and experience can be taken to be his central theme, Servilius might have been compelled to go back some distance. Perhaps even to the aftermath of Actium. Or perhaps, for the sake of continuity, putting his inception at A.D. 4, a decisive year, when Caesar Augustus designated his successor. The discomforts which soon arose for Cornelius Tacitus because of his choice of A.D. 14 were grievous and manifold.[3] However it be, nothing in the early chapters of Book I suggests that Tacitus was following closely and carefully an annalist who had dealt with the previous decade in an exemplary fashion.

Speculation need not be pursued further. Nor is there any sign where Servilius ended. If he went beyond the assassination of Caligula, the affair of Camillus Scribonianus was awkward—yet perhaps not unmanageable. But the annalist might soon have to stop, for good reasons of discretion. An attractive point would be the invasion of Britain in 43, or Claudius' censorship in 47 (which happened to coincide with the eighth century of the city).

Hazards and inhibitions of this nature ought not to be neglected when the projects or the performance of historians under the Caesars come under discussion. There are factors on the other side. Historians do not always survive to bring their tasks to the appointed end; and the recorder of recent or contemporary events, aware of the dangers and anxious for

---

[1] Based on Seneca, Suas. VI. 18; 23, on which see above, p. 102, n. 2.

[2] That was Mommsen's opinion, restated by W. Pelka, Rh. Mus. LXI (1906), 620 ff. It renders hazardous much 'Quellenforschung' on the reign of Claudius.

[3] Tacitus (1958), 370 f.

his repute with posterity, may prefer that his work be left for an heir or executor to publish in a safe and suitable season. Thus the elder Pliny (*NH, praef.* 20). His nephew testifies to the hazards inherent in the recording of recent transactions—'graves offensae, gratia levis' (*Epp.* v. 8. 12).

Tacitus in his preface pronounces a firm condemnation of the imperial annalists. According as the ruler were alive or dead, the narrations were 'ob metum falsae' or 'recentibus odiis compositae'. That being so, on what criterion was he to proceed? The structure and content of the first hexad reflects constant recourse to the *acta* of the Senate. That was his main source in many tracts (it can be argued), not merely the framework. But what of the transactions which no document disclosed? There precisely the historians, for all their defects, become useful. Also the writers of memoirs.

Servilius or Aufidius, this is not the place for discussing the vexed question of the main written sources used by Tacitus in the Tiberian books, by Cassius Dio and by Suetonius. Scholars exhibit a heavy predilection for Aufidius.[1] Instead of fixing upon a name it is better to deduce the type of source from the type of narration. None the less, if a name be sought at all costs, it is a fair assumption that Tacitus was drawn in preference to Servilius Nonianus, senator, orator, and consul. A member of the high assembly from the middle years of Tiberius Caesar, and having benefited no doubt from a living historical tradition in the person of his consular parent, Servilius possessed manifold sources of information, of a kind needed to supplement the bare record of senatorial business. Thus the account of the proceedings against the ex-wife of Sulpicius Quirinius (III. 22 f.). It goes beyond the context in which it occurs (where Tacitus appears to be using the *acta*), and it also adduces the name of Servilius' father (III. 22. 2).

In the first hexad as extant only subsidiary sources are cited by name, viz. the *Bella Germaniae* of Pliny (I. 69. 2) and the *Memoirs* of Agrippina (IV. 53. 2). However, Servilius or Aufidius might have been invoked somewhere on a clash of testimony when the author discussed events before or after the fall of Seianus. For the rest, one observes that Suetonius for an incident on Capreae adduces 'annalibus suis vir consularis' (*Tib.* 61. 6). Who but Servilius Nonianus? There might be a temptation to assign several episodes in Tacitus to this source. For example, when Cocceius Nerva, the only senator who went with Tiberius to the island, resolved to put an end to his life, those who knew his thoughts reported

---

[1] Thus Ph. Fabia, *Les sources de Tacite dans les* Histoires *et les* Annales (1893), 397.

his reasons (VI. 26. 2). Or for that matter, the suicide of L. Arruntius (VI. 48). Again, Servilius ought to have been able to produce revelations about the splendours, the follies and the perils of high society in the days of Caligula, not inferior to Pliny's biography of Pomponius Secundus, the consular dramatist.

It will not be expedient to plunge any further into the unverifiable. Another item, however, calls for mention in passing. Josephus presents a full narrative of the assassination of Caligula and its sequel, with an oration for the Republic delivered by the consul Sentius Saturninus. Style and sentiments reflect a Roman historian, in whom can be recognized a predecessor of Tacitus. The claimant most in favour has been Cluvius Rufus.[1] One might wonder about Servilius Nonianus.

IX. A consular annalist, that did not exhaust the value and significance of this man. Tacitus was composing the annals of decline and fall—not merely a dynasty but an aristocracy brought to ruin. As he looked back to the early imperial epoch, he might discover here and there, among the idle and vicious, the inept or the subservient, some aristocrat who maintained the dignity of his line in a changed world, combining personal honour with political sagacity. Thus M. Lepidus (cos. A.D. 6), whose comportment induced the historian to put in a word for the freedom of the will, despite fate and the astrologers (IV. 20. 3). Servilius belonged to an ancient stock, restored after long eclipse through the patronage of the Caesars. He made a more than adequate response, by 'bonae artes'. Some other nobiles, it is true, did not neglect the study of eloquence or the law. Aemilius Scaurus (suff. 21), the great-grandson of the princeps senatus, had splendid talents as an orator—which he put to an evil use, behaving like a prosecutor of low degree and disgracing his ancestry (III. 66. 2). Servilius Nonianus, however, was a historian as well as a public speaker. The senatorial annalist tends to be a novus homo, in the line of Cato, Sallust, Pollio. A nobilis is something of a paradox in that tradition.

Tacitus, who had himself passed from oratory to the writing of history, will have been alive to that paradox. The surviving noblemen in his own day could not compete.

Historians can be exploited as useful documents for social history; and the figure of Servilius opens guidance to the opinions and the personality

---

[1] Mommsen, Hermes IV (1870), 320 = Ges. Schr. VII (1909), 248. For a cautious assessment of the problem, see now D. Timpe, Historia IX (1960), 474 ff.; L. H. Feldman, Latomus XXI (1962), 320 ff. For a low view of Cluvius' quality as a historian, G. B. Townend, Hermes LXXXIX (1961), 248.

of Cornelius Tacitus. According to a widely held persuasion, this historian fell into disillusion, he grew ever grimmer with the years, and more rigorous in his moral standards.

It is hazardous to equate the writer and the man. The tone and colouring of the *Annales* is largely determined by a tradition of historiography, and by the transactions narrated. Indeed, it can be contended that Tacitus gained in tolerance as he went on, and even in humour.[1] Let there be cited that masterpiece of parody and gaiety, the oration in which L. Vitellius explained to the Senate why the Emperor ought to be joined in matrimony to his own niece (XII. 5 f.).

Tacitus admires the social graces no less than honour and dignity. Observe his sympathetic portrayal of the way Valerius Asiaticus ordered his end, whom Vitellius and Messallina destroyed, the dull Claudius concurring (XI. 3). That type of admiration shows a verifiable enhancement in his writings. Exalting poetry against oratory in the *Dialogus*, he matches Pomponius Secundus with Domitius Afer, the advantage going to the former because of 'dignitas vitae' (13. 3). At the first presentation of Pomponius in the *Annales* his prime quality has become 'elegantia morum' (V. 8. 2). Now it is precisely 'elegantia vitae' that sets off Servilius against Afer (XIV. 19).

That should suffice, even were there not the full and explicit portrayal of the 'elegantiae arbiter' himself, T. Petronius (XVI. 18 f.): a deterrent, it should seem, of conventional and schematic notions.

An unobtrusive item can be added to show how the historian's views broadened. From the outset he was ready to make concessions in favour of bad men if they had any active talent. In the *Historiae*, referring to Otho in Lusitania, the author states 'comiter administrata provincia' (I. 13. 4). Now 'comitas', an amicable term, might in a governor cover connivance or slackness. There is a wide gap between 'comitas' and Otho's conduct as registered in the *Annales*—'integre sancteque egit' (XIII. 46. 3).

'Elegantia vitae' therefore opens a path to the comprehension of Cornelius Tacitus. The reference to Servilius Nonianus is indeed summary —perhaps he had appeared somewhere in the lost books. Similarly, Domitius Afer. For parallel, the excellent Pomponius Secundus passes from the scene without any evocation. A previous tribute from the historian suffices, when he earned the *ornamenta triumphalia*: 'modica pars famae eius apud posteros in quis carminum gloria praecellit' (XII. 28. 2). Poetry is the supreme title to fame, better than the service of the State. Hence also, by implication, the writing of Roman history.

---

[1] As argued in *Tacitus* (1958), 476; 537; 539.

That was what Sallust meant when, firm and contemptuous, he said that anybody now can be praetor or consul (*Jug.* 4. 8).

It is sheer delight to have a historian's generous tribute to one of his predecessors in the class of senatorial annalists. And, something more. Servilius Nonianus has narrowly escaped oblivion. Otherwise there is only Quintilian's testimony, in his short list—for the anecdote in the younger Pliny does not state explicitly that Servilius was reciting from a historical composition.

Servilius finds no admittance to the various writings of Seneca.[1] But, for that matter, Pomponius Secundus is also absent. Ever and again, emphasis must come back to the gaps and hazards of documentation.

Further, a disturbing suspicion arises. Perhaps Tacitus, moved by a prepossession in no way mysterious or dishonourable, pitched too high his estimate of Servilius as an orator no less than as a historian. Quintilian, who knew his subject, has a plethora of information about Domitius Afer: tributes to the force of his eloquence, cases in which he was advocate, notable *dicta*. Servilius Nonianus secures admission to his pages only once, because he wrote history with an eloquent style.

In his selection of names and facts, and in his verdicts, Tacitus is alert to persons on public show in his own time. The descendants of Domitius Afer occupied a prominent place in society—and, in fact, they turn out to be one ancestral component of the Antonine dynasty. One must be on guard all the time. That is evident in another matter: characters with no posterity were liable to suffer obscuration and dispraisal. Has Tacitus made too much of the political rôle of Annaeus Seneca and Afranius Burrus? That can be suspected, not that it need stand to his discredit.

X. Epilogue. Nobody who examines the obituary notices in Tacitus ought to let pass a difficulty in the text of *Ann.* xiv. 19. As follows:

Sequuntur virorum illustrium mortes, Domitii Afri et M. Servilii, qui summis honoribus et multa eloquentia viguerant, ille orando causas, Servilius diu foro, mox tradendis rebus Romanis celebris et elegantia vitae, quam clariorem effecit, ut par ingenio, ita morum diversus.

A query enforces itself, about the phrase 'elegantia vitae quam clariorem effecit'. How understand it, and how translate? Patently, 'elegantia

---

[1] Seneca has Augustus rebuke the alleged conspirator Cinna as follows: 'cedo, si spes tuas solus impedio, Paulusne te et Fabius Maximus et Cossi et Servilii ferent?' (*De clem.* I. 9. 10). In that season Servilii do not deserve to be reckoned among names of splendour, potency and ambition. Perhaps Seneca was unconsciously influenced by the *nobilitas* of his coeval the historian.

vitae' can render one man more famous than another. But it is a quality in itself, which its happy possessor does not enhance (or, for that matter, diminish). Where, then, does the comparison obtain? Beatus Rhenanus saw a remedy long ago. It is simple enough. Read 'quae clariorem effecit'. That is to say, 'elegantia vitae' made Servilius superior in fame to Afer.

Further, an improvement in punctuation will help. The relative clause should either be put in brackets or followed by a colon.

That is not the end of the matter. Is the relative clause necessary? It explains, but it adds nothing. The distinctive virtue of Servilius Nonianus is 'elegantia vitae', and the contrast of his renown, greater than that of Domitius Afer, is adequately conveyed by the antithesis, 'ut par ingenio ita morum diversus'. It is not the habit of Tacitus to amplify the obvious.

Moreover, the clause is neither sharp nor elegant. *Efficio* is not a vigorous word, or one of Tacitus' favourites.[1] Perhaps, therefore, the clause is an interpolation. That was the verdict of Acidalius.

Perhaps another explanation avails. A change of style in the third hexad of the *Annales* has not failed to draw the attention of scholars. Various reasons are canvassed. The author may have died before his task was completed.[2] At the least, lack of revision can be postulated. Towards the end, various peculiarities in content and arrangement can be detected. Furthermore, a piling up of indistinctive words or compound verbs such as had been eschewed in the earlier manner. The style is looser than would be expected, with certain weaknesses or redundancies.[3] Indeed, an infelicity could be established at an earlier stage. There is an awkward passage describing what Roman officials did to natives in Britain— 'praecipui quique Icenorum, quasi cunctam regionem muneri accepissent, avitis bonis exuuntur' (XIV. 31. 1). Here it is no remedy to expunge (as some have proposed) the clause introduced by 'quasi'. Haste is the easier explanation.

Similarly, perhaps, the redundant clause about the fame of Servilius in the condensed obituary notice. All that Tacitus had said earlier about his rival, Domitius Afer, anticipating an obituary, that had occurred long before, in Book IV. Neither had been named in the third hexad. Tacitus, choosing to register summarily the decease of persons close to his pre-occupations, may have intended to revise the passage—and even to expand it. Something unsatisfactory, though not of the same kind, may

---

[1] With a double object, *efficio* occurs only three times in the *Annales*, all strangely in Book IV (1. 2; 12. 4; 50. 4). Further, if 'quae clariorem effecit' (Rhenanus) is to be commended, not everybody may like the ellipsis of the second object (*eum*).

[2] E. Koestermann, *Gnomon* XI (1935), 322.

[3] For the various suspect phenomena see *Tacitus* (1958), 740 ff.

be detected in the comments on Memmius Regulus, who likewise had been absent from the third hexad (XIV. 47).[1]

However that may be, the emendation 'quae' instead of 'quam' is easy and makes sense. Anybody might have thought of it, and it can stand on its own merits. Strange, therefore, that no modern edition of the *Annales* should deem Rhenanus worthy of recognition, at least in an *apparatus criticus*.[2]

By good fortune, support is to hand, even if not required. The manuscript used by R. Agricola and by Ryckius has recently been discovered and identified at Leyden.[3] It carries a number of remarkable and plausible variants. Indeed, one scholar argues firmly for *Leidensis* as independent and ancient tradition; and he admits some of its readings to his text.[4] Not, however, the variant in XIV. 19. *Leidensis* here produces 'quae clariorem Afro effecitque'. It is good to have 'quae' in place of 'quam'. The addition of Afer's name makes the meaning clear—perhaps superfluously so. As has been demonstrated above, the parenthetic explanation is feeble. A concise writer would do without it. Perhaps Acidalius was right.

---

[1] *Tacitus* (1958), 743 f.

[2] The passage troubled several of the editors and commentators in the sixteenth century: see the proposals registered in the *Variorum* edition of Gronovius (1685). The moderns have expressed no disquiet. When examining Tacitean obituaries [above, p. 89], I was impelled towards 'quae' instead of 'quam', but did not wish to overburden the article with textual argument. I was not at that time aware of Rhenanus' proposal.

[3] C. W. Mendell, *AJP* LXXII (1951), 337 ff.; LXXV (1954), 250 ff.; *Tacitus, the Man and his Work* (1957), 328 ff.

[4] E. Koestermann in the third edition of his Teubner text (1960), cf. his important article, *Philologus* CIV (1960), 92 ff. Against, H. Heubner, *Gnomon* XXVI (1964), 159 ff.; R. H. Martin, *CQ²* XIV (1964), 169 ff.

IX

THE FRIEND OF TACITUS*

THE ASPIRATION to fame being open, avowed, and honourable, it was no scandal if a Roman of consular rank insisted on a mention in books of history written by a friend and destined (it was clear) to undying renown. Pliny saw his chance (*Epp.* VII. 33). There was another way and device. By publishing his own correspondence, Pliny was able to put in circulation a kind of autobiography, subtle and unimpeachable. The collection carries no fewer than eleven letters to the address of Cornelius Tacitus, and he is referred to in four others. Pliny quietly established a claim to parity in the field of eloquence.

Posterity responds, recognizing Pliny as the especial friend of Tacitus. It has not sufficiently been observed that when Tacitus felt impelled to write about the condition of Roman oratory he chose to dedicate the treatise to somebody else, to L. Fabius Justus, consul suffect in 102. The person and the occasion deserve scrutiny. Evidence casual, heterogeneous, or neglected might be adduced to throw light on the career and occupations of Fabius Justus, and even to convey what manner of man he was.

His name first turns up in certain transactions shortly after the assassination of Domitian. The barrister Aquillius Regulus, fearing the enmity of Pliny, made approach to various persons in December of 96, among them Fabius Justus (I. 5. 8). Fabius is also the recipient of two letters—which seem never to have been properly exploited. The one (I. 11) has been dismissed as unimportant.[1] As for the other, addressed to a man called 'Iustus' (VII. 2), a doubt is expressed, whether the person be not perhaps Minicius Justus.[2] This was an elderly Roman knight, *praefectus castrorum* long ago in 69 but still extant, the husband of a lady called Corellia, hence related (it can be conjectured) to Pliny's third wife.[3]

---

* Reprinted from *JRS* XLVII (1957), 131–5.
[1] E. Groag, P-W VI. 1773.
[2] E. Groag, l.c., cf. *PIR*², F 41.
[3] *PIR*¹, M 436. His wife was the sister of the consular Q. Corellius Rufus (*Epp.* VII. 11. 3). Corellius' daughter was called Corellia Hispulla (*PIR*², C 1296), and a Calpurnia Hispulla is the aunt of Pliny's wife (C 329).

In the first letter Pliny deplores the fact that there is no news from Fabius Justus and goes on to evince some perturbation: 'fac sciam quid agas, quod sine sollicitudine summa nescire non possum' (I. 11. 2). Why should Pliny conceive extreme anxiety about this Roman senator? Is it not because he is absent in one of the military zones? Not necessarily involved in active warfare on the frontiers—and let it not be forgotten that in 97, Nerva being Princeps, there was danger of a civil war. For disquiet about a friend with the armies compare, a little later, the stronger language of the amicable complaint that Pliny addresses to Julius Servianus (*suff.* 90, *II ord.* 102): 'ipse valeo, si valere est suspensum et anxium vivere exspectantem in horas timentemque pro capite amicissimo quidquid accidere homini potest' (III. 17. 3). Pliny's assiduous fears prove what is nowhere else attested, that Julius Servianus was present, for a time at least, at the seat of war, with Trajan in the first two campaigns against the Dacians (101 and 102).[1]

In the second letter Pliny is sensible that Justus, although impeded by 'adsiduae occupationes', would like to have some of his writings (VII. 2. 1). The word 'occupationes' is suitably applied to the employments of a magistrate or official at Rome or a governor in the provinces. Thus, the 'occupationes' of which Pliny himself makes complaint (I. 10. 10; II. 8. 3)— presumably his business when *praefectus aerarii Saturni*. Compare further his missive to a certain Minicius: 'inter istas occupationes' (VII. 12. 5). That can perhaps be taken as a reference to the consulate of C. Minicius Fundanus in 107.[2] Or again, to the army-commander Sabinus: 'quia tuas occupationes verebar' (IX. 2. 1). There is something more in the letter to Justus. The author concedes that his correspondent will have an exacting and anxious summer but ought to enjoy leisure in winter, at least during the nights: 'patiar ergo aestatem inquietam vobis exercitamque transcurrere et hieme demum, cum credibile erit noctibus saltem vacare te posse, quaeram quid potissimum ex nugis meis tibi exhibeam' (VII. 2. 2). What is the business of this man? He looks like the commander of an army. Compare Tacitus, *Ann.* I. 17. 4: 'duras hiemes, exercitas aestates.' Here as elsewhere (it will be noted) the author of these elegant epistles never specifies the province of any consular legate he happens to be

---

[1] Groag (P-W X. 884) assigns the letter to the winter of 98/9 (when Trajan himself was on the Danube). Servianus had gone from Germania Superior (cf. HA, *Hadr.* 2. 5 f.) to take over the Pannonian command (*Epp.* VIII. 23. 5), presumably in 98. But Pliny's language (and the order of the letters) speaks rather for 101 or 102: that is, the Dacian War.

[2] Not adduced by Groag in his full and sympathetic discussion of this cultivated person (P-W XV. 1820 ff.). The letter proves that Fundanus preferred a style of oratory more chaste and restrained than that of Pliny: observe the plural in 'vestro iudicio' and 'tenuitas vestra' (4 f.). That is to say, he adhered to the 'Attic' school.

writing to. Observe, however, the plural of the pronoun, 'vobis,' and compare, to Sabinus, 'arma vestra' (IX. 2. 4); also, to a certain Mamilianus, 'inter aquilas vestras' (IX. 25. 3). Sabinus is patently governor of a consular province.[1] Likewise Mamilianus.[2] It can be surmised that Fabius Justus was somewhere with the troops c. 106.

Fact and inference converge without discomfort. Still at Rome in December, 96, Fabius Justus went out to command a legion in the provinces with no great delay, either before the adoption of Trajan (October, 97) or not long after. Whether or no he also held a praetorian province, as was normal (see further below), there is a chance that he saw active service in the first campaign against the Dacians. His consulate might suggest it. The *ordinarii* of 102, consuls for the second time, are the principal allies of Trajan—Julius Servianus and Licinius Sura. When Sura resigns the *fasces* on 1st March, if not earlier, Fabius steps into his place, to remain as colleague of Julius Servianus. Sura had played a conspicuous part in the operations of 101.[3]

Favour, capacity, or emergency could bring a command a year or two after the consulate. There are clear and contemporary instances, thus the *ordinarii* of 99, A. Cornelius Palma and Q. Sosius Senecio.[4] Fabius may

[1] Sabinus will be identified as P. Metilius Sabinus Nepos (*suff.* 103). That is, the Nepos who in 105 is 'maximae provinciae praefuturus' (*Epp.* IV. 26. 2). Groag, noticing that his son (or nephew), P. Metilius Secundus (*ILS* 1053), suffect consul in 123 or 124, was *tribunus* of X Gemina, conjectured that the province was Pannonia (P-W XV. 1401). Perhaps, however, an earlier command, before Pannonia (which now stood very high in the hierarchy of the consular commands).

[2] Mamilianus (also the recipient of IX. 16, which shows that he had been hunting) is clearly T. Pomponius Mamilianus (*suff.* 100). A certain '[T.] Pomponius T. f. Gal. Mamilianus Rufus Antistianus Funisulanus Vettonianus' sets up a dedication at Deva (*CIL* VII. 164, improved by Haverfield in *Eph. Ep.* IX. 535). Commonly assumed governor of Britain, but his title, 'leg. Aug.,' suggests rather the commander of XX Valeria Victrix: a recent entry in a standard work (P-W XXI. 2342) imports confusion—'Statthalter von Britannien und Kommandant der *leg.* [II *Augusta*]'. That work (it can be noted) omits T. Pomponius Antistianus, the *suffectus* of 120 (*PIR*[1], P 522), who as legate of Lycia-Pamphylia bears the nomenclature 'Pomponius Antistianus Funisulanus Vettonianus' (*IGR* III. 739, ch. 14).

[3] Dio LXVIII. 9. 2.

[4] Palma held Tarraconensis about 101 (Martial XII. 9. 1). Sosius was in a high command in 102 or 103, not at the beginning of his tenure, cf. 'multa beneficia in multos contulisti' (*Epp.* IV. 4. 3). Groag suggests a post that ended in 105 at the latest (P-W III A, 1183). Stein, who unfortunately failed to cite (or notice) the letter of Pliny, argues that Sosius was legate of Moesia Inferior, succeeding A. Caecilius Faustinus (*suff.* 99), who is attested in May, 105 (*CIL* XVI. 50). See, against this view, *JRS* XXXV (1945), 112. Sosius could have been legate of Moesia Superior after C. Cilnius Proculus (*suff.* 87) attested in 100 (*CIL* XVI. 46), and before L. Herennius Saturninus (*suff.* 100) whose tenure falls somewhere between 103 and 106 (*CIL* XVI. 54).

have acceded very quickly to a consular province, passing thence to a second command. In 106 or 107 (for such is the date that the chronological order of Pliny's Letters permits) he appears to be in active employ (VII. 2, quoted above). Two alternatives are open. First, governor of a province. Indeed, to push the argument, perhaps a province at the seat of war. Fabius could have been in charge of either of the provinces of Moesia at the time of the second war against the Dacians (105 and 106). That is to say, Moesia Superior, following L. Herennius Saturninus (*suff.* 100), whose tenure falls somewhere between 103 and 106;[1] or Moesia Inferior, after A. Caecilius Faustinus (*suff.* 99), who is attested in May, 105.[2] Second, not a governor but on Trajan's staff or commanding a separate army corps. Such a position was held in this war by C. Julius Quadratus Bassus (*suff.* 105).[3] It could also be conjectured for Sosius Senecio (*cos.* 99) by reason of the signal honour of his second consulate in 107, when he shared the *fasces* with the great Licinius Sura, *consul tertio*.[4]

If the above reconstruction be held valid, it can come as no surprise that Fabius Justus subsequently rose to the command of most ample historic prestige among the military provinces. A milestone set up near Palmyra in the year 109 shows him legate of Syria.[5] He took the place of Cornelius Palma (*cos.* 99) who departed to hold the *fasces* for the second time as *ordinarius* in 109.

Fabius occupies a high rank among the marshals of Trajan. Below M'. Laberius Maximus (*suff.* 89) and Q. Glitius Agricola (*suff.* 97), consuls for the second time in 103 (*ordinarius* and *suffectus* respectively), the one with splendid exploits to his credit in the campaign of 102, the other legate of Pannonia and honoured with consular military decorations.[6] But not perhaps so far below Palma and Senecio—or the mysterious L. Publilius Celsus (*suff.* 102, *II ord.* 113), of whom no provincial command stands on record. Palma, Senecio, and Celsus all had public statues.[7] As for iterated consulates, it will be noted that Trajan, as his reign progressed, became less generous—the last are Palma in 109, Celsus in 113. An early decease may (or may not) have annulled the prospects of Fabius Justus after his governorship of Syria. Another military man to miss the distinction is

---

[1] *CIL* XVI. 54 (cf. the preceding note).   [2] *CIL* XVI. 50.

[3] As shown by the inscription of Pergamum, cf. A. v. Premerstein, *Bayerische S-B* 1934, Heft 3, 15 f. For his identity (not Julius Bassus, the deliquent proconsul of Bithynia), see *JRS* XXXVI (1946), 162 f.

[4] cf. Groag, P-W III A, 1184 f.   [5] *AE* 1940, 210.

[6] For Maximus, who had been legate of Moesia Inferior in 100 (*SEG* I. 329, ll. 62 ff.), Dio LXVIII. 9. 4. For Agricola, *ILS* 1021a, cf. *CIL* XVI. 47.

[7] Dio LXVIII. 16. 2.

D. Terentius Scaurianus (whose consulate presumably falls either in 102 or 104): Scaurianus was the first governor of Trajan's new province of Dacia.[1]

Sura passed away in his prime, perhaps as early as 108, but Servianus lived on to reach the age of ninety and a melancholy end. Glitius Agricola became Prefect of the City, but Laberius Maximus incurred disgrace—at the death of Trajan he is found confined to an island. Senecio may still have been alive in 113, but leaves no trace thereafter. Palma and Celsus survived only to be summarily executed in the first year of the new reign, conjoined with two other consulars in the charge of treason and a plot against Hadrian (not very convincing).

Friendship and loyalty, discord or feud among the marshals of Trajan, that would be a theme worth exploration—and extremely hazardous. The facts are not adequate. However, Licinius Sura must have had a following, and curiosity might ask how his adherents fared after the decease of their friend and patron.

Local origins or alliances sometimes furnish a clue. Sura came from Hispania Citerior. Tarraco and Barcino bear witness to his munificence, though his origin is perhaps to be sought in some other city of the region, for his tribe is not the 'Galeria' but the 'Sergia'.[2] It is therefore reasonable to put a man of Barcino among his adherents, namely L. Minicius Natalis, suffect consul in 106 but not promoted to the command of an army until late in Trajan's reign.[3] Possibly also L. Fabius Justus. The *nomen* 'Fabius', with about 300 instances in *CIL* II, is the fourth most common name in Spain, attesting the *clientela* of the patrician Fabii in old days. Spain might thus seem plausible, Baetica as well as Tarraconensis.[4] But it would not be well to omit Gallia Narbonensis which, though it makes a poorer showing (about fifty in *CIL* XII), had also been in the ambit of the historic Fabii. One might cite 'L. Fabii' there, for example, half-a-dozen at the colonia of Narbo (mainly *liberti*).[5] There is a chance that Fabius Justus was a Narbonensian;[6] and it will suitably be recalled that some are prepared to argue that the 'patria' of Cornelius Tacitus lies somewhere in the 'provincia'....

[1] *CIL* XVI. 57, 160, 163.   [2] *CIL* II. 4282 (near Tarraco), cf. Groag, P-W XIII. 471.

[3] *ILS* 1029. His governorship of Pannonia Superior (attested in 116, *CIL* XVI. 64) lasted into the reign of Hadrian. Q. Pompeius Falco (*suff.* 108), the son-in-law of Sosius Senecio, is parallel—legate of Moesia Inferior in 116 and 117 (*CIL* III. 7537; 12470), transferred to Britain by Hadrian (*ILS* 1035).

[4] At Italica, the 'patria' of Trajan, there is a dedication to the Emperor, perhaps as '[hosp]iti', set up by two men, viz. ']s. L. f. Mae[c.' and ']ius Iustus' (*CIL* II. 1114).

[5] *CIL* XII. 4791, 4794–6, 4798, 5218.

[6] Possibly the unknown consular of the acephalous inscription at Nemausus (*CIL* XII. 3169), cf. below, p. 115, n. 6.

Also worth inspection are the paths that bring a man to his consulship. The study can prove variously remunerative. The praetorian provinces included in the portion of Caesar are of cardinal rank in the hierarchy, quick and sure for advancement. From an early date they furnish direct access to the consulate, and in the course of time notable instances can be discovered. Thus, Glitius Agricola coming from Belgica in 97.[1] Indeed, appointment to the post reveals an emperor's intentions and can be described as very much like a designation.[2] Further, the title 'cos. des.' will occur on inscriptions set up before a governor leaves his province, and it can happen that the *fasces* are held in absence.[3]

There is an especially favoured class of 'viri militares'—men who pass straight to the consulate after only two posts, viz. a legionary command and a praetorian province.[4] Examples abound in the time of Trajan. Among them are two *Ignoti* worth keeping in mind for various reasons. The first, revealed by an inscription at Rome, had been with Trajan when the Emperor 'gentem Dacor(um) et regem Decebalum bello superavit'; his honours were *ornamenta triumphalia* and two sets of consular military decorations; between praetorship and consulate he had been legate of I Minervia (in Germania Inferior) and governor of Belgica.[5] The second, at Nemausus, with consular decorations, had been a legionary legate under Nerva and Trajan, then governor of some praetorian province: hence consul not later than 102, one would expect.[6]

The normal tenure of each post was about three years, but not all of the 'viri militares' will have spent a full six years abroad. A season of crisis would bring abbreviations. Such may with propriety be surmised in the period 97–100—alert young men going out to command a legion under some prominent consular in Nerva's reign or gaining quick advancement after the adoption of Trajan.

Licinius Sura, so it is reported by a late epitomator, had an active part in Trajan's seizure of the power.[7] It is not clear what position he held in

---

[1] *ILS* 1021. The consulate is registered on the new fragment of the *Fasti Ostienses* (*AE* 1954, 220).

[2] Tacitus, *Agr.* 9. 1.

[3] cf. observations on this type of province in *JRS* XLIII (1953), 152 f.

[4] cf. E. Birley, *Roman Britain and the Roman Army* (1953), 4; *Proc. Brit. Ac.* XXXIX (1953), 203.

[5] *ILS* 1022 (Rome, the Mons Caelius).

[6] *CIL* XII. 3169. Perhaps D. Terentius Scaurianus, the first legate of Trajan's Dacia, as was suggested in *JRS* XXXVI (1946), 160: it can be argued that he came from Gallia Narbonensis (Groag, P-W v A, 669). Possibly, however, L. Fabius Justus.

[7] Pseudo-Victor, *Epit.* 13. 6: 'ob honorem Surae, cuius studio imperium arripuerat, lavacra condidit'.

summer and autumn of 97. Was he consul suffect in that year (late in the year)—or not perhaps in 93 (the only times that seem available or plausible)?[1] The acephalous *elogium* at Rome has commonly been assigned to Sura. The attribution is highly attractive, but not quite proved.[2] Sura's praetorian posts will therefore have to remain dubious. Nor is evidence abundant about the previous occupations of the other consular marshals. However it be, a prompt promotion could be conjectured for the first *ordinarii* of the new reign, Cornelius Palma and Sosius Senecio, consuls in 99.

Fabius Justus was absent from Rome not long after December, 96. Presumably as legate of a legion (*Epp.* I. 11). Pliny expresses anxiety. Warfare does not have to be invoked. There was, however, the insistent menace of a civil war in 97 when Nerva was ruler of Rome, precarious and ephemeral. Not only the threat (perhaps exaggerated) from the legate of Syria, which happens to stand on record:[3] the situation that compelled Nerva to adopt as his son and partner one of the army commanders has to be adduced and estimated.

If Fabius was a legionary legate in 97, there would be time for him to pass, before his consulship, to a praetorian province. Also time for a post on Trajan's staff in the first campaign against the Dacians, or for the command of a corps in the field.[4]

Changing rulers and a rapid turn of events could be propitious to retarded ambitions or forgotten men as well as to youthful opportunists. Not all of Trajan's generals in the first war derive from the company of recent consuls. Seniority and friendship, allies or coevals come into the reckoning. Thus, M'. Laberius Maximus, consul suffect in 89: the son of a powerful man, L. Laberius Maximus, who was promoted from the pre-

---

[1] The possibilities have narrowed. The consuls of 94–6 are known; also those of 98, if the pair P. Julius and Q. Fulvius Gillo belong, as is probable, to the last two months of 98 (cf. *JRS* XLIII (1953), 154); while 99 seems too late. As against 93, observe that Martial in a poem of 92 shows Sura recovering from a dangerous illness (VII. 47), with no sign that he is soon to be consul.

[2] Compare Groag's powerful arguments, discussing *ILS* 1022 (P-W XIII. 472 f.). A case could perhaps be made for Sosius Senecio: honours conferred for the Second Dacian War at least.

[3] *Epp.* IX. 13. 10 f. Note further the anomalous promotion of A. Larcius Priscus, quaestor of Asia, becoming 'legatus Augusti leg. IIII Scythicae/pro legato consulare provinc. Syriae' (*AE* 1908, 237, cf. *ILS* 1055). See *Philologus* XCI (1936), 238 ff.

[4] Thus perhaps C. Julius Quadratus Bassus (*suff.* 105). Some of the legionary detachments registered on his inscription might have been commanded by him in the First Dacian War; he had previously been legate of XI Claudia, which went from Vindonissa to the Danube *c.* 101 (E. Ritterling, P-W XII. 1697).

fecture of Egypt to the command of the Praetorian Guard in 84.[1] A *suffectus* of 102 taking over the *fasces* from Licinius Sura and duly promoted to the high military commands, is another matter. Everything speaks for youth.

The successful 'vir militaris', of the type already registered and defined, can reach the consulate a dozen years from his quaestorship, seven or eight from his praetorship. That is to say, he is consul at thirty-seven or thirty-eight. The odds are that the year of Fabius' birth is in the neighbourhood of 65. He is junior to Tacitus (*suff.* 97), born (it can be supposed) in 56 or 57, a little junior to Pliny (*suff.* 100), born either in 61 or 62. Fabius will be one of the eager youths who acclaimed and emulated the oratorical genius of Cornelius Tacitus when it flowered in the eighties of the first century A.D. Pliny, avowing himself a disciple, says that he was an 'adulescentulus' at that time (VII. 20. 4).

The presumed age of Fabius Justus has a bearing on the *Dialogus*. The dramatic date of the colloquy there reproduced should belong in 74 or 75, as is indicated by 'sextam iam felicis huius principatus stationem qua Vespasianus rem publicam fovet' (*Dial.* 18. 3). Perhaps 75 rather than 74, reckoning from the calendar years of Vespasian's effective rule at Rome, not from the artificial antedating to 1st July, 69. About the date of composition, lengthy controversies have obtained. One notion that still lingers, protected among the safe and accepted beliefs or consecrated in standard manuals, will have it that the *Dialogus* is the earliest of Tacitus' works, written under Titus, in or about A.D. 80. That notion ignored the propriety of style to the literary genre. The only argument was feeble, reposing on a fallacy: the neo-Ciceronian manner (it was postulated) could only belong to the first stage in the development of the Tacitean style.

Fabius Justus deals a blow in the flank, cruel and perhaps unnecessary. The choice products of a Roman education might be both precocious and pompous. But who shall believe that the young Tacitus, reporting a conversation that took place five or six years earlier, would describe himself as then having been 'adulescens admodum' (*Dial.* 1. 2), that he dedicated the treatise to a boy who had just assumed the 'toga virilis'?

It would be an easy assumption that the *Dialogus*, like sundry works of prose or verse in the literature of the Romans, was destined for a consul or a consul-designate—the Fourth Eclogue, the History of Velleius Paterculus, or the Twelfth Book of Martial.[2] Pliny in 101 and 102 was elaborating his consular 'actio gratiarum'. Flocks of fanciers came to the recitation

---

[1] *P. Berol.* 8334, as interpreted by A. Piganiol, *CRAI* 1947, 376 ff., cf. *JRS* XLIV (1954), 117.
[2] That date and occasion for the *Dialogus* was firmly postulated by W. Kappelmacher, *Wiener Studien* L (1932), 121 ff.

of the *Panegyricus*, they turned up in the foulest of weather, and some asked for more (*Epp.* III. 13; 18). Fabius Justus, an enlightened and cultivated person, had deserted eloquence for the career of provinces and armies. He belongs with Sosius Senecio, the friend of Plutarch, with Licinius Sura, who was an orator and patron of letters before chance or ambition swept him into war and politics.

Fabius took it as evident and manifest truth that there were no orators any more, only barristers, advocates, and the like (*Dial.* I. 1). The author of the *Dialogus* concurs. He furnishes a diagnosis, balanced and mature, with a historian's line of argument. Cornelius Tacitus had been among the leading speakers, if not the first of them all. No senatorial debate registers his name subsequent to the prosecution of Marius Priscus, which he conducted along with Pliny to its termination in January, 100. Tacitus had found the better way. He was writing history.[1]

[1] It must, however, be added that indications in the letters of Pliny point to a date later than 101 or 102. Thus, the reference to *Dial.* 9. 6, in *Epp.* IX. 10. 2: 'itaque poemata quiescunt quae tu inter nemora et lucos commodissime perfici putas'. Further, the book which Tacitus sent to Pliny for his comments (VII. 20). Tacitus in his covering missive wrote 'ut magistro magister' and 'ut discipulo discipulus' (VIII. 7. 1). The book should therefore be an oration or a treatise about oratory. What is the solution? Perhaps the *Dialogus*; and perhaps, originally designed for the consulship of Fabius Justus, it was being revised for publication *c.* 106. However it be, the age, character, and occupations of the dedicant retain their relevance.

X

THE POLITICAL OPINIONS OF TACITUS

THE ROMANS had an extreme distrust of abstract speculation, especially if it touched state and society. Political theory was foreign and Greek: idle and superfluous when not positively noxious. The Greeks had proved a failure in the arts of government. What could they offer? The Roman constitution is patently the best that any community had evolved. As Cato, a senator and a statesman, was in the habit of saying, the institutions of Greek cities were the product of individual legislators, whereas Rome had benefited from the sagacity of many men and the long process of the ages.

Such are the axioms stated by Cicero in the books *De re publica*. Apart from Cicero, the last epoch of the Roman Republic shows a dearth of political theory. But the governing class cannot have been destitute of political thinking and presuppositions. That must be allowed for. Language, attitudes and actions will repay examination.

Cicero by himself is not adequate for guidance. Nor, for that matter is Sallust, although he is a useful corrective, being angry and subversive where Cicero is complacent and edifying. And they labour under a common defect. Both look back to the past.

Cicero held that the ancestral constitution was the ideal. It might have to be modified and it could be improved, but only in part, not in essentials. The changes which he contemplates in the treatise *De legibus* are in fact modest enough—tribunes curbed and the office of censor made permanent. Cicero's gaze is fixed on the City and its institutions. He has not faced the problem provoked by the impact of empire abroad. How would the Roman aristocracy be able not only to maintain the old structure but also to manage the dominion of the world?

Similarly Sallust, for all their dissonances. He attacks the regiment of the oligarchy as restored by Sulla; but he has no faith in the People and its ostensible champions. He admired Caesar—but perhaps Cato more. They were 'ingenti virtute, diversis moribus'.[1] A blend of both was requisite to save the Commonwealth through their contrasted and complementary

[1] *Cat.* 53. 6.

virtues. But lesser men now had the arbitrament, and very nasty men: the Triumvirs, bringing back a despotism like Sulla's dictatorship, with proscription and confiscation.[1] Sallust valued liberty, but, like others of his class, yearned for order and concord in the Commonwealth. Stability, however, was not to be had, save by submitting to centralized authority. 'Cum domino pax ista venit', that was the only rational forecast.[2] The future was dark and menacing.

Writing under the Triumvirate, Sallust can with propriety be styled the earliest of the imperial authors. Subsequent historians in Rome of the Caesars would have to confront, or evade, a dilemma comparable to his. The main preoccupation of the senatorial historian is the relationship between Senate and Emperor. That was also the main problem of the Caesars themselves, for something like a century and a half, if not longer. Administration, the armies and foreign affairs are easy in comparison.

Tacitus is the primordial document. Doubly so—for the season of his own career as a senator and for that earlier epoch which he portrayed in his second historical work, the *Annales*: the reigns of the successors of Caesar Augustus in the line of Julii and Claudii.

When Nero fell, it was the end of a dynasty that had subsisted for a hundred years from the Battle of Actium: a long stability, with acquiescence passing into habit, and even a loyalty to ruler as well as to system of government. It is therefore not vain to ask what were the sentiments and attitudes of the senatorial class. And it will be an advantage if some kind of answer can be furnished without having to draw in the first instance, or mainly, on the testimony of Cornelius Tacitus.

Centralized government arose out of the Civil Wars, and its continuance was imposed by the necessity of concord at home and dominion abroad. The aristocracy had to accept the verdict and the victor. Not always with sorrow or reluctance. The descendants of consuls discovered signal benefits in the 'novus status'. Ruinous competition being now abated, the *nobiles* acquire the consulship by prerogative of birth and prosper in the alliance of Caesar. The monarchy itself is an aristocractic faction, and to the dynasty are linked other houses not only noble but patrician, such as Fabii, Valerii, and Aemilii. On the other hand, patronage opens careers to the municipal gentry of Italy and the provinces of the Roman West. *Novi homines* tended to be traditionalist in sentiment; and the profiteers of the Revolution were eager to become respectable through the painless process of social mimesis.

---

[1] It is here assumed that Sallust wrote his first monograph in 42.   [2] Lucan I. 670.

To be sure, the heirs of a great and glorious past will not gladly acclaim a system that curbs their freedom, or frankly avow the benefits that accrue from obedience. However, there was an easy path of automatic persuasion. The government by the use of Republican language facilitated the acceptance of the new dispensation. Imperial propaganda in its varied arts and aspects need not be denied. But, on the whole, the educated classes were left to devise their own apologia.

Some persons, such as Velleius Paterculus, affected to believe that the ancient Republic had in truth been restored by Caesar Augustus.[1] Others were more honest—or more subtle. Though next to nothing survives of Augustan prose literature, some of the arguments that were current can perhaps be divined. One of them would be the appeal to change and development in the history of Rome. The City being destined to endure for ever, new forms of authority, 'nova imperia', would inevitably arise through the ages. Those are the words of a tribune in an early book of Livy.[2] Again, the vast bulk of empire that threatened to collapse under its own weight: the 'corpus imperii' could only be held together by the mind and direction of a single governor.[3] That is Florus, an epitomator who might have found the idea already in Livy. Further, the ruler is a 'first citizen', a 'guardian' or 'president' of the Commonwealth—not, of course, king or tyrant. That obvious and necessary antithesis is stated by the poet Ovid in a crisp and personal form when contrasting Romulus (the Founder, but of dubious repute) with Augustus:

> vis tibi grata fuit: florent sub Caesare leges.
> tu domini nomen, principis ille tenet.[4]

Perhaps the most significant formula evolved in defence of the Principate is the 'Middle Path'. Rome now enjoyed 'order without enslavement, liberty but not licence'. That important truth is enounced among the comments which the Romans made when assessing the reign of Augustus after the funeral ceremony. Not in the version of Tacitus, but in that of Cassius Dio, writing a century after Tacitus.[5] Now Dio, it is plausible if not patent, went back to the predecessors of Tacitus, because they were closer

---

[1] Velleius II. 89. 4: 'prisca illa et antiqua rei publicae forma revocata'.

[2] Livy IV. 4. 4: 'quis dubitat quin in aeternum urbe condita, in immensum crescente, nova imperia sacerdotia iura gentium hominumque instituantur ?'

[3] Florus II. 14. 5 f.: 'perculsum undique ac perturbatum ordinavit imperii corpus, quod haud dubie numquam coire et consentire potuisset nisi unius praesidis nutu quasi anima et mente regeretur'.

[4] Ovid, Fasti II. 141 f.

[5] Dio LVI. 43. 4: βασιλευομένους τε ἄνευ δουλείας καὶ δημοκρατουμένους ἄνευ διχοστασίας.

to the events, if for no other reason. A helpful formulation of this type and tenor could have emerged at a quite early date—even before the decease of Caesar Augustus. It happens to occur for the first time (but that is no objection) in the oration of Galba, as invented by Tacitus in the *Historiae* (I. 16. 4).

On this showing, Rome had the advantage both ways: Republic and Monarchy, each in its beneficial aspect. Furthermore, it could be argued (and it was true), Caesar had one portion in government, Senate and magistrates another, since 27 B.C. Their respective spheres were duly de-limited by Seneca in the speech he composed for Nero on his accession (*Ann.* XIII. 4). So far, but only so far, the modern term 'dyarchy' is admissible. It must be added that in the strict letter of the law there was only one source of authority ultimately, namely Senatus Populusque delegating power to the emperor. That is to say, in different language the rule of the Caesars can be defined summarily and properly as absolutism parading under legal forms.

However that may be, the educated classes had been able (as has been shown) to produce a theory of the Principate, representing it as a kind of constitutional monarchy. That was comforting. The Caesars paid necessary homage, not always feigned, for some of them disliked monarchy (notably Tiberius) or shared the normal reverence for the past of Rome; and the appropriate language was artfully employed by their ministers, or echoed by senators not always insincerely.

This edifying comportment had an unfortunate sequel. Once a theory had formed, the government lay open to criticism for having deserted its public professions; and Caesar by unguarded behaviour might all too easily lapse from the rôle and label of a true 'princeps', disclosing the despot.

The ruler thus became vulnerable, but not the institution. With Tiberius, the system withstood various shocks and strains: discord in the dynasty, the removal of the great minister Aelius Seianus and the ruler's long absence from the capital. On his decease, no discomfort, but the succession of Caligula no less easy for his not being associated previously in the imperial powers.

The assassination of that prince provoked a brief crisis. Sovereignty lapsed to Senate and People (that is, to the Senate), and the consuls took charge. One of the consuls spoke, advocating a restoration of the Republic; but aristocratic candidates quickly put up their claims for the power. One of them would presumably have been chosen by vote of the Senate;[1] but the Guard discovered and proclaimed a forgotten member of the dynasty

[1] Josephus, *BJ* II. 205: κρινεῖν ψήφῳ τὸν ἄξιον τῆς ἡγεμονίας.

and the Senate acquiesced. That was the first occasion (and the last) when a return to the Republic was the subject of open discussion.

It is not clear that everybody had realized what such a change would entail: free competition for the consulate, and the Senate put in control of finance, armies and foreign policy. Brief reflection would show that it was impossible to abolish a system of government that had lasted for a good seventy years. Nor was that the intention when in the second year of Claudius the legate of Dalmatia raised rebellion, duly invoking the names of Senate and People.[1] This pretender, Arruntius Camillus Scribonianus, had a dynastic claim to set in rivalry against Julii and Claudii—he was a descendant of Pompeius Magnus on the female side.[2]

The efflux of time reinforced loyalty and confirmed the advantages of a hereditary succession. Seneca devised for his pupil in the purple the necessary and 'constitutional' language to use in addressing the Senate. But Seneca not long afterwards, when exhorting Nero to practise clemency, did not hesitate to start from the axiom that Nero's power was regal and absolute. In that treatise Seneca coolly disregarded the conventional distinction between 'princeps' and 'rex'.[3] The two types of discourse employed by the minister reveal and show up the essential duplicity of the Principate.

So strong, therefore, and so widely conceded were the arguments in favour of the new government and the existing order. Who could oppose, who cared to criticize? Dislike of an emperor is another matter. Growing distaste for Nero produced—in the eleventh year of his reign—a great conspiracy, with the attempt to put an aristocrat, C. Piso, in his place. At the same time, and independent of that venture, a body of reasoned criticism had been taking shape. It is associated with, and concentrates on, the person of Thrasea Paetus: not a scion of the old nobility but a new man from Patavium in Transpadane Italy.

An important question challenges enquiry. What in fact were the ideals of Thrasea and his friends—for this was a group, and even (as to be expected at Rome) a family faction, with continuity before and after, with a tradition, and, so it seemed, a common doctrine? Its most conspicuous members owed allegiance to the teachings of the Stoics; and that creed is duly indicted by their enemies.[4]

[1] Dio LX. 15. 3.   [2] PIR², A 1140.

[3] Seneca, De clem. I. 4. 3: 'principes regesque et quocumque alio nomine sunt tutores status publici'.

[4] Ann. XVI. 22—the deliberately exaggerated denunciation put into the mouth of Cossutianus Capito.

Caution is requisite if one tries to assess the influence of doctrines on Roman political behaviour, in this instance as earlier with Cassius and Brutus, the one of the Epicurean persuasion, the other not Stoic but Academic. Thrasea Paetus, in the words of Tacitus, was 'Virtus ipsa' (XVI. 21. 1).[1] Now that 'virtus' which Thrasea was deemed to embody was a Roman, Republican and aristocratic quality: it does not imply that Thrasea or any of his allies advocated the Republican form of government. Their Republicanism was moral, not political. But, as they stood for the 'libertas' and 'dignitas' of the senator and the senatorial order, this attitude, sharpened by their disapprobation of Nero, forced them into an opposition that could be construed as treason by a prosecutor or a tyrant. Thrasea himself was anything but a fanatic, in truth a humane and judicious man.[2] Not all of his allies were so sensible.

Thrasea even had a policy, of a sort. When the government made fair professions (as in Nero's oration at the outset), nothing was lost and something might be gained if in ostensible faith one tried to take them seriously. It might be possible to vindicate for the Senate a modest function of cooperation with the ruler. The first few years of Nero's reign had passed without conflicts. When Thrasea spoke in the Senate he kept off the sphere of Caesar in government and did not touch his provinces and armies.

Thrasea Paetus was destroyed, with death or exile for his adherents. Educated opinion being now alienated, Nero was faced with the danger of a proclamation from one of the generals, sympathetic to the discontented at Rome or even in close touch with them. As it happened, the movement started in one of the unarmed provinces (the causes are obscure) when Julius Vindex, the legate of Gallia Lugdunensis, rose in revolt. Vindex was defeated by Verginius Rufus, who held the command on the upper Rhine, but that victory did not avail to save Nero from a series of accidents and misunderstandings—and from his own incompetence. The power came paradoxically to Sulpicius Galba, the legate of Tarraconensis.

Civil wars ensued quickly, Vespasian prevailing, who had sons and could establish a dynasty. The years 68 and 69 re-enact the lessons of a century earlier and enforce the claims of stability. And, be it recalled, the chief problems inherent in the Principate had been manifested during the rule of the Julian and Claudian House, likewise the standard attitudes adopted by senators. It remains to trace briefly the evolution of government in the next forty years or so.

[1] cf. Velleius II. 35. 2 on Cato—'homo Virtuti simillimus'. Thrasea had in fact written a life of Cato (Plutarch, Cato 25).

[2] cf. Thrasea's maxim, 'qui vitia odit homines odit' (cited in Pliny, Epp. VIII. 22. 3).

The imperial power continued to grow steadily at the expense of the Senate in every field and aspect, Trajan continuing the methods of the Flavian emperors and bequeathing them to his successor. The line of development is so clear that one might be tempted to regard the crisis under Domitian as no less an interlude than the brief anarchy under Nerva and consequently put at A.D. 70 the inception of the Antonine era.

The old forms and institutions subsisted as necessary relics, but void of content or changed in function. The decadence of the high assembly stands revealed in the items reported by Pliny in the letters of a consular orator giving a friendly portrayal of contemporary society: several trials of proconsuls, it is true, but for the rest a miscellany of the trivial or tedious. The season for eloquence was over—no great orators any more, but only petty advocates.[1] Intelligent men drew the moral and turned their talents to an active career in the provinces of Caesar. Such was Fabius Justus, governor of Moesia Inferior and of Syria.[2] It may be observed that none of the especial friends of the Emperor among the consular legates, such as Julius Servianus or Licinius Sura, is registered by Pliny as present at any debate in the Senate.

Nor were many still extant of the 'magna nomina' that recalled the Republic and had once adorned the Senate of the early imperial epoch. The old aristocracy was all but extinct, victims of the Caesars and of their fatally illustrious pedigrees; and the survivors were sparse of their first successors, the families ennobled by the Triumvirs and by Caesar Augustus. Instead, ever newer stocks, and they tend to monopolize the high consular commands. The Emperor now controls promotion of every kind more overtly than before. Trajan did not bother to take the power of censor. He admitted new senators and created new patricians by mere prerogative.

And the recruitment of the Senate had been widening all the time. It was no surprise that after Spain and Narbonensis Roman colonies in other regions showed their consuls in due course, such as Cirta or even distant Pisidian Antioch.[3] But, before Domitian's reign ends it exhibits two men from cities of western Asia Minor, namely Julius Celsus and Julius Quadratus;[4] and, soon after, C. Julius Quadratus Bassus, belonging to a nexus of dynastic families that traced their descent from kings and

---

[1] *Dial.* I. 1: 'causidici et advocati et patroni et quidvis potius quam oratores vocantur'.
[2] For Syria, *AE* 1940, 210 (near Palmyra); for Moesia Inferior, Pliny, *Epp.* VII. 2. 2 along with BM Papyrus 2851, col. II. 25, as elucidated in *JRS* XLIX (1959), 26 ff.
[3] *ILS* 1001; 9485.
[4] *ILS* 8971 (Ephesus); 8819 (Pergamum).

tetrarchs, commands a Roman army in the second war against the Dacians.[1]

The primacy of Italy was waning fast. The fear was expressed that the senators of extraneous origin might regard it merely as a temporary place of sojourn, not as their new home.[2] Italy in fact was reduced very much to the condition of a province, if an imperial legate can be found in charge of the Transpadane zone.[3] That seems to foreshadow Hadrian's institution of four consular regions in Italy.

The emperor also encroaches on the sphere of the Senate abroad by sending imperial commissioners to its provinces. The bureaucracy swells everywhere, with many new posts for equestrian agents. It was a truth revealed long ago that knights by the friendship of Caesar or the quality of their employment might stand at parity with consulars, or even in front of them. The prestige of the higher knights is now advertised when a Prefect of the Guard can pass into the Senate and become consul almost at once.[4]

So far the system of government, accepted and unshakeable. Next, the feud between the ruler and educated opinion, which broke out in the later years of Nero, died away at last. But not without having caused strain and annoyance to Vespasian and to Domitian. The party of Thrasea Paetus was still there, led by his son-in-law Helvidius Priscus, a man of indomitable character and rigid principles. After a quarrel with Vespasian, Priscus was sent into exile and there put to death. Priscus, it appears, had not only been loud in praise of the old Republic. He had allowed himself incautiously to bring hereditary succession into question. At least Vespasian (it is reported) after an altercation with Priscus went out of the Senate exclaiming 'my sons shall succeed me, or no man shall'.[5]

The group is not heard of again for a long time. In 93, when Domitian had been in occupancy of the power for twelve years, it was brought to ruin in a sequence of prosecutions for high treason. The causes are not wholly clear. Accident, personal feuds and the eager ambition of prosecutors must be allowed for; and the emperor was insecure and suspicious.

After the assassination of Domitian, the exiles came back. Faithful friends

---

[1] *AE* 1933, 268 (Pergamum), as corrected by A. v. Premerstein, *Bayerische S-B* 1934, Heft 3. But observe that he is not the same person as Julius Bassus, the delinquent proconsul of Bithynia (Pliny, *Epp.* IV. 9). For his kinsfolk, *OGIS* 544 (Ancyra).

[2] Pliny, *Epp.* VI. 19. 4: 'urbem Italiamque non pro patria sed pro hospitio aut stabulo quasi peregrinantes habere'.

[3] *ILS* 1040 (Antium).   [4] Sex. Attius Suburanus, *cos. suff.* 101, II *ord.* 104.

[5] Dio LXVI. 12, cf. Suetonius, *Divus Vesp.* 25.

or opportunistic allies duly raised a great clamour for vengeance on the agents of the previous regime.[1] However, Nerva, though not a strong man, was astute. The plea of concord and good sense was heard, their zeal was baffled. Under Nerva's successor, anger and criticism abated utterly. Educated opinion is reconciled to the government, and philosophers acclaim his rule as that of the best man. Senators now enjoy 'securitas' and in return are happy to practise 'obsequium', or rational obedience.[2]

Trajan came to the power through the act and choice of Nerva, ostensibly a free choice but in truth imposed in a season of crisis; and Trajan happened to have no son. Those facts supplied a consolation to the ingrained anti-dynastic prejudices of the senatorial order. Hence laudatory effusions extolling the ideal of adoption from men who in other circumstances would have been no less ready to acclaim the manifest validity of succession in the blood and family.

The comportment of Trajan himself appeared to flatter those notions. Next in male kin was Aelius Hadrianus, the son of a cousin; and, soon after Trajan's accession the young man took to wife the grand-niece, Vibia Sabina. Trajan, however, gave no further sign of his intentions, nor did he take any step to associate Hadrian with himself in the imperial powers.

If Trajan thereby paid tribute to a theory of the Principate, he was scrupulous to excess, or even perverse. He cannot earn approbation from men of understanding. Rather perhaps can he be held deserving of censure. The Senate and the Senate alone could confer the power legally. That is clear. But was it not the plain duty of a Princeps to discover and designate a successor, as Augustus had done? Otherwise his decease might provoke a catastrophe. It would be criminal negligence to make no provision for continuity of rule or abandon the choice to the arbitrament of a body like the Roman Senate, about whose character and capacity there is adequate information in this age. Nothing short of a felicitous accident would avert dissension, rivalry, and the menace of civil war.

Emperor and Senate, such was their situation when Cornelius Tacitus, some years intervening since his *Historiae*, set himself to the composition of a second great work. The imperial system had come to full and defined maturity. Looking backwards in time, a man might contemplate a long development. It was a question where he would put the inception of the

---

[1] Pliny, *Epp.* IX. 13.

[2] For 'obsequium', cf. *Agr.* 8. 1; 42. 5; *Dial.* 41. 3. Pliny helps to illustrate the word, cf. *Epp.* VIII. 23. 5; X. 3a. 3; X. 100; *Pan.* 9. 3 and 5; 78. 1.

story. Tacitus decided to begin with Tiberius Caesar. A mistake, as he came to see before he was far forward with the *Annales*. It was too late to modify his design—but if he lived he would go back again and deal with Caesar Augustus (III. 24. 3).

It will now be expedient to discuss the writer's opinions in the light of his life and times. Born in 56 or 57, Tacitus owed to Vespasian his admission to the career of honours. In 88 he reached the praetorship. By that year he was *XV vir sacris faciundis* (XI. 11. 1). A fact of exceptional value. This priesthood, to which the normal *novus homo* can hardly aspire before his consulship, indicates loyal service to the ruler of Rome or high favour with the dispensers of patronage. Soon after the praetorship supervened a period of three or four years abroad (perhaps the command of a legion). Then, in 97, Tacitus became consul suffect, at some time in the second half of the year, perhaps not before September. It would be hasty to assume that he owed that honour to Nerva—he may already have been designated by Domitian.

His first published writing was a biography of his deceased father-in-law, Julius Agricola. The monograph is something more than a delayed commemoration. It stands (so one can maintain) in close relation to the events of the year 97. Next, and quickly, the *Germania*, not without some relevance to Trajan's presence on the Rhine. As for the *Dialogus*, that treatise, which assumes and demonstrates that there is no place any more for public oratory at Rome, can be assigned an appropriate date early in the reign of Trajan. Perhaps in 101, as a pointed epilogue on the *Panegyricus* of Pliny, perhaps a few years later.

Meanwhile Tacitus had embarked on a full-length history of his own time. Announced in the *Agricola* in words that imply a narration of the reign of Domitian (3. 3), the project was modified. Tacitus took the point of departure back to January 1st, 69, and he may not have begun at once. The earliest repercussions of the historian's work in progress are discovered in certain letters of his friend Pliny. It may be supposed without discomfort that he brought the twelve books of the *Historiae* to completion towards the year 109. That is to say, a good decade from the original announcement. There is no sign that Tacitus turned at once to a second project. Obedient to duty, station, or curiosity, he went out to Asia as proconsul in 112 when the year of his eligibility arrived.[1]

The date at which Tacitus began the writing of the *Annales* is a matter in dispute. A digression in Book II that expatiates on empires in the eastern

---

[1] The proconsulate is attested by *OGIS* 487 (Mylasa). The year of office 112/13 is all but certain. There is only a very faint chance that it could have been 113/14.

lands concludes with a sentence in elevated language alluding to the present extent of Rome's dominion in the Orient. The author describes Elephantine and Syene as 'claustra olim Romani imperii, quod nunc rubrum ad mare patescit' (II. 61. 2). Justus Lipsius saw a clear reference to the high peak of Trajan's conquests in 116. Context and style speak in favour of 'rubrum mare' as the Indian Ocean—Livy can be adduced in support.[1] Now the sentence might be a subsequent insertion of the author. If so, when did he put it in ?[2] But the sentence looks integral to its context, and a climax. Therefore it would appear that the author did not get very far with his enterprise of eighteen books (in three hexads) before the death of Trajan in 117.

A variety of perspectives offers. On the most modest count it can hardly be denied that Tacitus was writing the Neronian books under Hadrian. However that may be, the question, though important, may be waived in this place. The date may not matter much for Tacitus' opinions about the central problem: Republic and Empire, senator and emperor.

Let those opinions therefore be scrutinized. Sound method would enjoin one to look first at the author's own words. But there might be a temptation to proceed a priori, and even some advantage. Well before the end of the first dynasty the typical attitudes of a senator had emerged, and the appropriate language. The true sentiments of the upper order do not wholly evade enquiry. And the next epoch brings a clarification.

The Republic was now a distant memory, purified, exalted, and harmless. Nobody could fail to pay homage to the glorious past of Rome. But that allegiance was not political, only moral and social: under Trajan it did not denote any hostility to the Caesars. The cult of the old ways and the ancestral virtues had long been established form among the Romans. Anything that could be labelled 'priscus' was irresistible in appeal. Serious men responded. The state religion of the Romans lacked dogma and imposed no claims on belief. Here, then, was a faith to fill the gap. And hypocrisy, which must find an outlet somewhere, duly exploited the language and

[1] Livy XXXVI. 17. 15; XLII. 52. 14; XLV. 9. 3. These are all passages in elevated language referring to wide conquest or dominion in the Orient. Observe also the Livian phrase 'crescentibus iam provinciis et latius patescente imperio' (XXXII. 27. 6). For these reasons (if for no others) it is not likely that Tacitus can have been referring to the Red Sea and a small accession of territory either on the Nabataean or the Egyptian littoral. The kingdom of the Nabataean Arabs was annexed in 105 or 106.

[2] The sentence might have been inserted when the author had completed I–III or I–VI. It is surely illicit to suppose it to have been inserted after the completion of the whole work—and hence date the publication of the *Annales* to 117 (as some do). It is far from certain, moreover, that the author lived to terminate the third hexad. . . .

the heroes of the Free State. That, it may be said, was the religion of the educated class—and notably of new arrivals and parvenus. The conspicuous document is a person who had statues of Cato, of Brutus, of Cassius in his house. Not even a senator but a knight in the imperial secretariat, continuous in employment when rulers changed.[1]

There was thus a normal and conventional ambiguity. How far did Tacitus participate in it? A new man, owing advancement to the Caesars, he would none the less honour the traditional virtues bequeathed by the Republic; but his studies in the history of eloquence since the epoch of the Republic would render him aware of change and development. Furthermore, his experience as a senator, with multiple advantages. He had been abroad in the provinces; he had lived under the tyranny of Domitian; and in the year of his consulship he had witnessed the distintegration of a government, with the menace of an armed proclamation against Nerva.

So far so good. Tacitus seems not altogether unpredictable. It might be possible to construct a plausible framework of beliefs, not peculiar to him alone but shared with many of his age and class.

But there are his writings, of various dates. The exegesis is bound up with certain hazards. First, and obvious, did the author's convictions undergo change in the course of Trajan's reign? Second, and fundamental, the whole relation between the writer and his material. History is dramatic narration. The author's presentation is coloured by the theme, the events, and the characters. Did not Livy, recounting ancient history, make the proper and honourable avowal of that influence? He says 'nescio quo pacto antiquus fit animus'.[2]

Much of the *Annales* was ancient history to Cornelius Tacitus, writing a century after the accession of Tiberius Caesar. That emperor was archaic in character and aspirations—and even in his language, as skilfully reproduced by the alert historian.[3] And in the principate of Tiberius there subsisted 'quaedam imago rei publicae'. Again, though Nero became more or less contemporary to Tacitus, and disquieting, for he prefigured Hadrian in his philhellenism, Thrasea Paetus and his friends belonged to a past epoch of heroism and tragedy, not conceivably recurrent under Trajan or in the early years of Hadrian.

Third, the tradition of Roman historiography. Sallust, the great originator, ordained the tone and manner: truculent, censorious, and subversive. Tacitus acknowledges his precursor, even had he not paid the compliment,

---

[1] Namely, Titinius Capito (Pliny, *Epp.* II. 17. 3). For his career, *ILS* 1448.
[2] Livy XLIII. 13. 1.
[3] Observe the forms 'duint' and 'hominum officia fungi' in a Tiberian oration (IV. 38).

with one of his rare superlatives, to 'rerum Romanarum florentissimus auctor' (III. 30. 2). Tacitus exploits, or rather assimilates, the Sallustian idiosyncrasy.

The approach therefore has to be conducted with caution and discrimination. The dramatic presentation of men and events discloses the author's devices and preoccupations, not his innermost sentiments. The speeches, though often a clue by their selection and emphasis, cannot safely be invoked to register his own opinions. And finally, as often and inevitably, save in the most direct and elementary forms of literary exposition, the man and the writer are not the same person.[1]

Tacitus is a subtle and sophisticated writer, heir to a long tradition, and writing for men of understanding. The situations he describes are permeated with all the ambiguities of high politics—and of human nature—in any age. His manner is majestic and reticent. Perhaps in himself a complicated character, perhaps not. Who can say? Remote, austere and enigmatic, on a surface view, yet perhaps in no way a problem in his comportment towards Rome and the Caesars.

With this necessary proviso and warning, let the writings be briefly examined. The *Agricola* expounds and eulogizes the career of a good man who served the state under a bad emperor. It is a laudation of Agricola and an attack on Domitian. But it is something more. The author interpolates violent language to the detriment of unnamed persons, those who tend to admire that which is wrong—'inlicita mirari' (42. 4). He reads them a lesson. He condemns perilous conduct and ostentatious deaths with no benefit to the Commonwealth.[2] Alluding thus to the victims of the Domitianic tyranny, Tacitus turns a sharp edge against their friends and would-be avengers in 97. That is not all. Defending Agricola, Tacitus defends his own conduct and that of others who had kept aloof from futile, doctrinaire and fractious opposition. Among them the reader could divine Trajan who, like Agricola, practised the sober virtue of 'obsequium' and served the State in the command of provinces and armies. The link and parallel is made explicit—Agricola (it is alleged) saw Trajan as a future emperor.[3]

---

[1] That has not, unfortunately, impeded the reconstruction of a poet's character and biography from his poems—for example, the satirist Juvenal.

[2] *Agr.* 42. 4: 'sciant quibus moris est inlicita mirari posse etiam sub malis principibus magnos viros esse, obsequiumque ac modestiam, si industria ac vigor adsint, eo laudis excedere quo plerique per abrupta sed in nullum rei publicae usum ambitiosa morte inclaruerunt'.

[3] *Agr.* 44. 5: 'quod augurio votisque apud nostras aures ominabatur'.

Nor need the *Dialogus* be baffling to interpretation. The debate is summed up by Curiatius Maternus, who had abandoned public speaking for poetry, in fact historical drama, his most recent work being a *Cato*. Oratory, he points out, changes with the condition of state and society. The great orators of the past were a product of freedom—or rather, of anarchy. One cannot have both oratory and a well-ordered Commonwealth. The choice and moral is plain. Eloquence is obsolete.[1]

That is to say, the diagnosis of Maternus plainly accepts the present dispensation. Some would go further and deduce an enthusiastic acceptance of monarchy. That notion hardly makes sufficient allowance for gentle irony in the alert author. When he commends civic obedience and deprecates long speeches in the Senate, he employs the axiom that the best men come quickly to unanimity. And the ruler has the decision now, not the People, and rightly, for he is 'sapientissimus et unus'.[2] So elevated an estimate of Senate and Emperor is too simple-minded to reflect the judgement of Curiatius Maternus, or of Cornelius Tacitus—or, for that matter, of Fabius Justus, to whom the treatise is dedicated.

Agricola and *Dialogus*, therefore, each in its own fashion, discountenance opposition, the one using the arguments of a politician, the other from the standpoint of a historian (and not a mere historian of Roman eloquence). Opposition was now a foolish anachronism, and perhaps dangerous. To men of judgement, what matters is the quality of a ruler and the spirit of his regime. He must be genuinely 'capax imperii'—and not decline in the sequel. In comparison, the way he has in fact acquired legitimation is subordinate: hereditary succession, an adoption, or even a *coup d'état*.

One of those ways, however, is it not the sovereign remedy and ideal, namely adoption? 'Optimum quemque adoptio inveniet'. That maxim comes early in the *Historiae*. It is enounced by Galba in his oration when selecting Piso Licinianus for son and successor (I. 15 f.). Galba indicts the dynasty of Julii and Claudii. Rome has been for too long 'unius familiae quasi hereditas'. If the stability of the empire did not demand a single regent, Galba might initiate a republic. The next best thing will be the new practice of a ruler freely chosen—'loco libertatis erit quod eligi coepimus'.

---

[1] *Dial.* 41. 5: 'nunc, quoniam nemo eodem tempore adsequi potest magnam famam et magnam quietem, bono saeculi sui quisque citra obtrectationem alterius utatur'.

[2] *Dial.* 41. 4: 'quid enim opus est longis in senatu sententiis, cum optimi cito consentiant? quid multis apud populum contionibus, cum de re publica non imperiti et multi deliberent sed sapientissimus et unus?'

Galba terminates by invoking the doctrine of the middle path—Romans cannot endure the extremes of either liberty or enslavement.[1] The speech is a free composition of Cornelius Tacitus, deliberately put in sharp prominence. Surely therefore it deserves to be exploited to the full. This precious document is nothing less than the historian's own confession of a political creed.

So at least a number of scholars assume. The assumption is hasty and incautious. Orations in Tacitus are not always exempt from ambiguity. They have to be carefully examined for their language—and set against the context of the situation. One observes Galba's phraseology, highly conventional and therefore suspect. It resembles the legends advertised on the coinage. Passing lightly over the facts Galba boldly asserts that he was summoned to empire 'deorum hominumque consensu'.[2] And there is the inevitable appeal to Augustus, but the orator goes further, claiming to excel Augustus: 'sed Augustus in domo successorem quaesivit, ego in re publica'.

Galba was trapped in a sorry predicament. Adoption was 'unicum remedium', so the historian pertinently states (I. 14. 1). Seen in the light of that predicament, the speech as devised by Tacitus takes on a slightly different coloration, exhibiting that contrast between words and facts which is the constant preoccupation of a historian. One is drawn to compare the noble oration in which Otho, an emperor created by the armed insurrection of the Praetorian Guard, extols the virtues of discipline and patriotism (I. 83 f.). In peroration Otho asserts that Rome and the Senate are on his side. Rome is no mere fortuitous collection of edifices; on the Senate depend 'aeternitas rerum et pax gentium'; the Senate is perpetual from the Kings to the Caesars; soldiers of the Guard can become senators, and senators can become emperors.[3]

All too noble; and the historian a few pages later quietly discloses a disturbing fact. Otho's eloquence was not his own (men believed), but borrowed, and the manner of a notorious practitioner, Galerius Trachalus, could be detected, pompous and resonant.[4]

---

[1] *Hist.* I. 16. 4: 'imperaturus es hominibus qui nec totam servitutem pati possunt nec totam libertatem'.

[2] *Hist.* I. 15. 1, cf. I. 30. 2 (Piso's address to the Praetorian Guard).

[3] *Hist.* I. 84. 4: 'muta ista et inanima intercidere ac reparari promisca sunt: aeternitas rerum et pax gentium et mea cum vestra salus incolumitate senatus firmatur. hunc auspicato a parente et conditore urbis nostrae institutum et a regibus usque ad principes continuum et immortalem, sicut a maioribus accepimus, sic posteris tradamus. nam ut ex vobis senatores ita ex senatoribus principes nascuntur'.

[4] *Hist.* I. 90. 2: 'et erant qui genus ipsum orandi noscerent, crebro fori usu celebre et ad implendas populi aures latum et sonans'.

These orations, it will appear, illustrate the historian's deadly and demo-litionary technique. His portrayal of Galba's character and actions lacks sympathy. If that person was indicated as 'omnium consensu capax im-perii',[1] the 'consensus' was quickly shown to be an illusion. Galba was a dull disciplinarian, rigid yet liable to be swayed by his entourage. When he made a decision, it proved to be calamitous. He chose pedigree and the negative virtues. Piso's descent advertised an illustrious Republican line-age, but he had lived in exile for long years, he knew nothing of empire and its problems.

To Tacitus' treatment of Galba and the theme of adoption, the events of 97 stand in close and strict relation. Nerva chose a man who was patently 'capax imperii'. It may well be doubted, however, whether he was a free agent in the crisis of October, 97. The Guard had risen and dominated Rome; there had been rumours earlier in the year about one of the army commanders;[2] and Trajan's elevation (if the facts were known) may have resembled a *coup d'état*.

Transmission of the power through adoption therefore acquired a start-ling relevance when Tacitus wrote, and subsequent events were to keep the theme in prominence. Nor is there any mystery. It had been a normal method of perpetuating a family in the Roman aristocracy, an heir being sought among kinsfolk, political allies, or houses of social parity. In turn Trajan, Hadrian and Antoninus Pius lacked sons; but Marcus Aurelius left it in no doubt that Commodus was to succeed him. Adoption, it can be argued, is not the response to a theory of government but merely the next best thing to hereditary succession.

A ruler without a son might (or might not) enjoy a certain freedom in selection, and the practice naturally gave rise to edifying language about the 'choice of the best man'. Each time the circumstances and the person have to be watched. Tacitus in the oration of Galba furnishes the plea in favour, but not unequivocally. He is also careful to demonstrate that an adoption could be foolish or disastrous. Men of understanding may already have been asking what line of conduct Trajan would follow—or what would happen if Trajan died.

The new regime appeared to open under good auspices (after a sharp threat of catastrophe and civil war). Nerva achieved a harmony between 'principatus' and 'libertas', and, with every day that passed his adopted son was augmenting the felicity of the age. So Tacitus in the *Agricola* (3. 1).

---

[1] In the damning obituary notice (I. 49. 4).
[2] cf. Pliny, *Epp.* IX. 13. 11.

'Felicitas temporum' was no exaggeration after the tyranny of Domitian's last years. Then, in the preface to the *Historiae* Tacitus makes an announcement. If life be vouchsafed, he will go on and narrate that happy period in which freedom of thought and freedom of speech obtain (I. I. 4).

He did not carry out that promise, if promise it should be styled, and not a normal and necessary compliment to the new regime. Instead, the *Annales*, sombre and murderous. Where lies the explanation? Brief reflection suggests a ready answer. The truth about certain transactions of the year 97 could not safely be told. Nor was Trajan's reign practicable while Trajan lived. And it could not have been an attractive subject. Dull urban annals and a successful war of conquest across the Danube, whereas Tacitus had already found scope for his especial talents in narrating tyranny at home and the defeats sustained by Roman armies, the vicissitudes of warfare or the imperfect victories.

None the less, perplexity has been felt, a question has been put and earnestly debated. Tacitus at first hailed with sincere enthusiasm the epoch of felicity inaugurated by Nerva and Trajan. Later on his opinions underwent a change. He conceived disappointment with Trajan. Or perhaps his historical studies made him perspicacious and pessimistic. Or again, it might be suggested, he came to discern the grave moral and political dangers inherent in autocracy even at its best. Benevolent despotism evades criticism, blunts the intelligence and enfeebles the will. 'Obsequium' is not an exhilarating way of life. Tyranny, however, had acted as a tonic, not unproductive of energy and talent. It was not Domitian, perhaps, who killed oratory, but Trajan.

The notion that the political attitude of an author changed in this way is not to be repulsed. To be welcomed rather—especially if that author began with an ingenuous acquiescence in the existing order or faith in governmental professions. That is a hazardous assumption for any Roman senator. For Tacitus, it depends on a surface interpretation of the *Agricola*, the *Dialogus*—and a single speech in the first book of the *Historiae*—set against the testimony of the *Annales*. But, it must be added, the *Annales* may turn out to be not at all plain and unequivocal, and the decisive books of the *Historiae* are not extant. Perhaps Tacitus did not modify the main lines of his political thinking. Once again, caution must interpose, adducing various factors: the type of history writing to which Tacitus conformed, the nature of the transactions he chronicled, and a perhaps transient influence from the contemporary situation.

The *Historiae*, opening with armed proclamations and civil wars, went on to narrate how a dynasty degenerated in the years of peace. The theme of the *Annales* presents a parallel—the decline and fall of the Julian and Claudian line, dragging with it to destruction ancient families of the aristocracy, but also (and worse) destroying freedom of speech and human dignity.

Tacitus is hostile to tyranny—yet not always a champion of its enemies and its victims. Commending in the *Agricola* the patriotic discretion of his father-in-law, Tacitus goes out of his way to condemn those who sought ostentatious renown, with no benefit to the Commonwealth (42. 4). The language is admonitory, violent, emotional. Language of that kind can be a valuable clue, as is elsewhere evident in Tacitus.[1] This instance avows its source. Under Nerva excessive praise of the martyrs became an annoyance, revenge a menace to the proper conduct of government. The anger of Tacitus abated in the sequel, so it appears. One of the main themes of the *Historiae* is the conflict between authority and opinion. It is introduced early in Book IV in the person of Helvidius Priscus. Tacitus has nothing but praise for his character and his principles. The only doubt is faint enough and expressed in brief epilogue—some held that Priscus was over-anxious for personal renown.[2]

Nor would Tacitus fail in the *Annales* to offer a sympathetic portrayal of Thrasea Paetus. And who could approve Nero or the prosecutors who contrived the ruin of this excellent man?

Thrasea stood for 'dignitas' and 'libertas'. Political terminology changes with the times. The old words subsist, the content is different. Of 'libertas' the most valuable survival was freedom of speech. In defence of that ideal, Tacitus is unequivocal and fervid. The historian's avowal is instructive, no less his artistic device. After a notable digression on history and politics, comparing past and present (IV. 32 f.), the next item is the prosecution of Cremutius Cordus, senator and historian. Tacitus invents an oration, splendid, vigorous, and coherent. And he subjoins in his own person a withering comment: how can one sufficiently deride the brute stupidity of those who think they can suppress opinion?[3]

---

[1] Thus the violent outburst in *Germ.* 33. 2: 'maneat, quaeso, duretque gentibus, si non amor nostri at certe odium sui, quando urgentibus imperii fatis nihil iam praestare fortuna maius potest quam hostium discordiam'. Also the attack on the Greeks because their histories ignored Arminius—'Graecorum annalibus ignotus, qui sua tantum mirantur' (*Ann.* II. 80. 3).

[2] *Hist.* IV. 6. 1: 'erant quibus adpetentior famae videretur, quando etiam sapientibus cupido gloriae novissima exuitur'. Nor is severe censure to be discovered in the historian's comment on Thrasea—'sueta firmitudine animi et ne gloria intercideret' (*Ann.* XIV. 49. 3).

[3] *Ann.* IV. 35. 5: 'quo magis socordiam eorum inridere libet qui praesenti potentia credunt exstingui posse etiam sequentis aevi memoriam. nam contra punitis ingeniis gliscit auctoritas, neque aliud externi reges aut qui eadem saevitia usi sunt nisi dedecus sibi atque illis gloriam peperere'.

Tacitus cannot but admire the moral qualities of the Republican tradition. Is he guilty of excess in this direction—perhaps a late convert, as it were? Some claim that as he went on Tacitus became more and more the prisoner of a narrow and moralistic attitude. He was now less a historian than a preacher. And, a further refinement. He was nearly sixty when he began to compose the *Annales*. The onset of old age made him gloomy and hopeless.

Notions of this kind are a pure assumption. To dispel them, appeal can be made to various passages in the *Annales* which indicate that, if anything, Tacitus went the other way, his moral standards becoming more tolerant and humane.

From *Historiae* to *Annales* the style tightens and hardens, the manner is more austere and ferocious. The historian was growing to full awareness of his talent for the grim and subversive. And from his frequentation with Tiberius Caesar, his sarcasm took on a sharper edge. But Claudius broadened his sense of humour. Tacitus exhibits gaiety and goes in for parody. When a wife must be found for Claudius, the freedmen of the palace produce and argue the names and qualities of noble ladies (XII. I. f.). That is travesty of a cabinet council. Agrippina's claims prevailing, L. Vitellius addresses the Senate, using and abusing conventional language (and much verbal malice from the historian) to persuade them that the emperor should marry his own niece (XII. 5 f.).[1]

These transactions were a fit occasion for mockery. But Tacitus goes further. He does not exempt from criticism the votaries of ancestral virtue. They can be histrionic, hypocritical, or detrimental. 'Severitas' was laudable. But it can pass into harshness or rigour, even in men whom Tacitus admires, such as the jurist Cassius Longinus.[2] And the ostentation of strict discipline in an army commander may be only a mask for incompetence or may go with subservience to the emperor.[3]

On the other hand, the social graces win the approbation of the austere historian. Tacitus singles out two men for their 'elegantia vitae', namely Pomponius Secundus, the dramatic poet, and Servilius Nonianus, orator and historian (V. 8. 2; XIV, 19). Like the author himself, not merely men of letters. Pomponius as legate of Germania Superior earned the

---

[1] Note the choice language: 'maritandum principem', which recalls the title of an Augustan law; the 'sanctimonia' of Agrippina, a word elsewhere applied by Tacitus only to elderly Vestal Virgins; and the fact that she is providentially a widow, 'provisu deum' (it was alleged that she had poisoned her previous husband, Passienus Crispus).

[2] *Ann.* XIII. 48. This is relevant to the estimate of his speech urging that all the slaves in the household of Pedanius Secundus should be put to death (XIV. 43 f.).

[3] Thus the verdict on Q. Veranius (XIV. 29. 1).

ornamenta triumphalia (XII. 28. 2); and Servilius had been proconsul of Africa.[1]

Further, a courtier, a flatterer, and a minister of Claudius Caesar can be dispassionately estimated: L. Vitellius behaved with 'prisca virtus' in the governance of provinces (VI. 32. 4). Even a voluptuary earns indulgence if he can show ability, even Otho. His conduct as governor of Lusitania is described in the *Historiae* as 'comiter administrata provincia' (I. 13. 4). In the *Annales*, however, it earns the high and surprising award: 'integre sancteque egit' (XIII. 46. 3).

Above all will be noted the generous space and appraisal accorded to the 'elegantiae arbiter' in person, namely Petronius—who, the historian adds, showed capacity as proconsul of Bithynia and as consul (XVI. 18. 2). Petronius in his last hours looked for comfort not to philosophers and discourse on the immortality of the soul but to verse and song (XVI. 19. 2).

The graceful end of Petronius is intended to stand in artistic contrast to dramatic or even pompous exits like that of Seneca. But it would be an error to suppose that Tacitus means any depreciation of Seneca. He accords him a proper recognition—the much-maligned who none the less did his best in an impossible situation. Tacitus in fact shields the conduct of Seneca. It is not the philosopher that excites his interest and sympathy, but the statesman. Tacitus knew that compromise is the essence of civil government.

That theme recurs in various presentations all through the writings of Tacitus. Not only with Agricola—one observes a parallel in the reign of Tiberius. An aristocrat, Marcus Lepidus, steered a safe course, avoiding the extremes of defiance and subservience. His example encouraged the historian to conceive grave doubts about fatalism and predestination: the human will can count.[2]

On a lower key, a speaker in the *Historiae*, parading as a plain honest man, proclaims a salutary doctrine: one can admire the past, but one ought to keep in step with the present, pray for a good emperor but put up with what comes along.[3] That argument is put into the mouth of Eprius Marcellus, a character far from admirable—in fact the man who prosecuted

---

[1] *CIL* VIII. 24585a and *AE* 1932, 24.

[2] *Ann.* IV. 20. 3: 'unde dubitare cogor, fato et sorte nascendi ut cetera ita principum inclinatio in hos, offensio in illos, an sit aliquid in consiliis nostris liceatque inter abruptam contumaciam et deforme obsequium pergere iter ambitione ac periculis vacuum'.

[3] *Hist.* IV. 8. 2: 'se meminisse temporum quibus natus sit, quam civitatis formam patres avique instituerint; ulteriora mirari, praesentia sequi; bonos imperatores voto expetere, qualescumque tolerare'.

Thrasea Paetus and who (the reader would divine) was going to be responsible for the destruction of Helvidius Priscus.

The irony is typical of Cornelius Tacitus. If challenged, would he not have been compelled to confess that such were the principles of expedience which he and others had followed under Domitian? Tacitus' views on men and government are ambiguous, necessarily so, for they reflect the historical situation. And, let it be maintained, they are not peculiar to himself, but for the most part obvious and predictable.

Tacitus is elusive, and he affects the reticent manner proper to a historian. It is rare and remarkable when he introduces a personal avowal. Few among the Romans had the strength, the honesty, or the insight to liberate themselves from obsession with the past. If it was not the Republic that caught and hampered them, it was the epoch of Caesar Augustus. Discussing Roman morals from the War of Actium to his own day, Tacitus, while coolly dismissing the Augustan programme of reform, traces the process of change and adds a testimony in conclusion: not all things were better in the old time.[1] That is a quiet and masterly understatement.

Elsewhere, in an episode deliberately selected for high relief, the historian makes his own contribution to a theme of perennial interest that goes back to Cato's pronouncement: the long development of the Roman State through the ages.

Claudius Caesar proposed to bring into the Senate tribal chieftains from that Gaul which Julius Caesar had subjugated. The imperial counsellors were hostile. Tacitus invents their objections, shows them up as the product of narrow prejudice, and makes them ridiculous (XI. 23). On the other hand, he improves the oration of Claudius Caesar in various ways, an emperor for whom he otherwise lacks respect and tolerance. This time Claudius speaks as the Imperator should, embodying and declaring the majesty of Rome (XI. 24).

Impersonating Claudius, the historian neatly inserts a reference to the first senators that came from Spain and Narbonensis, and proceeds: 'their descendants are in our company, they are not inferior to us in devotion to Rome'.[2]

---

[1] *Ann.* IV. 55. 5: 'nec omnia apud priores meliora, sed nostra quoque aetas multa laudis et artium imitanda posteris tulit'. Let it also be added that this is a historian who deprecated excessive zeal for ancient history—'dum vetera extollimus recentium incuriosi' (II. 88. 3).

[2] *Ann.* XI. 24. 3: 'num paenitet Balbos ex Hispania nec minus insignes viros e Gallia Narbonensi transivisse? manent posteri eorum nec amore in hanc patriam nobis concedunt'. This emphatic pronouncement concludes the first half of the Claudian oration—and ought to be printed as the end of a paragraph.

Tacitus speaks for the new imperial aristocracy of the western provinces, for Trajan and Hadrian as for Agricola—and for himself. The avowal is proud and unobtrusive. Cornelius Tacitus is not a descendant of the patrician Cornelii, but a *novus homo*, like his predecessors in the line of the senatorial historians (Cato, Sallust, Pollio); and further, not an Italian (it can be conjectured) but deriving from some town of Narbonensis.

ADDENDA

FOR the text of the *Annales* see the latest of the successive editions by E. Koestermann (Teubner, 1934, 1952, 1960, 1965). For a number of passages his full commentary will be consulted, now brought felicitously to its conclusion in four volumes (1963 to 1968). Further, and in general, S. Borzsák, 'P. Cornelius Tacitus', P-W, Supp. XI (1968), 373–512.

Ch. I, p. 10. For the Narbonensian *patria* of the historian, briefly alluded to in two other places in this volume, see *Tacitus* (1958), 611 ff. The case for Transpadane Italy has recently been argued by E. Koestermann, *Athenaeum* XLIII (1965), 167 ff.

Ch. II, p. 11. The historian as a late beginner. The reference is to E. Kornemann, *Tacitus* (Wiesbaden, 1947), 16; 45.

p. 12. Sallust's gardens on the Esquiline. Better to be assigned to his opulent grand-nephew, cf. *Sallust* (1964), 283.

p. 12. The date of Livy's birth. I have a decided preference for 64 B.C., cf. *Tacitus*, 137, with the arguments adduced in *Harvard Studies* LXIV (1959), 40 ff.

p. 13. The purpose of the *Agricola*. See the lucid discussion in the edition of R. M. Ogilvie and I. A. Richmond (1967), 16 ff.

Ch. III, p. 24, n.2. The inscription of Julius Classicianus is now *RIB* 12.

p. 26. The oration of Claudius Caesar. See further *Tacitus*, 317 ff.; 461 ff.; 623 f.

p. 27. The paucity of Gallic senators. See *Tacitus*, 462; 799.

p. 27. The rising of Julius Vindex. Given its origin and supporters 'it quickly took the form of a native insurrection'. That the city of Vienna in Narbonensis espoused the cause of Vindex is a clue to his aspirations, cf. *Tacitus*, 463. For discussion about this affair (lengthy), see M. Raoss, *Epigraphica* XX (1958), 46 ff.; XXII (1960), 39 ff.; P. A. Brunt, *Latomus* XVIII (1959), 531 ff.; J. B. Hainsworth, *Historia* XI (1962), 86 ff.

Ch. IV, p. 31, n. 5. That the Lepidus who gave testimony in 65 B.C. is Mam. Lepidus Livianus (*cos.* 77 B.C.) has been argued by G. V. Sumner, *JRS* LIV (1964), 41 ff. If so, the last appearance of this elderly person who had not been on prominence anywhere since his consulship.

p. 32. Persons called 'Q. Lepidus'. See, discussing Pliny, *NH* VII. 181, the paper 'Missing Senators', *Historia* IV (1955), 54 f.

p. 33. Descendants of Pompeius. See, in reference to the mysterious M. Livius Drusus Libo (*cos.* 15 B.C.), the long and valuable paper of E. J. Weinrib, *Harvard Studies* LXXII (1968), 247 ff., with a new *stemma*, in two versions, 274 f.

p. 34. The marriages of Paullus Aemilius Lepidus (*suff.* 34 B.C.). The younger Marcella is denied him by E. Bayer, *Historia* XVII (1968), 118 ff. He suggests that on the death of her first husband, in 12 B.C. (conjectured to be the consul Messalla Barbatus Appianus), she was consigned to the youthful L. Aemilius Paullus (*cos.* A.D. 1). The supposed offspring of the match are Paullus Aemilius Regillus, the quaestor of Ti. Caesar (*ILS* 949: Saguntum) and the *frater arvalis* L. Paullus who died in A.D. 14 (*ILS* 5026).

p. 34. The 'conspiracy' of L. Aemilius Paullus (*cos.* A.D. 1). This important transaction clearly falls in A.D. 8, as assumed in *Rom. Rev.* (1939), 432. A valid clue, discounting A.D. 1, is furnished by Suetonius, *Divus Claudius* 26. 1 (neglected by many scholars, including myself). Claudius, when 'admodum adulescens', was betrothed to an Aemilia Lepida, whom he was compelled to forfeit 'quod parentes eius Augustum offenderant'. Claudius was born in 10 B.C.

p. 35. M. Lepidus as governor of Dalmatia. Add the fragmentary name in fine lettering (*CIL* III. 13885, Gradac), adduced long ago by C. Patsch.

p. 35. Lepidus as governor of Tarraconensis. He was certainly back in Rome by the year 17 (*Ann.* II. 48. 1). The presumed predecessor is Cn. Calpurnius Piso, whom I detect in the erasure on the monumental inscription from Cabo Torres (near Gijón in Asturias), bearing the date 9/10 by the *tribunicia potestas* of Augustus (*CIL* II. 2703). See a forthcoming paper; and also G. Alföldy, *Fasti Hispanienses* (1969), 10.

p. 36. Sex. Pompeius (*cos.* 14). He became proconsul of Asia in the sequel (24/5 or 25/6), and had for companion a loyal client, the writer Valerius Maximus (II. 6. 8). R. Hanslik suggested 'nach dem J. 27' (P-W XXI. 2267), R. Helm 'etwa 27' (VIII A. 90). The tenure 26–8 is occupied by M. Lepidus (above, p. 43).

p. 44. The African proconsulate of M. Silanus (*cos.* 19). Compare *PIR²*, J 839.

p. 44, n. 3. The consuls of 13. In *JRS* LVI (1966), 55 ff. I adduced arguments in support of the view of the Gordons, viz. that 'C. Silius A. Caecina Largus' is two people: C. Silius the *ordinarius* as colleague of L. Munatius Plancus, the other a *consul suffectus*. However, about the same time, A. Ferrua produced a document which, first published in 1923, had escaped even the notice of Attilio Degrassi: a small funeral tablet with the consular date 'L. Planco C. Caec.' (*Bull. Com..* LXXIX (1966), 94 ff., whence *AE* 1966, 16). Therefore the remarkable and suspect *polyonymus* is redeemed.

p. 47, n. 1. The 'capaces imperii' (*Ann.* I. 13. 2 f.). The phrase 'a later addition by the author' might be modified. Rather 'an insertion on the basic text'. It is annotation, interrupting the debate in the Senate. The item, though attractive, is absent from Suetonius and from Dio. Presumably therefore from a subsidiary source, or sources, and perhaps from the *Memoirs* of Agrippina (cf. IV. 53. 2). That lady would not miss an anecdote damaging to Tiberius, the enemy of her parents. For the two passages about Tiberius on Rhodes (I. 4. 4; IV. 57. 2), which by contrast can safely be claimed as insertions on revision, see *Tacitus*, 695 f.

p. 47. Cn. Piso in Tarraconensis. For the date, of some importance, cf. above.

p. 47. L. Arruntius as absentee legate of Tarraconensis. For the date of his appointment, probably just before the death of Drusus in October of 23, see *Tacitus*, 443.

p. 48. The children of M. Lepidus. There is no evidence about the identity of his wife (or perhaps wives). L. (Aemilius) Paullus, the *frater arvalis* deceased in 14 (*ILS* 5026), might be a son.

p. 49, n. 3. The 'capaces imperii', cf. above on p. 47 n. 1. See further *Tacitus*, 485, where the item is described as 'perhaps an insertion, when Tacitus was revising Book 1'. For the relevance of the fate of the Four Consulars, cf. ib. 694. However, there is no necessity to regard the passage as a later insertion. Many parallels of situation or events between the years 14 and 117 are natural or fortuitous. Compare further 'more things than one in the early books of the *Annales* quickly acquired a sharp and contemporary relevance' (ib. 771).

Ch. V, p. 54. The 'L. P⟨lancio⟩' emendation is adopted by Koestermann.

p. 55. 'Q. Veranius' is adopted by Koestermann.

p. 56. L. Piso in Tarraconensis. See now G. Alföldy, *Fasti Hispanienses* (1969), 14; 67.

p. 57. The tenure of L. Arruntius. See further *Tacitus*, 443.

p. 57. The *stemmata* of the Pisones. See 'Piso Frugi and Crassus Frugi', *JRS* L (1960), 12 ff. It is there conjectured that M. Crassus Frugi (*cos.* 14 B.C.) is a grandson of M. Pupius Piso Frugi (*cos.* 61 B.C.), adopted by M. Licinius Crassus (*cos.* 30 B.C.).

Ch. VI, p. 58. For rare or unique local *nomina* see also 'Senators, Tribes, and Towns', *Historia* XIII (1964), 105 ff.; for the emending of personal names, 'People in Pliny', *JRS* LVIII (1968), 139 f.

p. 61. 'M. Aletus' (*Ann.* II. 47. 4). It can be conjectured that this senator was a M. Aedius from Allifae, cf. the fragments *CIL* IX. 2341; 2344. See above, p. 98.

p. 61. The Ateii Capitones. 'Voltinia' as the tribe of Castrum Novum is preferred by L. R. Taylor, *The Voting Districts of the Roman Republic* (1960), 89, cf. 276.

p. 63. The mother of C. Junius Silanus, consul A.D. 10 (III. 68. 2). Presumably Appia, cf. U. Weidemann, *Acta Classica* VI (1963), 138 ff. The consul's son is C. Appius Junius Silanus, the consul of 28 (*PIR²*, J 822), his niece Junia Claudia (857). Approved in *PIR²*, J 824 f.

p. 66. Caesilianus (VI. 7. 1). Now restored to the text by Koestermann.

p. 68. Falanius (I. 73. 1; 2). Retained by Koestermann. As for the *nomen* on the bronze tablet at Asculum (*CIL* VI. 37045), Degrassi prints 'M?]aia[ni(us)]', and mentions 'Faianius' (*ILLRP* 515).

p. 70. Latinii and Lucanii. Koestermann now prints the names as given by the *Codex Mediceus*. In favour of 'Lucanius', it can be conjectured that the source of VI. 4. 1 is the *Acta Senatus* (*Tacitus*, 277).

p. 71. The *delator* Romanius Hispo (I. 74. 1). Koestermann keeps 'Romanus'.

p. 72. The polyonymous Caepio Hispo (*PIR²*, E 83), consul suffect *c.* 101. For his nomenclature and origin see *JRS* LVIII (1968), 144; 146.

p. 73. Q. Corellius Rufus (*suff.* 78). Presumably from Laus Pompeia, cf. *Tacitus* 58; *JRS* LVIII (1968), 147.

p. 73. The Sanquinii. For the tribe of Caere, L. R. Taylor prefers the 'Voturia, (o.c. 89; 276). But see *Historia* XIII (1964), 106; E. Badian, *JRS* LII (1962), 208.

p. 78. The Volcacii. See further 'Missing Persons III', *Historia* XI (1962), 152; 'Ten Tribunes', *JRS* LIII (1963), 60. The inscription cited as 'from Priene' (*OGIS* 458) is in fact composite; and a new fragment from Apamea discloses the title of proconsul before the name of L. Volcacius Tullus (Ehrenberg-Jones, *Documents²*, etc. (1955), 98; *SEG* XV. 454). For his nephew, G. W. Bowersock, *Augustus and the Greek World* (1965), 21; 79.

Ch. VII, p. 82, n. 7. For Sex. Pompeius (*cos.* 14), above, pp. 36–41. He is mentioned as dead by Valerius Maximus (IV. 7, *Ext.* 2)—and might therefore have qualified for an obituary notice in the *Annales*, Book V. The person alluded to by Seneca is presumably a son, not otherwise attested.

p. 83. For peculiarities in the treatment of Memmius Regulus, see *Tacitus*, 486; 743 f.; 787.

p. 84. For the notion that the historian did not survive to complete the work, cf.

Tacitus, 361 f.; 742 ff.; Koestermann in his annotation on XVI. 35. 2.

p. 87, n. 2. Tiberius on Rhodes. See the *Addendum* to p. 47, n.1.

p. 88. Obituary notices on Augustan *novi homines*. See *Tacitus*, 580 f.

p. 89. Servilius Nonianus, See further above, p. 107.

Ch. VIII, p. 91. For an appreciation of the predecessors of Tacitus, see F. Klingner, *Mus. Helv.* XV (1958), 194 ff.

p. 105, n. 7. Cluvius Rufus. For his employment in the *Historiae*, G. B. Townend, *AJP* LXXXV (1964), 337 ff.

p. 107. The obituary notice (XIV. 19). See now the commentary of Koestermann. H. Fuchs proposed not only to expunge 'quam clariorem effecit' but to add 'clarus' after 'elegantia vitae' (*Mus. Helv.* XXII (1965), 115 f.). But 'clarus', coming soon after 'celebris' might be dispensed with. Fuchs states 'Syme allerdings hielt es für möglich, dass Tacitus selbst die Worte *quae clariorem effecit* hinzugefügt habe' (ib. 115, n. 3). An insertion by Tacitus? Not at all my meaning. Neither scholar appears to assess properly my objections (including the weak verb 'effecit'), or grasp the line of my argument—which concludes with 'the parenthetic explanation is feeble. A concise writer would do without it. Perhaps Acidalius was right'. Eschewing the remedy 'clarus', I would put instead a colon after 'elegantia vitae'.

Ch. IX, p. 113. A Danubian command for Fabius Justus. The British Museum papyrus known as 'Hunt's *Pridianum*' on the revised reading of R. O. Fink disclosed 'singulares fabi useti lega...' (Col. II. 25). Therefore, patently, Fabius is legate of Moesia Inferior: from 105, succeeding A. Caecilius Faustinus (*suff.* 99), until 108. For the argument, 'The Lower Danube under Trajan', *JRS* XLIX (1959), 26 ff. On the document see further J. F. Gilliam, *Hommages Grenier* (1962), 747 ff. The new knowledge has been slow to spread. No trace, for example, in A. N. Sherwin-White, *The Letters of Pliny. A Historical and Social Commentary* (1966), or in the article 'M. Ulpius Traianus' by R. Hanslik, P-W, Supp. X (1965), 1032 ff.

p. 112, n. 2. The Sabinus of Pliny, *Epp.* IX. 2. 4. The identification with P. Metilius Sabinus Nepos (*suff.* 103) is disputed by Sherwin-White, who prefers Statius Sabinus (IV. 10), held the same person as Sabinus of Firmum (VI. 18).

p. 113. Army commanders during the Dacian Wars. See *Tacitus*, 52 f., with App. 14; 'Pliny and the Dacian Wars', *Latomus* XXIII (1964), 750 ff.

p. 113. The governorship of Syria. His name is revealed on another milestone, published in *Ann. Arch. Syrie* X (1960), 159 ff. Trajan's titles are given as *cos.* VI (112 or after), *imp.* VII (114), but *trib. pot.* XIII (108) is discordant.

p. 116. Fabius' occupation in 97. For the situation in Syria see *Tacitus*, 631 f.

p. 117. The date of the *Dialogus*. See further *Tacitus*, 670 ff.

Ch. X, p. 129. The date of the *Annales*. For the interpretation of II. 61. 2, see *Tacitus*, 470 ff.; 768 ff.; and, in concordance, Koestermann in his commentary, also in his latest edition (1965), XXVIII. For the controversy (Indian Ocean or Red Sea), see the full account of S. Borzsák, P-W, Supp. XI (1968), 467 ff.

The passage runs 'exin ventum Elephantinen ac Syenen, claustra olim Romani imperii, quod nunc rubrum ad mare patescit'. The notion that this emphatic sentence refers not to the conquests of Trajan but to the annexation of a vassal kingdom in 105/6 (the Nabataean Arabs) finds fresh and vigorous advocates. For example, J. Beaujeu, *Rev. ét. lat.* XXXVIII (1960), 200 ff.; C. Questa, *Riv. di cultura cl. e med.* III

(1961), 390; F. Grosso, *Epigraphica* XVI (1964), 146; G. B. Townend, *CR²* XIV (1964), 54 (in review of the second edition, unchanged, of Paratore's *Tacito*); S. Mazzarino, *Il pensiere storico classico* II. 1 (1966), 456; II. 2 (1966), 391; R. Häussler, *Tacitus und die historische Bewusstlichkeit* (1966), 277 f. Hence the conclusion that Tacitus began his second historical work at an early date. Thus Beaujeu, suggesting even 108 or 109 (o.c. 232). That is well before his proconsulate of Asia (112/13), which experience, it may be contended, has left various traces in early books of the *Annales* (*Tacitus*, 466 ff.).

It may be noted that not all of the champions of the Nabataean hypothesis were well served. Paratore neglected to cite Livy, whose language shows what 'rubrum mare' might convey to a Roman historian; and, on Virgil, *Aen.* VIII. 686: 'victor ab Aurorae populis et litore rubro', he asserted: 'allusione non alla spedizione di Antonio contro i Parti, ma alla sua campagna vittoriosa contro i Nabatei' (*Tacito* (1951), 624). No such expedition of Antonius occurred. Further, Questa has the 'reduzione a provincia romana dell' Arabia Felice' (*Maia* IX (1957), 293).

Few have adopted a sceptical or negatory stance. Momigliano, however, issued a firm pronouncement in this line. He states that *Ann.* II. 61. 2 'lässt sich in keiner Richtung auswerten'. Further 'tatsächlich wissen wir nicht, was Tacitus mit *mare rubrum* gemeint hat' (*Gnomon* XXXIII (1961), 56).

Must we then renounce, holding it beyond ascertainment what the historian meant by 'rubrum ad mare' (note the position of the adjective, as in 'Romani imperii')? A paradox in a writer who, like Tiberius Caesar, was 'validus sensibus aut consulto ambiguus' (*Ann.* XIII. 3. 2). Tacitus is ambiguous when he decides to be, when the theme demands. The same holds for his use of bathos. None is more careful in the choice of words; and he has a marvellous gift for structure and for transitions. For these reasons and for others I continue to stand by the interpretation that commended itself to Justus Lipsius—and to Edward Gibbon.

p. 129, n. 2. The structure of the Claudian oration. Modern paragraphing sometimes has to be modified, cf. *Sallust* (1964), 80, n. 83. For example, the last sentence of *Ann. I.* 10, marking a shift of scene, should be transferred to the next chapter.

p. 140. Tacitus as the spokesman of the new Romans of the West. It is desirable to avoid misconceptions about this theme of high and imperial significance. Momigliano affirms 'dass die Quellen nichts über Tacitus' gallischen Ursprung aussagen. Seine Schriften verraten keinen provinziellen Standpunkt' (o.c. 56). Two observations are called for. First, I do not assign a 'Gallic origin' to the historian. All through I draw the sharp and necessary contrast between Tres Galliae and Narbonensis, which is 'Italia verius quam provincia'. And I firmly discount 'ultima origo', stating 'it is all vanity. The things that matter are education and national spirit, wealth and energy, and rank' (*Tacitus*, 618).

Second, the term 'provinzieller Standpunkt' is vague and misleading. Tacitus shows deep understanding of the provinces. But the mind of the Roman consular, like the manner of his writing, is in no way provincial or parochial.

INDEX

Emperors, members of dynasties, and classical authors are registered by their conventional English names. With the exception of Barea Soranus, Piso Licinianus and Thrasea Paetus, senators are classified by *gentilicia*, with *praenomen* and rank appended where possible. Certain *polyonymi* are abbreviated.

The Index comprises names in the footnotes and *Addenda* as well as in the text.